A Lasting Relationship

A LASTING RELATIONSHIP

PARENTS AND CHILDREN OVER THREE CENTURIES

LINDA POLLOCK

FOURTH ESTATE · LONDON

First published in Great Britain in 1987 by
Fourth Estate Ltd
113 Westbourne Grove
London W2 4UP
Telephone: 01–727 8993/243 1382

British Library Cataloguing in Publication Data

A Lasting relationship: parents and children over three centuries.
1. Family — Great Britain — History
2. Family — United States — History
I. Pollock, Linda A.
306.8'5'0941   HQ613
ISBN 0–947795–25–1

Design by Mark Hosker
Phototypeset in 10/11 Palatino by
Falcon Graphic Arts Limited
Lavender Vale, Wallington, Surrey SM6 9QS
Printed and bound by
The Bath Press, Lower Bristol Road, Bath BA2 3BL

for my mother

CONTENTS

CONTENTS

Acknowledgements

I would like to thank Keith Wrightson, Richard Wall, Roy Porter and Peter Laslett, who all read parts of the anthology, for their helpful comments and suggestions. I would also like to thank William Radzinowicz of Fourth Estate for his help and patience. The selection and compilation process was facilitated by the loan of a portable computer from the Cambridge Group for the History of Population and Social Structure, greatly simplifying the transcription of archive material, and by the research facilities provided by Churchill College, Cambridge. I also appreciate the interest of Kevin Ward, archivist at Northampton Record Office, who drew the text books of John Bach and H. Bonham to my attention.

I wish to thank the following for permission to reproduce material from their publications or collections. I have endeavoured to trace all copyright holders. Allen and Unwin for extracts from *The Amberley Papers* ed. Bertrand Russell (Russell); Berham and Co. for extracts from *The Oxley Parker Papers* by J. Oxley Parker; Bodleian Library for extracts from the Heber and Henry manuscripts; British Academy for extracts from 'The Diary of Ralph Josselin' ed. Alan Macfarlane; British Library for extracts from the Brockman, Carew, Hamilton-Gordon, Hatton and Oxinden manuscripts; A. Brown and Sons for extracts from *Leaves from a Family Tree* ed. J. Grimston (Grimston); Buckinghamshire Record Office for extracts from the Chester and Johnson manuscripts; Cambridge University Press for extracts from *The Autobiography of Francis Place* ed. Mary Thrale; Jonathan Cape for extracts from *The Capel Letters* ed. the Marquess of Angelsey; De Capo Press for extracts from *Memoirs of Aaron Burr with Miscellaneous Selections from His Correspondence* ed. Matthew Davis; Clarendon Press and Oxford University Press, Oxford, for extracts from *The Letters of Sydney Smith* ed. Nowell Smith; Colonel Williamsburg Inc. and the University Press of Virginia for extracts from *The Journal and Letters of Philip Vickers Fithian* ed. Hunter Parish; Derbyshire Record Office and the Rector of Ashover parish, Derbyshire for extracts from the Revill manuscripts; Essex Record Office, for extracts from the Mildmay manuscripts; Evans Brothers, now Bell and Hyman, for extracts from *Queen Victoria: Dearest Child* ed. Roger Fulford; Gregg International Publishers for extracts from *The Lives of the Norths* by Roger North; Hamish Hamilton, part of Chapman and Hall, for extracts from *The Ladies of Alderley* ed. Nancy Mitford (Stanley), (reprinted by permission of A. D. Peters and Co.); Hertfordshire Record Office for extracts from the Cowper, Lawes-Wittewronge and Martin-Leake manuscripts (Lady Ravensdale granted permission to quote from the Cowper papers);

Iowa State University Press for extracts from *The Letters of A. Bronson Alcott* ed. R. Herrnstadt; History of Childhood Quarterly for extracts from 'A Transcendentalist Father' by Charles Strickland; Kent Archive Office for extracts from the Barrell and Dering manuscripts; Lambeth Palace Library for extracts from the Talbot manuscripts; Longman Group for extracts from *Admiral's Wife* ed. C. Aspinall-Oglander; National Library of Scotland for extracts from the Maxwell, Fleming, Fletcher, Gordon-Cummings, Steuart and Sutherland manuscripts; Mitre Press/Charles Skilton for extracts from *The Journal of John Gabriel Stedman* ed. Stanbury Thompson; Massachusetts Historical Society for extracts from 'The Saltonstall Papers' ed. Robert Moody; John Murray for extracts from *Lady Charlotte Guest: Extracts from Her Journal* ed. Earl of Bessborough; Northampton Record Office and the respective owners for extracts from the Bach, Bonham, Brooke, Dryden, Hatton and Isham manuscripts; Nottingham University Library for extracts from the Portland letters (Cavendish); Peter Owen for extracts from *Mrs Longfellow. Selected Letters and Journals of Fanny Appleton Longfellow* ed. Edward Wagenknecht; Oxford University Press, New York, for extracts from *Not so long ago* by Cecil Drinker; St Martin's Press for extracts from *The Quaker Family in Colonial America. A Portrait of the Society of Friends* by J. William Frost; Scottish History Society for extracts from 'The Lauderdale Letters'; Secker and Warburg for extracts from *Lying Awake* by Catherine Carswell (reprinted by permission of MBA Literary Agents); Peter Smith for extracts from *The Works of Anne Bradstreet in Prose and Verse* ed. John Ellis; Scottish Record Office and the Controller of HM Stationery Office for extracts from the Dunbar, Leith and Melville manuscripts (the Leven and Melville documents are cited by permission of the Rt Hon the Earl of Leven); Somerset Record Office for extracts from the Phelips manuscripts; Strathclyde Regional Archives and Mr Archibald Stirling for extracts from the Stirling Papers; Staple Press and Mrs FitzGerald for extracts from *Emily Duchess of Leinster 1731–1814. A Study of Her Life and Times* by Brian FitzGerald (Kildare); University of North Carolina Press for extracts from *William Fitzhugh and His Chesapeake World: The Fitzhugh Letters and Other Documents, 1676–1701* ed. Richard B. Davis; University Press of Virginia for extracts from *The Diary of Colonel Landon Carter* ed. Jack Greene and *The Correspondence of the Three William Byrds of Westover* ed. Marion Tinling; Warwick Record Office and Sir Richard Hamilton for extracts from the Mordaunt manuscripts.

Introduction

The history of childhood has become an embattled topic. The emotion it engenders in specialists and non-specialists alike, as well as the problems of evidence it sets for those endeavouring to understand child life in the past, have combined to render it an area of inquiry rife with controversy, but far from replete with knowledge. Despite the limitations of the material unearthed so far, confident assertions on the miserable conditions of child life, and the inadequacies of parental care in previous centuries, have lacked neither promulgaters nor supporters. The main thrust of the most influential works in the field has been to argue that good parental care has evolved through the centuries. It is claimed that before the eighteenth century parents subjected their children to a strict, often severe, disciplinary regime; relations between parents and children were formal and distant, and parents were purportedly unmoved at the death of any of their children. Instead of childhood being regarded as a special time of life, children were considered to be merely adults in miniature, thus precluding any recognition of or allowance for their immaturity. According to this stance, childhood in the past was emphatically a time to be 'endured and not enjoyed'. This interpretation has not received wholesale approval among historians, but the view that child rearing has progressively improved as the centuries passed by – 'modernisation theory', as it may be called – has proved to be a most influential thesis. It has been used as the starting-point for twentieth-century theories of child development, and to support the view that the maternal instinct is a myth. Since bad maternal care was the norm in the past, so the argument goes, mothers today should not feel guilty if they are inept at mothering.

Interest in the history of childhood as a subject worthy of historical investigations began with the publication of Philippe Ariès' ambitious survey *L'Enfant et la vie familiale dans l'ancien regime*, translated into English in 1962 as *Centuries of Childhood*. However, it was not till the mid-1970s that research on the topic burgeoned. Many of the books on childhood which began to appear in that decade reflect this sudden and massive upsurge of interest, being characterised more by the construction of grandiose theory, and premature attempts at synthesis, than by attention to the requirements of scholarship. Ariès argued that there was no concept of childhood before about the seventeenth century: as soon as children could leave the care of the nursery, they entered the adult world. He thus seemed to demonstrate a world of thought and culture quite unlike that of today, and later scholars employed his argument to depict a world in which children were not only adjudged to be little adults, but one in which they were frequently subject to neglect and cruelty.

Many of the premises of these historians have now been shown to be ill-founded. The cherished belief in the prevalence of the extended family system, used to explain the ease with which children mixed with the adult world, has been demolished. English households in the past generally consisted of parents, children and servants, and rarely included grandparents and adult siblings. Neither were they large: the mean household size for the seventeenth century was 4·18, for the eighteenth 4·57, and for the nineteenth 4·21, demonstrating a remarkable constancy through these centuries. The widespread conviction that people married very young in the past, even in their early teens, has also been exposed as a myth. Demographers have conclusively shown that the average age of first marriage was commonly in the late twenties for men, and the mid-twenties for woman. It was perhaps a few years earlier for the upper classes.

It has been argued, too, that parents were often indifferent to the death of their offspring because so many children died. They have been regarded as either so familiar with childhood death that they had become resigned to the situation, or as having taken steps to protect themselves by refusing to become too emotionally in- volved with their children. In fact, the evidence suggests that the childhood mortality rate was not constant in the past. It rose during the period 1650 – 1750, when it reached 265 deaths per 1000, and peaked in the nineteenth century at 288 deaths per 1000. One child out of every four born would die before the age of nine, an undoubtedly high rate but one which is lower than that of many 'third world' countries today. What is more important, though, is that three out of four children would live. This makes it unlikely that parents, even if they did consciously work out the life-expectancy of their infants and adapted their emotional reac- tion accordingly, would focus on the death rate rather than the survival rate of children.

There has recently been a volte-face in the historiography of family life. Historians, rather than insisting on the differences between modern and past techniques of parenting, emphasize instead the continuities in modes of parental care. Most parents, we are now told, did indeed love and care for their offspring to the best of their ability. Unfortunately, this change of direction places would-be historians of childhood in something of a quandary: if nothing has altered throughout the centuries then we have *no* history of childhood. At the very least, it raises the question of where do we go from here? How should the history of childhood be approached? The answer may be that we should not seize too eagerly upon theories of fundamental change in parental attitudes over time, but that we should cultivate a sense of proportion in our interpretation of change. In particular, we should keep in mind that there are some basic features of human experience which are not subject to change, and use this as a context within which to pursue our analysis of those dimensions of childhood which have altered. Change and continuity should be investigated simultaneously, the one concept informing the other. Instead of searching for the existence or absence of emotions such as love, grief, or anger, we should concede that these emotions will be present in all cultures and in all communities, and seek instead for the varied ways in which they were perceived and expressed in particular societies. At the same time, however, we should beware of being blinkered by the concept of continuity: of allowing it to deaden our sensitivity to those slow and often subtle shifts in social, economic and cultural contexts which have modified the lived realities of parenthood and childhood through the centuries.

It seems unlikely that either side in the debate will agree, both sets of protagonists being convinced of the accuracy of their assertions. Rather than trying to discover some way of reconciling the two points of view, it may be more fruitful and instructive to begin our examination of the history of childhood afresh. This anthology is a collection of new source material on the home life of children from 1600 to 1900. By utilising diaries, memoirs, autobiographies, letters and account books, it permits the exploration – as far as is possible – of what it was like to be a child and a parent in past times. It deals with attitudes to and experience of childbirth, the physical care of children in sickness and in health, the world of childhood pastimes, the regulation and socialisation of children and the sometimes stormy relationship between parents and children as the latter approached adulthood. The evidence presented supports the interpretation that most parents in the classes and countries represented here were acutely aware of and concerned for their children. They tended them when sick, lamented their deaths, fretted over the appropriate way to deal with disciplinary problems, pondered how to ensure for them the best possible education, and worried about their future. The extracts highlight the differences in the upbringing of sons and daughters, differences which appear to intensify in the nineteenth century as girls were more and more secluded in the home. They also unveil the attention which fathers paid to their children and the active part they took in looking after them.

The anthology is above all a series of signposts, making it possible for diverse facets of the history of childhood to be scrutinised. Scholars of the history of childhood to date have mainly concentrated on those aspects of the upbringing of children which are considered to be of importance today, rather than studying what past generations of parents held to be vital in the rearing of children. It is time to ask new questions. The quotations enable us to analyse hitherto neglected themes: for example, the selections in Chapter Three allow us to enter into a world of pain and suffering in the realm of childhood illness and death, and to learn something of the remedies used to treat childhood ailments; those in Chapter Six make us aware of the intensity of religious preparation for a great many children in previous centuries. Furthermore, because of the nature of the sources quoted from in this selection, it is possible to appreciate these subjects from the perspective of the parents and children themselves.

Anthologies are, however, problematic source books. The compiler can convey a sense of what has been written but not of the silences in the documents. Quotations have generally to be of a reasonable length; otherwise the book becomes too piecemeal. As a result the short sentences of half articulated thoughts, asides, and brief allusions are invariably excluded. The process of selection risks becoming a carving up of history, wrenching evidence from its context and dislocating the framework required to give it substance, cohesion and meaning. Inevitably, the quotations are abstracted from their cultural and material world. Moreover, even if the compiler is satisfied that the extracts given are representative of the documents available, he or she cannot surmount the biases inherent in the evidence itself. The diaries, account and commonplace books, and letters upon which this anthology is based are drawn from the middling and upwards strata of English, Scottish, and American society. This is not a source book for the 'lower orders'. Due to the painstaking detective work of John Burnett and David Vincent in their quest for working-class autobiographies of the nineteenth century, it would be possible to include domestic material on the nineteenth-century working – class family. Unfortunately, such material is not readily available for the period 1600 – 1800 and thus its inclusion for the nineteenth century would lead to an imbalance in the anthology. The history of the working-class child through the centuries has yet to be written.

These caveats notwithstanding, the value of works such as this lies in the range and variety of material they reproduce. The selections contained in *A Lasting Relationship* are derived from my extensive reading in the primary sources. It has been exceptionally thorough, drawing the quotations from several hundred such texts covering a wide-ranging geographical area and time span. The documents cited from are not easily accessible: many of the extracts are from rare books, possessed by only a few libraries, or from manuscript collections deposited in county record offices up and down the country. These are difficult to obtain and the latter can be laborious to read. To unearth the amount of material presented in this anthology demands much painstaking research: a great deal of sifting and time-consuming reading has to be undertaken before an apt quotation comes to light. To the general public, students and academics without the time or the facilities to delve into such sources, this book furnishes them with the opportunity to appreciate parenting, as it was experienced, in the period covered.

The extracts introduce the general reader to the fascinating world of parenting from 1600 to 1900, providing an insight into many aspects of parental care and child life. They also provide the specialist with new evidence to incorporate into a synthesis, and supply new points to ponder. The sources used are highly personal, vividly bringing to life the experience of many generations of parents as they groped their way towards an understanding of the children they had brought into the world, and struggled both to fit and equip them for society. The selections are illuminating, at times surprising, occasionally harrowing and always absorbing. All of us have passed through the stage of childhood, and many of us go on to become parents. *A Lasting Relationship* highlights the uniqueness of the parent-child relationship and provides an enduring testimony to the strength of the parent-child bond.

How To Use This Book

The material is presented chronologically within each section. Married daughters in the seventeenth and eighteenth centuries were commonly referred to by their husband's name, thus 'my daughter Christopher' signifies the wife of Mr Christophers. The spelling has been altered to conform to present day usage and punctuation has been amended where this has been necessary to clarify the sense of the extract. Unfamiliar words, in those cases in which it has been possible to trace them, will be found in the Glossary.

Each quotation is headed by one name in bold script. This refers to the Sources where an entry will be found under this name, together with a few details of the family concerned. These details are taken from the *Dictionary of National Biography*, *Dictionary of American Biography*, from the bibliographies on diaries compiled by William Matthews or from the published edition of the diary. The source of each extract is also identified. The page or folio numbers of each extract are given at the end of every quotation. There is a personal name index at the end of the volume.

Introduction

The process of reproduction, if not completely shrouded in mystery, was not well understood in past times. Up till about 1700 it was accepted that there was no difference between the genitalia of the sexes – except that women's were internal – and that both men and women had to produce a seed if conception were to take place. Those seeds, it was held, could be emitted only during orgasm. With the discovery of ova and spermatozoa in the late seventeenth century the two seeds theory was gradually superseded by the ovum theory in which the egg was seen as inert, shaken into life by the sperm. Women, therefore, were assigned a more passive role in the reproductive process than hitherto, this belief paving the way for the concept of female sexuality – or lack of it – prevalent in the nineteenth century.

Accurate diagnosis of pregnancy was difficult in the seventeenth century (Edward Conway, p. 23). The function of menstrual blood was not appreciated and thus the cessation of menstruation was not regarded as particularly important. This altered during by the eighteenth century when the signs of pregnancy relied upon were similar to those used today. There was also a great deal of uncertainty about the length of gestation. The egg was thought to contain a fully formed infant and so conception and gestation were a matter of enlargement and not creation. Pregnancy up to about 1750 was considered to be comparable to a disease and expectant women were treated accordingly, for example by being let blood. Medical opinion was divided over the suitability of this procedure but as the extracts given here demonstrate, some women at least had faith in the efficacy of the method (Frances Boscawen, p. 25).

Childbirth itself was not an event that many anticipated with confidence. Pregnancy for some women was uncomfortable and many became increasingly frightened as the onset of their labour drew near (Susan Magoffin, p. 26, and Mary Walker, p. 40). Even if the delivery was problem-free, there were still hazards from infection, haemorrhaging and eclampsia to negotiate, and before the introduction of chloroform and ether in the mid-nineteenth century (Fanny Longfellow, p. 40, and Henrietta Stanley, p. 40), there were no effective methods of pain relief. The most recent estimates we have of the maternal mortality rate suggest that it varied from about 10 per thousand in the first half of the seventeenth century, rising sharply to about 16 per thousand in the later seventeenth century, falling thereafter to about 8 per thousand in the later eighteenth century and then to between 5 and 6 per thousand in the early nineteenth century. This may seem lower than might have been expected, but it did affect a large number of women, and childbirth was a leading cause of death among women of child-bearing age. To women and their husbands the possibility of dying in childbirth seemed very real. Arrangements for an approaching confinement thus included not only organizing a midwife, a nurse and baby clothes, but also a period of mental preparation for the ordeal which lay ahead (Mary Timms, p. 29). Some expectant mothers, for example Elizabeth Joceline, (p. 27), and Elizabeth Stirling (p.29), envisaging the worst, made provision for the care of their child if they did not survive the birth.

Up till about 1800, childbirth was very much a female affair, with the proceedings enveloped in the aura of ritual. Although male midwives and doctors were used in the seventeenth century, they were called upon to assist during difficult labours. The midwife and the doctor in this period thus had different roles – the midwife to deliver a live child and the doctor, almost invariably, a dead one. Husbands for the most part were not present, though they were usually not far away; indeed, as Endymion Porter's letter to his wife shows (p. 27), they were expected to be near at hand. Women were delivered at home, normally with a number of female friends and neighbours in attendance. A variety of birthing positions was employed, including using a birthing stool or accoucheur's chair (Samuel Sewall, p.33) but from about 1700 onwards bed delivery became increasingly common. A room was made ready for the lying-in by excluding fresh air and light, and a spiced water gruel laced with alcohol known as caudle was prepared. After the birth, the woman was expected to spend two weeks in bed and a further two weeks in the house before resuming her normal work and social life. Throughout the eighteenth century these preparations were going out of fashion (Francis Place, p.36) and childbirth was no longer likened to a serious illness.

Midwives may have been criticized, by John Locke (p. 33) for instance, for meddling unnecessarily in the birthing process. However, provided the confinement was normal – as about 94 per cent of all births were – their skills were adequate. Grave problems arose, though, if the foetus was obstructed. Until the invention of forceps (the discovery was published in 1733) there was no way of delivering an obstructed child alive. Instruments were used to remove a dead infant and so save the mother. It was difficult to ascertain foetal death and this, coupled with the knowledge that bringing in the doctor would almost inevitably mean the death of the child, ensured a delay in sending for help, a delay which often proved fatal to the mother as well, as in the case of Elizabeth Tufton (p. 32). No successful caesarean section was performed on a living woman in England till 1793, and the operation was not really safe till the 1830s, following the discovery of anaesthetics, developments in surgical techniques and the introduction of antiseptic principles. The innovation of forceps brought about an increased participation of men in childbirth, and since men possessed more knowledge and skill than the midwife concerning difficult deliveries, their attendance at normal confinements became more and more common.

It has been argued by some that children in the past were not welcomed into the world. As the material presented here shows they were, on the contrary, received into the world with relief, with joy and with pleasure. It is undoubtedly true that sons were very much desired, and in families in which daughter after daughter arrived the pressure on the wife to produce a son could be immense (Frances Hatton, p. 44). For the landed classes the desire for male heirs had an extra dimension of urgency since the number of families who produced no male heir rose to 52 per cent by 1750. However, it would be an exaggeration to argue that daughters were not welcomed and, moreover, a family full of sons was considered to be as much a disaster as one with no sons at all. Occasionally mothers (Elizabeth Fry, p. 45, and Elizabeth Prentiss, p. 45) experienced post-natal depression, though from the accounts given here, it seems to have been mild.

The last section of this chapter reveals that many parents, especially mothers, did not want too large a family. There were various contraceptive measures at their disposal: sponges, sheaths made from animal intestines, and coitus interuptus. None of these methods were very efficient, and all too often, women found themselves carrying a child they would have preferred to have been without. As the quotes from the Countess of Wemyss (p. 48) and Henrietta Stanley (p. 49) reveal, abortion was resorted to, often successfully.

Pregnancy

England, 1608 *Anne, Countess of Arundel, writes to Gilbert **Talbot** apologising for his daughter Alethea who, at almost four months pregnant, is too ill to visit him.*

Indeed I assure your Lordship she is not fit to travel, as I have writ to my lady and withall she hath an uncertain disposition to a fever these divers days which I forbear to write to her Ladyship so causing her fear, but think fit to let your Lordship understand how it is. Yet doubt I not, with God's grace, but she will do well with rest and quiet for all children are not bred alike.

To Mary Talbot.

My good daughter and yours is not so well as I hoped to have written unto you of, for when I last writ in haste to my honourable good brother my daughter had been less well some small time than usual. Of late she hath been but, good sister, going out to take a little air. Yesterday after her long sickly keeping-in, she grew so much distempered this last night as she could not stir out of her bed all day but she is something better this night. But I do now leave hoping of any continuance of ease till God send her quick with child which I think will be about some three weeks or a month. I beseech our Lord send her much comfort of her children for she breeds them very painfully. [*MS3205, ff. 139, 141*]

England, 1652 *Alice **Thornton** recollects her physical and mental health during pregnancy.*

With her first child.

About seven weeks after I married it pleased God to give me the blessing of conception. The first quarter I was exceeding sickly in breeding, till I was with quick child; after which I was very strong and healthy, I bless God, only much hotter than formerly, as is usual in such cases from a natural cause, insomuch that my nose bled much when I was about half gone, by reason of the increase in heat. [*p. 84*]

1665.

It pleased God to give me a new hopes of comfort of bearing Mr Thornton another child, although these are accompanied with thorny cares and troubles, and more to me than others. But yet I was continued in much health and strength, after I had given suck to Robin, all along while I was with child, and till about a fortnight before my delivery, when my travail began upon me, and then the pangs of child-bearing, often remembering me of that sad estate I was to pass, and dangerous perils my soul was to find, even by the gates of death. [*pp. 144–5*]

Edward **Conway** *writes to his brother about his wife Anne.*   *England, 1658*

When I wrote you last what the sad condition my wife was in, I held it impossible the next letter would not impart the worst news; she was also resigned. It is no wonder I should be mistaken in providence, who am so perfectly ignorant of the truth of that which I am about to write, though it appears evident to sense. However, I hold myself to thank God that we have yet ground to hope she may do well, and that the violent extremity she was then in, tended not to the concluding of her own life, but to the giving life to another. We have had thoughts oftentimes in my wife's sickness, perhaps she may be breeding; but the excessive increase of her distemper, with many other reasons, so interrupted it, that they served only to torment. At last seeking but sincerely her satisfaction, we had recourse to the best doctors and midwives to be resolved, but they have plunged us into the greatest uncertainty; for they assured us with much confidence that, according to their art, she is not so. On the other side, my wife finding herself quick, and with such a motion as they say is not compatible with any disease – for I myself and others have felt it, just like a fit of the ague, and besides many outward signs. They have directed remedies which could nothing prove, no not so much as against melancholy thoughts. But it is concluded on all hands, that if she be with child, she must expect as hard labour as any woman in the world ever had; the shape of her body, as well as the incidents of this sickness, necessitate caution. She hears that my Lord Chichester's former Lady had got an eagle's stone esteemed of great virtue in hard labour, and it's her wish [to have it]. Few people be aware I write to you for it: therefore possibly without telling the person, they shall not choose but to trust you with it, if they are not induced to part with it. Mr Hill saw the stone, and hath another: but she prefers it, if it may be had. I will willingly be at the charge of an express messenger rather than not get it with all care and speed. We keep this as private as it is possible, till we have more assurance, that we may not be made a town-talk, and I hope you will do so too. My thoughts were long since sealed against any impetuous desires after children, and my mind disposed to that which was more diffusive than gathering together an estate for an heir, and this will not alter me. [*pp. 152–3*]

Their son, Heneage, was born four months later.

England, 1678   Frances **Hatton** *writes to her husband Christopher as she awaits the birth of their child.*

20 April.

My last letter [*31 March*] I write you word that I had apprehension that my labour was beginning which Mrs Allen assured me it would prove, so my pains continued till seven o'clock at night but afterwards went off. I have never been well since. I hope you will hear suddenly I am well brought abed. Mrs Allen believes that I have a very great child but I am apt to think I have two I am so exceeding big.

21 April.

Every hour in expectation of my labour . . . my condition ties me to my bed and chamber above this three weeks. Mrs Allen will not let me stir out of it I am so extreme big. [*Hatton (b), add, MSS 29571, ff. 459, 463*]

Their daughter was born on 14 May and Frances survived the birth.

Scotland, 1695   Margaret, Countess of Wemyss, to her pregnant daughter Anne. The letters are in the **Melville** collection.

I long to hear if you be grown big yet and if you keep your meat well. I hope you will grow stronger and be better and better with every child till all the twenty be born that you used to wish for . [*GD26/13/401/21*]

I am very sorry you are still so much troubled with the colic. I fear you eat too much fruit or heavy meats both which are very ill for you. I never found any thing to me so much good as a gentle glister which they never stand to give after one is with quick child. You never told me if you used to vomit your meat. I entreat you strive against it for it destroys your stomach and gives you perpetual pains. [*GD26/13/401/22*]

My sister writes me word that you look very well. I pray God it may continue. There is nothing so good for you and the child both as to be merry, so I entreat you let not any thing that falls out disquiet and vex you for it never alters the matter that troubles us and does much displease and dishonour God. [*GD26/13/401/23*]

I am sorry to hear you are so oft troubled with pains but I trust in God it will make your labour the more easy. [*GD26/13/401/28*]

Anne successfully gave birth to a son.

*From William **Byrd**'s diary.* *America, 1709*

We had nothing extraordinary happen in our journey but only that my wife had a pain in her belly which made me afraid she would miscarry. However, we made shift to get her home and after some rest she recovered.

Two weeks later.

I was out of humour at my wife's climbing over the pales of the garden, now she is with child. [*Byrd (a), pp. 31, 38*]

*Frances **Boscawen**, pregnant with her third child, writes to her* *England, 1747*
husband.

The near approach of my labour terrifies me and sinks my spirits to a degree that you would be sorry to be witness of. Indeed, were you here, if would not be thus. I frequently get no sleep of nights, and not through indulging in a morning, for I do not breakfast in bed, nor continue there longer than nine – seldom so long. I was obliged to send for Sandys, and he ordered me to be blooded, which I was, and on sight of the blood he said I had very great occasion for it. [*pp. 40–1*]

*Molly **Tilghman** writes to her friend Polly Pearce about her sister* *America, 1785*
Henrietta, who is four months pregnant.

O this Henny of ours is the saddest creature you can conceive. If she drags her bloated self to the Wind Mill, she thinks so prodigious an exertion entitles her to groan and complain the whole evening, till nine o'clock when she departs, and is seen no more till the next morning. Now is it not a melancholy thing to see a young person give themselves up to such horrid ways, because they are married? I declare it robs me of all patience. [*pp. 130–1*]

*Edward **Fitzgerald** writes to his mother about his wife Pamela, who is* *England, 1794*
five months pregnant.

Pam is as well as possible, better than ever; the only inconvenience she finds is great fullness, for which she was bled this morning and it has done her a great deal of good. [*p. 72*]

*Sydney **Smith** writes to Francis Jefferey about his wife.* *England, 1805*

I have been expecting that she would be brought to bed every night for the last eight days, but to the amazement of the obstetric world she is still as pregnant as the Trojan Horse. [*vol. 1. p.101*]

England, 1815 *Caroline* **Capel***, carrying her thirteenth child, writes to her mother.*

I am perfectly well, and have no thought *of it* before the end of *June* which is later than I mentioned to Jane by a month. [*p. 94*]

It will not I am certain take place sooner than the first week in July – and you know how apt I am to go even beyond the last period that has been fixed for me on these occasions. [*p. 107*]

The child was born on 16 July.

America, 1846 *Susan* **Magoffin** *records in her diary.*

In a few short months I should have been a happy mother and made the heart of a father glad, but the ruling hand of a mighty providence has interposed and by an abortion deprived us of the hope of mortals. [*p. 67*]

The next year she is pregnant again.

I do think a woman em beraso has a hard time of it, some sickness all the time, heart-burn, head-ache, cramp, etcetera. After all this thing of marrying is not what it is cracked up to be. [*p. 245*]

England, 1858 *Queen* **Victoria** *to her daughter Vicky, who is expecting her first child.*

I also send you some soothing tincture (which Mr Saunders prescribed) which will do you great good; put a teaspoonful of it into water, and hold it in your mouth, when you have pain and it will allay it. I suffered also this way. Mr Saunders is going to Germany and is most anxious to see you, and he is so sensible and clever and always managed your teeth so well – (and the German dentists are not famous and the German teeth are so bad) you ought to see him, for teeth suffer much from your condition, some people lose one every child they have, and you will require to have them carefully looked at. [*Victoria (a), p. 119*]

Six months later.

I sent you today a bottle of camphor lozenges which I always have standing on my night table near my bed, wherever I go – since they were first recommended to me by Sir C. Locock when I was so restless before you were born, and I found them very soothing. They are perfectly simple and innocent; he said he found them the answer with ladies – and so have I; taking one in your mouth when you can't sleep does real good, at all times. [*Victoria (a), p. 152*]

Preparations for Childbirth

*Bridget **Willoughby** writes to her pregnant daughter, Elizabeth Gell.*   *England, 1614*

I have sent you a chair which I ordinarily used and liked myself.
[D258 box 41/31v]

*Elizabeth Raleigh writes to her brother Nicholas **Carew**.*   *England, c.1620*

I pray thank my sister for the nurse. I like the woman very well but
that she hath but one breast and of three children she hath but one
living, all them she nursed herself as she sayeth. I pray say that I
was in certainty with another before, and no other dislike: but
indeed I fear the haughtiness of this woman. [*add. MSS 29598, f.9*]

*Endymion **Porter** writes to his wife shortly before the birth of their*   *England, 1620*
child.

My dear Olive, – God of heaven bless thee and send thee a very
safe delivery; my lord will by no means consent that I should come
unto you, which grieves me extremely, and for God's sake believe
it, there never happened a thing that doth so much trouble me.
Good sweetheart, show thy love to me now in excusing to thyself
the wrong I do thee to thyself, in not leaving the commands of a
master to see so good a wife, at such a time. [*p. 22*]

*Elizabeth **Joceline**, pregnant with her first child, writes to her husband.*   *England, 1622*

Mine own dear love, – I no sooner conceived an hope that I should
be made a mother by thee, but with it entered the consideration of
a mother's duty, and shortly after followed the apprehension of
danger that might prevent me from executing that care I so
exceedingly desired, I mean in religious training our child. And in
truth death appearing in this shape, was doubly terrible unto me.
First, in respect of the painfulness of that kind of death, and next
of the loss my little one should have in wanting me. [*Preface*]

*Elizabeth composed a book instructing how she wished her child to be
brought up if she died in childbirth (see Chapter Five, p.174). Her sense
of foreboding proved correct and she died nine days after the birth of
her daughter, probably from puerperal fever.*

*Elizabeth **Hatton** writes to her son Christopher about his wife.*   *England, c.1668*

If my guess be true tell her if she will make me a grandmother I
have a little shirt and head clothes and biggin which I have kept
by me that was the first that my mother wore and that I wore, and I

am very sure that you wore and have ever since laid it up carefully for your wife. [*Hatton (b), add. MSS 29571, f. 54*]

England, 1699   *Penelope* **Mordaunt** *writes to husband. (Pen is their young daughter.)*

I grow very uneasy nowadays as well as night which has made me this day send to Mrs Barnes for blankets and things for the child, lest I should be caught; and if I be Pen must be nurse for I have none yet; the woman I write to you about has not given me her answer yet. I like her the best . . . Mr and Mrs Morres dined with me yesterday . . . the nurse she hath is young and it is her first child which I do not like. If I can mend my self, I am to see her this week; she lives with an aunt that nurses children so she may have more experience upon that account. [*CR1368, vol. 1, f. 21*]

England, 1700   *Lady* **Massingberd** *writes to her daughter.*

Child, – You now draw near your time for child bed . . . I hope you will do very well, yet none can foresee how it may please the Lord to deal with you. The safe delivery in childbirth is God's own work. Pray spare as much time as you can for meditation and prayer to acquaint your self with God . . . I will come to you immediately if you send for me and will stay with you as long as you please. [*MS B/1*]

England, 1704   *Nicholas* **Blundell** *records in his diary.*

23 January.

My wife sent to Doctor Fabius, he said she was with child. [*(a) vol. 1, p.50*]

1 July.

I went to Liverpool, brought home a cradle etcetera, which was bought at Chester fair, [*(a) vol. 1, p.60*]

7 July.

I opened a box of baby clothes which was sent to my wife by my Lady Webb. [*(a) vol. 1, p.61*]

23 July.

Margaret Bullen who is to be nurse to my first child proposed me to bet one quarter's wages if she was delivered of a child within thirty weeks after she had declared to my wife that she was with child and promised to declare that she was with child if it should prove so whilst she was a Nurse. [*(a) vol. 1, p. 62*]

A daughter was born on 22 September.

*Thomas **Jefferson** writes to his daughter Mary, who is expecting her second child.*   *America, 1779*

Not knowing the time destined for your expected indisposition, I am anxious on your account. You are prepared to meet it with courage, I hope. Some female friend of your mamma's (I forgot whom) used to say it was no more than a jog of the elbow. The material thing is to have scientific aid in readiness, that if any thing uncommon takes place it may be redressed on the spot, and not be made serious by delay. It is a case which least of all will wait for doctors to be sent for; therefore with this single precaution nothing is ever to be feared. [*p. 199*]

Mary died two months after the birth of this child; her mother too had died in childbirth.

*Elizabeth **Stirling** writes to her husband.*   *Scotland, 1816*

My dearest husband, – As it may perhaps be the unerring will of God that your wife should die in giving birth to her child, I feel it an incumbent duty to address a few lines to you on the most important subject. The care of the soul of our infant and your own eternal interests . . . We all need pardon which God is willing to extend to us for his blessed son, we all need holiness of heart and life which is also received through Him . . . I beseech you my dearest husband to impress these saving truths *early* on the soul of our child. Let the word of God be the daily study of both. [*T-SK/13/7*]

*Mary **Timms** returned to her parental home for the birth of her first child and feared she would never see her marital home again.*   *England, 1833*

Sometimes I think I shall never again enter this house, death may have marked me for his prey . . . The hour of trial is approaching. Nature shrinks. O for grace – for patience – for resignation to the will of my heavenly Father, that I may be enabled to bear all that my God sees fit to lay upon me. Thousands have been supported; may the strength of the Lord be perfected in my weakness; and if my life be spared, I trust it will be to glorify him. [*pp. 84–5*]

She was safely delivered of a daughter.

Scotland, 1833   *Helenora* **Maxwell** *receives the following instructions from her mother.*

I have neither an expectation nor an idea my beloved child, that you will require any particular doctor or aid in the performance of Nature's job but still I deem it prudent and desirable to build your straw nest, within reach of a wise man and of those who know your constitution, Posy, and I do finally hope and trust that you and your dearie will cheerfully consent to the proposal of little Billy being born in Childs Becky. My plan is that we should take a quiet house in the near neigbourhood of no. 12 Shandwich Place, to enter to it about the 23rd or 24th February where Mammy will join you from hence.

You ought now to commence bathing your nipples night and morning regularly with spirits and water to harden the skin and so prevent them becoming tender or sore when your precious baby draws nourishment from the natural fountain of existence.

Now read and ponder over the enclosed and consult with your better half and weigh all the moral and intrinsic merits of Mrs Maxwell whose personal appearance, is that of a clean-looking, healthy, sensible, active, middle-sized female between thirty and forty not the least pretty or in any way handsome or even good looking and very much like what a child's maid should be . . . with respect to her non-infantine experience I understand that she had had repeatedly the care of her new-born nephews and nieces and as Mrs Campbell of Sagemouth's nurse is engaged for six weeks she can instruct both theory and practically. [MS 7043/21]

England, 1858   *Queen* **Victoria** *commiserates with her pregnant daughter Vicky. (Fritz is Victoria's husband, and Bertie her brother.)*

I hope Fritz is duly shocked at your sufferings, for those very selfish men would not bear for a minute what we poor slaves have to endure. But don't dread the denouement; there is no need of it; and don't talk to ladies about it, as they will only alarm you, particularly abroad, where so much more fuss is made of a very natural and usual thing. [*Victoria (a), p. 141*]

I cannot bear to think Bertie is going to you and I can't – and when I look at the baby things, and feel I shall not be, where every other mother is – and I ought to be and can't – it makes me sick and almost frantic. Why in the world did you manage to choose a time when we could not be with you? [*Victoria (a), p. 144*]

Delivery

*Mary **Verney** writes to her husband Ralph, three weeks after the birth of her son.*

Our poor child was so extreme sick that every body thought it would have died, but now I praise God 'tis beyond everybody's expectation strangely recovered. I intend to send it down the beginning of the next week; for my self I am so very weak that until yesterday, since I was brought to bed, I have never been able to sit up an hour at a time; I am so tormented with pains in my head, that if I hold it down but half a quarter of an hour, it puts me into such sweats that I am not able to endure it. But yet I trust in God if this pain in my head were but gone, I should recover my strength apace, for the Dr makes me eat good broth. [(a) v 1 p. 360]

*Charles Cheyne writes to his brother-in-law relating his wife's safe delivery. (The letter is in the **Portland** collection.)*

On Sunday last the 18 of May she was well and safely brought to bed of a daughter; some signs of near labour began upon her about two of the clock in the morning, but no hard pains till between eleven and twelve. Those continued but with some cheerful intermissions, I praise God, till half an hour past three and were endured with a very great patience and courage; we were all surprised with the unexpected coming, but I am confident she went her full time, though it was short of the first reckoning about ten days. The child, is, I thank God, though little and weak born, now well and thriving, its weakness made us give it presently a sprinkling of Christianity under much confusion; she hath been I praise God ever since well. [PW1/84]

*Ralph **Josselin** describes in his diary his wife's confinement.*

January 12.

At night the midwife with us, my wife thinking she might use her, but, being sent for, my wife let her go, [so] that another that was in present need might be helpen, and it was a mercy to us so to dispose my wife's heart, her going tending to save a poor woman's life; but within half an hour, as soon as I had done family prayer, my wife had so sure a sign of her labour and speedy that put us all to a plunge. I sent two messengers after her and it was at least four hours before she came. Mr R. H.'s man fetched her, but she came time enough for us, God be praised. My wife was wonderfully afraid and amazed but help was speedily with her and in particular young Mrs Harlakenden, who put forth her self to the utmost to help her, and her presence was much to my wife.

January 13.

Her pains ceased, the labour very strange to her, which set her heart, but her eye was towards him who is the helper. My faith was up for her. She judged at the labour it would be a daughter contrary to all her former experience and thought; prayer was for her; we commended her to God and her warm bed early and all to their rests, none watching this night as formerly. Her sleep was comfort to her mixed with pain and fear which made her quake and tremble.

January 14.

And so increased on her by two of the clock in this morning that I called up the midwife, and nurse, got fires and all ready, and then her labour came on so strongly and speedily that the child was born. Only two or three women more got to her but God supplied all, young Mrs Harlakenden got up to us very speedily, and some others. My wife's labour was different from all former, exceeding sharp. She judged her midwife did not do her part, but God did all, and hath given us a new experience of his goodness. The child was dead when born [*stillborn*], I bless God who recovered it to life. We baptized it this day by the name of Mary, young Mrs Harlakenden holding it in my wife's place. God hath evened my number and made up the three which he took from me. My heart was very lightsome and joyful in the God of my mercies. [*p. 415*]

England, c.1670   *Elizabeth Tufton to Cicelea* **Hatton**, *informing her of the death of her sister Frances Drax in childbirth.*

On Monday my sister was pleased to send for me. I since am told that she had pains a Saturday, and Sunday, but Mrs Baker believed it was not her labour, and so made nothing of it. When I came a Monday morning I found her in great pain, which continued till night. Then her water broke, and the midwife said the child came wrong; I had prevailed with Mr Drax to send to Canterbury, for Doctor Peters, who is very famous for his skill, and he was in the house ready, if there were occasion, but we were desirous if possible to save the life of the child by not using forcible means till it needs must. But her pains continuing all Monday night, without any profit to her labour, and the midwife finding by some tokens that the child was dead, she desired Doctors Peters would make use of his skill, for it was past hers. My poor sister seemed content that he should, only desired him to put her to as little pain as he could, and seemed very little discouraged but prayed as she had done all along, that God would enable her; in the afternoon the Doctor began to make use of his means, and we prayed either in the same room, or the next to it, all the while he continued his endeavours till ten o'clock at night, and we were forced to give her cordials almost every minute. But, at last, no passage being made for her delivery, though the man protested he tried all the way he could imagine, though in vain, and she growing faint and light-headed, begged of the Doctor for Christ's sake, to let her die at rest. Her condition being desperate we got her to bed, where she continued all that night without any rest, her spirits being spent by the flood of those things that came from her, as well after the Doctor left handling her as before, and the child dead within her made her never lie still one moment. On Wednesday morning the Doctor having told me that all hopes of her life was gone, I desired the minister to advertise her of her end, which he discoursed to her in a very pious manner. She told him she was willing to die and hoped God would receive her . . . The day after she died she was opened, and the child lay right at the birth, but the Doctor said he had forced it to that place, but when she was opened her bones within, especially her back bone, was so bowed, as he said it was impossible to make passage so much for a limb of the child. [*Hatton (a), 4412*]

*Samuel **Sewall** writes in his diary about the birth of his first child.*   *America, 1677*

About two of the clock at night I waked and perceived my wife ill: asked her to call Mother. She said I should go to prayer, then she would tell me. Then I rose, lighted a candle at Father's fire, that had been raked up from Saturday night, kindled a fire in the chamber, and after five when our folks up, went and gave Mother warning. She came and bade me call the Midwife, Goodwife Weeden, which I did. But my wife's pains went away in a great measure after she was up; toward night came on again, and about a quarter of an hour after ten at night, April 2, Father and I sitting in the great Hall, heard the child cry, whereas we were afraid 'twould have been twelve before she would have been brought to bed. Went home with the Midwife about two o'clock, carrying her stool, whose parts were included in a bag. [*vol. 5, p. 40*]

*John Locke advises Henry **Fletcher** on the safe delivery of his wife.*   *Scotland, late 17th century*

When the time of birth draws near [let her?, MS torn] not be forward to put her self into labour, nor let her midwife to be too busy with her. Those for the most part are meddling but ignorant women, who think they must be doing something (that they may not appear useless and unskilful) though it be generally to the prejudice of the great-bellied woman who by the officiousness of the midwife being put upon labour before the child is full ripe for the birth, have their strength wasted before the time that they should bring forth and so Mother or Child or both perish under it. The natural birth is a work only of nature which only knows when the fruit of the womb is full ripe, and if it be let alone till that time, it drops as it were of it self; 'tis certain it comes easiest . . .

At the time of labour the room is not [to] be crowded with useless women. So many and no more as will be of use to the woman in labour are all [that] should be there. All the rest hurt, hinder one another and spoil the air of the room which is the great refreshment of the woman in labour. As the open air is of great use to a breeding woman so [is] nothing so dangerous to her as soon as she is delivered and therefore should be immediately had to bed, nay the best way is to be delivered in bed but the fashions of country are not easy to be altered. [*MS17851/132*]

England, 1701 Thomas **Boston** *describes the birth of his daughter.*

On the 24 May, about two or three o'clock in the morning, my wife after long and sore labour brought forth her first child, a daughter, called Katharine; having, at the holy and just pleasure of the sovereign Former of all things, a double hare-lip whereby she was rendered incapable of sucking. My wife having a great terror of the pains of child-bearing had aforehand laid her accounts with death, as she always I think did on that occasion thereafter, having at the same sovereign pleasure an uncommon share of these pains, the remembrance whereof to this day makes my heart to shrink. When I, understanding her to be delivered and preserved, was coming towards the chamber to see her, Mrs Dauson above mentioned meeting me, intimated to me the case of the child; with which my heart was struck, like a bird shot and falling from a tree. Howbeit I bore it gravely; and my afflicted wife carried the trial very christianly and wisely, after her manner. Thus it pleased my God, to correct me for my sins; to balance my enjoyment; and to teach to acknowledge Him in the formation of children in the womb. The child being weak, was baptized by Mr Dauson the same day; and was for a long time watched in the night, through the summer. In that dear child's case, I had a singularly experience of tender love melted down in pity; as considering her teeth set on edge through the parent's eating of the sour grape. [*p. 137*]

Katharine died in late September of that year.

America, 1709 William **Byrd** *on his wife's second labour.*

My wife was much out of order and had frequent returns of her pains . . . In the evening I took a walk about the plantation and when I returned I found my wife very bad. I sent for Mrs Hamlin and my cousin Harrison about nine o'clock and I said my prayers heartily for my wife's safe delivery, and had good health, good thoughts, and good humour, thanks be to God Almighty. I went to bed about ten o'clock and left the women full of expectation with my wife.

About one o'clock this morning my wife was happily delivered of a son thanks be to God Almighty. [*Byrd (a), p. 79*]

*James **Boswell**, already father of two daughters, on the birth of his eldest son.*   Scotland, 1775

My wife having been seized with her pains in the night, I got up about three o'clock, and between four and five Dr Young came. He and I sat upstairs mostly till between three and four, when, after we had dined, her labour became violent. I was full of expectation, and meditated curiously on the thought that it was already certain of what sex the child was, but that I could not have the least guess on which side the probability was. Miss Preston attended my wife close. Lady Preston came several times to inquire, but did not go into the room. I did not feel so much anxiety about my wife now as on former occasions, being better used to an inlying. Yet the danger was as great now as ever. I was easier from the same deception which affects a soldier who has escaped several battles. She was very ill. Between seven and eight I went into the room. She was just delivered. I heard her say, 'God be thanked for whatever he sends.' I supposed that the child was a daughter. But she herself had not then seen it. Miss Preston said, 'Is it a daughter?' 'No', said Mrs Forrest the nursekeeper, 'It's a son.' [*vol. 10, p. 235*]

*William **Jones** writes of his feelings while his wife is in labour.*   England, 1782

My heart was anxious and uneasy, day and night, relative to that dearest of all human beings, my dearest Theodosia, who was then pregnant. The 6th of June arrived – and I may almost as well attempt to describe fully the miseries of the damned, as to express the horrible pain, the anguish with which I was racked during her labour. I am astonished, and shudder at the bare recollection of it. May it never be erased from my memory; but may it always engage me to treat her with grateful tenderness, and to consult her inclination on all occasions! [*Jones (2), pp. 90–91*]

At the birth of his second child, 1784.

My dearest, dearest Theodosia is now on the rack. I scarce know what my hands are doing, while I attempt to write. May Heaven preserve her, and, as much as possible, mitigate her sufferings! Her cries and groans do tear and rend my very soul. Now she has been for some time silent, – I was going to say – 'what a happy respite does my soul enjoy! – when, beyond my most sanguine expectations, Alice came down to inform me that all was happily over. [Jones (2), p.94]

England, 1794   *Francis* **Place** *recollects the birth of his children.*

On the 28 of April 1794 my wife had her second child, a girl whom we named after her Elizabeth. We had been hard at work all day and I had been out at business in the evening, my wife had been putting the room in order when she was taken in labour, and when I came home I found her in that state. At her first lying-in she was attended by a woman, but as we were not quite satisfied with her treatment, we resolved to have a man of some reputation, and one had been engaged, two guineas were laid by for him, and as good clothes had been provided for the child as any working man could reasonably desire. She was delivered at two o'clock in the morning. Our room was on the second floor, the landlady of the house was with my wife, and I was invited to sit in the room on the first floor. [p. 126]

On the 28 June 1798 my eldest son Francis was born. After the birth of our first child as has been related we employed a medical man in good practice, he had two guineas for his first attendance and a guinea for each of the succeeding two. This guinea was always carefully saved and immediately paid. As my wife was young, strong and healthy, as none of the absurdities of nursing and feeding were indulged in, as there were no curtains to the bed, no candle, nor heating and stimulating messes, we had no occasion for a regular nurse, some assistance was indispensable and this was easily procured. My wife remained in bed not more and seldom as much as two days, on the third day she got up to dinner and in a few days went about as usual, only refraining from any laborious employment. [p. 184]

America, 1795   *Elizabeth* **Drinker** *records in her diary the labour endured by her daughter, Sally Downing.*

April 5.

I came to Jacob Downing's after tea, found Sally complaining, she has pains, which probably, will not go off 'till worse comes on. We have sent Dr Shippen word that she is unwell. Sister has been out again this evening looking for a Nurse, but has not yet found one to our mind. Poor Sally is gone to bed, but I fear not to sleep, I am going to do the same in a back room with Eliza: rain this evening with thunder and lightning.

April 6.

There was a time, that if either of my beloved children were in the situation that my dear Sally is at present, I could not have found in my heart to have made a memorandum; is it that as we grow in years our feelings become blunted and callous? or does pain and experience cause resignation? 'tis now past eleven at night, my dear afflicted Child has just taken anodyne from Dr Shippen, she has been all this evening in afflictive pain though unprofitable. I came here yesterday afternoon, went to bed at eleven o'clock. Jacob called me up after two this morning when I had just fallen asleep, Sally being rather worse; before four o'clock Jacob went for Hannah Yerkes. After breakfast we sent for Dr Shippen, he felt her pulse, said he hoped she was in a good way – he dined with us and, as Sally did not wish his stay, he left us, saying he would return in the evening. She continued in pain at times, all day, was worse towards evening. Neighbour Waln, H. Yerkes and Sister with us – sent for the Doctor who soon came, towards night we perceived that all things were not right. I did not venture to question the Doctor, but poor Sally was not sparing in that particular. She suffered much to little purpose, when the anodyne was given, two opium pills, the Doctor went to lay down, when all was quiet for a short time, but poor Sally who instead of being composed grew worse. The Dr was called, when he came I quitted the room, knowing that matters must ere long come to a crisis. I was downstairs in back parlor by myself an hour and half as near as I can judge, when observing that my dear child ceased her lamentation and a bustle ensued – with a fluttering heart I went upstairs, in a state of suspense, not knowing if the child was born, or Sally in a fit, as I heard no crying of a child. It was mercifully born; the Doctor blowing in its mouth and slapping it, it came to and cried. The Doctor then told us, that a wrong presentation had taken place; which with poor Sally's usual difficulties called for his skill more particularly; by good management he brought on a footling labour, which though severe, was terminated by divine favour, I trust safely.

April 7.

Sally is this morning as well as can be, all things considered – the effects of the anodyne not gone off. Neighbour Waln, Hannah Yerkes and Dr Shippen left us after breakfast – no Nurse as yet obtained to our mind. The little one seems heart whole, though the blood is much settled in his legs, feet, etcetera, his feet almost as blue as indigo. Sally sleeps sweetly this afternoon, her cough very hard when she awoke, the child put to the breast this evening. He is, as the Nurses say, very handy at the business – Patty Mullen came this evening very opportunely, she nursed Sally with her two first children . . .

England, 1798   *Elizabeth* **Wynne** *on the birth of her children.*

Her first child.

I woke in great pain this morning, continued poorly all day, but minded it as little as possible. To my no small happiness and everybody's surprise I was brought to bed by seven o'clock in the evening of a boy, before Dr Savage had time to come, the nurse delivered me. A small child but a sweet boy. [*vol. 2, p. 203*]

On her second labour.

I was surprised and frightened at being taken ill in the middle of the night as I did not expect to be brought to bed till the end of the month and my nurse was not to come till the twentieth – I called up the women at four o'clock in the morning and sent immediately for Dr Tooky – it was all over a little after six. The *cook* was *headnurse* and dressed the child. It is a nice little girl but owing to her being born three weeks before her time is very delicate and small. [*vol. 3, p. 10*]

America, 1806   *Peggy* **Dow** *writes in her journal of her first confinement.*

The time arrived that I must pass through the trial, and my Lorenzo was at the doctor's. But those that attended on me would not suffer him to come into the room where I was – which gave him much pain. I did not know at that time how much he was hurt – but after my child was born which was on the 16th of September, between three and four o'clock, he was permitted to come in, and he had a white handkerchief on his hand and his face was as white as the handkerchief. [*p. 618*]

England, 1813   *Thomas* **Moore** *describes his wife's experience on the birth of their second daughter.*

After six o'clock this morning my Bessy produced a little girl about the size of a twopenny wax doll. Nothing could be more favourable than the whole proceeding, and the mamma is now eating buttered toast and drinking tea, as if nothing happened . . . I have been up all night and am too fagged to write more. [*vol. 1, p. 337*]

One week later.

On Sunday morning last, as I was at breakfast in my study, there came a tap at the room-door and in entered Bessy, with her hair in curl, and smiling as gaily as possible. It quite frightened me, for I never heard of any one coming downstairs so soon, but she was so cheerful about it, that I could hardly scold her, and I do not think she has in the least suffered for it. [*vol. 1, p. 342*]

Charlotte **Guest** *relates the ease with which she produced her numer-*   *England, 1833*
ous progeny, three weeks after the birth of her first child.

I have to thank God that my hour of trial is over, and that I am now fast recovering, for which mercy also I ought to be very grateful after having suffered about as little as was possible ... I had written home, and had got half way through a long letter at twelve o'clock, when I was taken ill. At two my dear child was born. I was soon pretty well. Merthyr had gone to the House soon after eleven, and did not return till past three. No one had told him of the little one till he reached the top of the stairs, when Mamma met him and told him that he had a little girl. He was quite overcome when he entered my room immediately after and he kissed me and our dear infant. [*pp. 31–2*]

On the birth of her eighth child, 1843.

Dear Ivor had strewed my room with the toys his father had bought for them all at Cardiff, and with the acquisition of which he was delighted. I let him stay a little while, then got him and my dear husband to go to luncheon, without however giving any hint that I was otherwise than quite well. However I went to bed as soon as they had left me, and in a very few minutes Merthyr came up again to see why I had not followed them down. I tranquillized him as well as I could and he again went out of the room, but only to be recalled almost immediately to see the eighth child to which, thank God, I had given birth with as little pain as I suppose it is possible to suffer on such occasions. She was born at a quarter past four p.m. being only three quarters of an hour from the moment of my having finished writing and dated my journal ... Merthyr sent for Mr White to see me when it was all over. I then lay quietly down and went to sleep, and slept most of the evening, which however did not prevent my afterwards having a very good night's rest. Now as regards myself and the child I have nothing else to say. I have been confined now upwards of a fortnight and hitherto have neither felt ache nor pain, nor any illness or inconvenience whatever. [*pp. 153–4*]

America, 1838   *Mary* **Walker** *on the onset of her first labour.*

Began to feel discouraged, felt as if I almost wished I had never been married. But there was no retreating; meet it I must . . . Soon I forgot my misery in the joy of possessing a proper child. [*p. 134*]

America, 1847   *Fanny* **Longfellow** *writes to her sister-in-law after the birth of her third child. Fanny was the first woman in America to give birth under the influence of ether. Ether had been used successfully to extract a tooth in September 1846 by William Morton in America.*

I am very sorry you all thought me so rash and naughty in trying the ether. Henry's [her husband] faith gave me courage, and I had heard such a thing had succeeded abroad, where the surgeons extend this great blessing much more boldly and universally than our timid doctors. Two other ladies, I know have since followed my example successfully, and I feel proud to be the pioneer to less suffering for poor, weak womankind. This is certainly the greatest blessing of this age, and I am glad to have lived at the time of its coming and in the country which gives it to the world. [*Longfellow (b), pp. 129–30*]

England, 1848   *Henrietta* **Stanley** *writes to her husband informing him of the innovation of chloroform. This had been introduced as an anaesthetic agent in obstetrics by James Simpson, in Edinburgh, November 1847.*

I went to see Emma Mainwaring yesterday who was full of her intention to be delivered without knowing it. She has been collecting information from many quarters and been encouraged by several medical men as well as by Mrs Middleton Biddulph who has practised it with the greatest success. Mrs Russell is another. I think in her case she *appeared* to suffer, and screamed, but had no recollection of anything afterwards and recovered particularly well – but in general people wake in about ten minutes after all is over in perfect ease and comfort.

Mr Dean and Mr Harrison of Chester who have both attended Emma in her confinements strongly advise her to try and I think she told me that Dr Locock either had made use of chloroform or had expressed approbation of it as a boon not to be rejected. She has large children and always suffers very much in her labours. [*pp. 151–2*]

In the event Emma decided not to use chloroform.

England, 1850   *Maria Josepha, Lady* **Stanley** *writes to her daughter-in-law, Henrietta. (Ally is the daughter of Lady Stanley.)*

You will have heard from Ally – but I must write to say how happy

I am though you can *guess* that without being told. I can hardly believe the full extent of what I have heard – not very long suffering, a live, fat, blue-eyed *beautiful* girl, as Ally says, as if a new born baby was ever beautiful, ugly little red things, but I *can* imagine she as well as Emmy would think it beautiful. Ally called it IT all through her letter – but luckily Albert said it was a girl, not that I cared nor they either, I daresay, *which* it was. Poor Albert how very happy he must have been, and it was so nice that he happened to be dining out, and so escaped the two hours of real labour, returning only just before the final, for Ally says it was not serious before nine o'clock and born at half past eleven. If you have heard all this and more you must excuse it, as it is so pleasant to relate and dwell upon it. [*p. 241*]

Rutherford **Hayes** *on the death of his sister after childbirth.*   *America, 1856*

It was not a sudden, unexpected blow. We have felt anxious about her for several months. On the 16th of June she gave birth to twins – both dead or nearly so when born. Fanny barely survived. Her fine constitution alone enabled her to rally after the severest and most exhausting trial which her experienced physicians had ever seen. She remained in a critical situation, sometimes apparently recovering and again sinking until her death on 16th July. [*vol. 1, p. 498*]

Queen **Victoria** *to her daughter Vicky, after the birth of Vicky's first*   *England, 1859* *child.*

I pitied you so! It is indeed too hard and dreadful what we have to go through and men ought to have an adoration for one, and indeed to do everything to make up, for what after all they alone are the cause of! I must say it is a bad arrangement, but we must calmly, patiently bear it, and feel that we can't help it and therefore we must forget it, and the more we retain our pure, modest feelings, the easier it is to get over it all afterwards. [*Victoria (a), pp. 165–6*]

One month after the birth.

Occasional lowness and tendency to cry you must expect. You of all people would be inclined to this; and I am quite agreeably surprised to hear from Sir James how little you suffered with this; for it is what every lady suffers with more or less and what I during my first two confinements, suffered dreadfully with. [*Victoria (a), p. 162*]

*Kate **Russell** describes her second confinement.*

I was suddenly taken ill at about 5.30 in the drawing room with the water breaking. I was carried upstairs at once and Amberley went for Miss Garrett. She came soon and we thought of moving to Little Fife House if Mr Burn would allow it; we only had it from March 5. Mama went to see if I could go in but when she returned the pains were too rapid and sharp for me to move. On finding it was a foot presentation Miss Garrett sent for Dr Priestley but he was out, so did not come. The first child was born about 7.15 and the other about quarter of an hour after, both foot presentations; the second never breathed but its heart beat for some time and Mama did all in her power to bring it to life and so did Miss Garrett but they did not succeed. I saw it one moment in Maude's arms but not again as I did not wish it at the time; but ever since I have been very sorry I did not see it and so grieved it did not live but at the time I felt I had one and did not at all realize I had lost anything. I hear it was the largest of the two and very dark and like Amberley – Lizzy dressed it in a nightgown and Mama had it sent down to Alderley unknown to me and buried in dear old Wee's grave. Mama did not tell me till some time after as she waited for me to say something and I never liked to mention the subject. I was very glad that I knew where it was. Lizzie was with me during my confinement and Mama and Amberley all the time. Maude also kept going in and out to get everything as of course nothing was ready and no nurse there; she was telegraphed for at once. Lizzie dressed the baby the first time. It was very small and thin and weighed 5½ pounds only; it is very dark, everyone says it is very pretty and very like Amberley. We settled to call it 'Rachel Lucretia' after Mrs Mott. Lady Russell was dining out when the news came to her and came at once to see the baby; she was very unhappy at one being dead. Miss Garrett, I heard afterwards, shocked them rather by not caring enough about the loss of one; she shocked me by saying she supposed Amberley did not mind as he was so Malthusian. He did not mind he told me. I hear it looked lovely when laid out. Mama sat up with me all the first night; and Lizzie too in the next room. I slept and felt very well. My nurse (Mrs Oakshott) came on the 3rd.

The next day.

I saw Papa and he met Miss Garrett in my room, he had been very angry at my having only her. I nursed the baby the first time. Lizzie had been drawing my breasts for some time as they were very full and much swollen and made me very uncomfortable. [*vol. 2, pp. 84–5*]

Reactions to the Birth of a Child

John Jemmat to Carew **Mildmay**.

I rejoice and praise God with you for this pledge of his love sent from heaven. The Lord hath given you the second great temporal blessing unto you that you had before, you cannot any way be answerable to the mind of the donor, but by giving it to him again: be not so overjoyed with the gift as to have your thoughts or affection in any measure drawn from the giver. Give it him by mental thankfulness, give it him by prayer, give it him by baptism, give it him by an humble resignation of it into the hands of his providence and casting of it upon him from the womb; you are not able to keep it your self, but he and his angels will; once more, give it him by careful education and fashioning it even from the tender years for the service of the temple . . . You shall prevent yourself much woe, and your poor child many a cross by a mindful performance of these things to the glory of that God, who by this blessing intends to animate and encourage you in his ways. [*Mildmay (1), D/DMS/C4/1*]

Hugh Smyth writes to Edward **Phelips**. *England, 1641*

I hope the news that my wife was this night delivered of our sixth daughter will settle my dear cousin's mind in that we shall now suddenly dispatch away her midwife: who hopes to be with her the end or very beginning of next week. If my issue had been masculine, I would have revenged on you for the journey I took this time twelve months to see your son, Thomas, receiving the superstitious sign of the cross. But now I'll forbear you until I have once more tried my skill for another boy. [*DDPH 224/33*]

Francis Thornbaugh writes to Oliver **St John**. *England, 1674*

I could not but signify unto you, my very great joy I received at the news of my sister's safe delivery, and that God will still continue good unto her in the restoring of her to her former strength is my earnest praise, Sir I wish you much comfort in your fair daughter. [*J/1469*]

Mary **Hatton** *to her brother Christopher after the birth of another daughter*. *England, 1676*

Though a son would have been more welcome I am confident, both to your Lordship and all your relations, yet I am very well assured you was very glad to have a daughter and my sister comes so quick that you have great reason to hope within a year to have a son which God grant you may. [*Hatton (b), add. MSS 29571, f. 341*]

England, 1678   *Charles* **Hatton** *informs his brother Christopher that he is the father of another girl.*

My sister Hatton is safely delivered but am not a little concerned that the number of your daughters should be increased. But thought I know your lordship hath great reason (as truly all that are of or love your family ought) to be troubled that you have not a son, yet I am certain you will be much satisfied to hear that my sister is very well and the child a lusty girl. [*Hatton (b), add. MSS 29571 f. 472*]

England, 1730   *John* **Byrom** *writes to his friend.*

If you had been brought to bed (your lady I mean) of a son, I suppose you would have mentioned it in your letter; but because it was a daughter, I suspect your taciturnity arises from that; whereas you ought to have communicated this to me as well as that, seeing that I rejoice in your female as your masculine felicities. [*vol. 34, p. 483*]

America, 1745   *Eliza* **Pinckney** *to her friend Miss Bartlett.*

Since my last Heaven has blessed us with a fine little boy, and would you think it? I could flatter myself so much as to believe I can discover all his Papa's virtues already dawning in him or would you imagine I could really be so fond a Mama so soon of a little babe of three months old, that I could go on to describe his fine black eyes with a thousand beauties more till I filled my paper and tired you. [*p. 109*]

Scotland, 1775   *James* **Boswell** *reacts with anxiety to the birth of his first son, Alexander.*

When I had seen the little man I said that I should now be so anxious that probably I should never again have an easy hour. I said to Dr Young with great seriousness, 'Doctor, Doctor, Let no man set his heart upon any thing in this world but land or heritable bonds; for he has no security that anything else will last as long as himself.' My anxiety subdued a flutter of joy which was in my breast. I wrote several letters to announce my son's birth. I indulged some imaginations that he might perhaps be a Great Man. [*vol. 10, pp. 235–6*]

Melesina **Trench** *recalls her delight at the birth of her first child.*   *England, 1787*

I had not long attained my nineteenth year, when I became a mother. The delight of that moment would counterbalance the miseries of years. When I looked in my boy's face, when I heard him breathe, when I felt the pressure of his little fingers, I understood the full force of Voltaire's declaration 'Le chef-d'oeuvre d'amour est le coeur d'une mère' ['Love's masterpiece is a mother's heart'] . . . My husband's delight in the birth of his son nearly equalled mine. My love for *him*, the father of my child, grew in strength, and I looked on myself as one of the happiest of women. [*p. 16*]

Elizabeth **Fry** *writing a month after the birth of her first child.*   *England, 1801*

I have hardly had time or strength, as yet, to describe the events I have lately passed through. I did not experience that joy which some women describe, when my husband first brought me my little babe, little darling! I hardly knew what I felt for it, but my body and spirits were so extremely weak, I could only just bear to look at those I loved. I felt the dear baby at first a quiet source of pleasure, but she early became a subject for my weakness and low spirits to dwell upon, so that I almost wept when she cried; but I hope, as bodily strength recovers, strength of mind will come with it. [*p. 92*]

Eight days later.

I have now pretty much recovered. I was at Meeting this morning; there appears great cause for my being thankful to have got through so great a trial, and to have a dear little living girl; but we are not always sensible of the blessings we enjoy. [*p. 93*]

On the birth of her second daughter, 1803.

My heart abounded with joy and gratitude, when my dear little girl was born, perfect and lovely. Words are not equal to express my feelings, for I was most mercifully dealt with, my soul was so quiet, and so much supported. [*p. 100*]

Ann **Grant** *writes to the Rev. Dr Hook.*   *Scotland, 1808*

A thousand thanks for your delightful intelligence, which would communicate to your friends a sensation of delight, only inferior to what you felt at the moment when you found yourself the father of a daughter: – a daughter I always insisted it would be, and therefore not only rejoiced in your joy, but triumphed in my own prescience. Now what, my dear sir, farther can I wish you, blest as you are in your family and connections, – rich in this additional blessing of the most endeared and tender kind, in the rising sunshine of worldy prosperity, and, more peculiarly, 'a cheerful heart, that tastes those gifts with joy'? I can only wish you a long continuance of them, and that the children whom God has given you may adopt your attachments, and share your emotions, with as much sensibility as mine do in those I feel. [*Grant (1) (b), vol. 1, p. 145*]

America, 1812   *Leverett **Saltonstall** writes to his father, Nathaniel.*

Honored Father, – It is with much happiness that I inform you that at five o'clock this morning we were blessed with a daughter, – a fine, healthy child, and that Mary is very comfortable. I need not explain to you the mingled emotions I feel in my new situation as a Father, which yet I can scarcely realize. Mary desires me to mention the name, which we think we have concluded on for our little one – Anna-Eliza or Elisabeth, the names of her two Grand-mothers. [*vol. 2, p. 510*]

England, 1815   *Georgiana **Capel** writes to her grandmother about her expectant mother, Caroline.*

Poor little Mama walks very well indeed and looks beautiful; we all hope she will have a boy because we have settled such a pretty name for him. [*p. 126*]

After the birth of her eighth sister.

The moment the child was born she kissed it and said 'Poor little thing I forgive you for being a Girl!' which is more than we do. [*p. 129*]

Caroline Capel to her mother, after this birth.

I am as well as the little *Girl*, who I am rather provoked is not a young *Hero* as you had predicted. However I suppose it is right as it is; and I am too happy to have it over. [*pp. 129–30*]

England, 1842   *Maria Josepha **Stanley** rejoices with her son.*

Your news was most welcome on every account – a girl is better than a boy as you have plenty of the latter and there is less trouble and expense in setting up the former forward in the world, let alone their being often greater comforts to parents, whereby I mean no reflection however. [*pp. 28–9*]

Elizabeth **Prentiss** *after the arrival of her first child.* *America, 1846*

What a world of new sensations and emotions come with the first child! I was quite unprepared for the rush of strange feelings – still more so for the saddening and chastening effect. Why should the world seem more than ever empty when one has just gained the treasure of a living and darling child? [*p. 102*]

To Miss Thurston, two months after the birth.

I dare say the idea of *Lizzy Payson* with a *baby* seems quite funny to you, as it does to many of the Portland girls; but I assure you it doesn't seem in the least funny to me, but as natural as life and I may add, as wonderful, almost. She is a nice little plump creature, with a fine head of dark hair which I take some comfort in brushing round a quill to make it curl, and a pair of intelligent eyes, either black or blue, nobody knows which. I find the care of her very wearing and have cried ever so many times from fatigue and anxiety, but now I am getting a little better and she pays me for all I do. She is a sweet, good little thing, her chief fault being a tendency to dissipation and sitting up late o'nights. The ladies of our church have made her a beautiful little wardrobe, fortunately for me. [*p. 102*]

Rutherford **Hayes** *on his first-born.* *America, 1853*

I hoped, and had a presentiment almost, that the little one would be a boy. How I love Lucy, the mother of my boy! Sweetheart and wife, she had been before, loved tenderly and strongly as such, but the new feeling is more 'home-felt', quiet, substantial and satisfying. For the 'lad' my feeling has yet to grow a great deal. I prize him and rejoiced to have him, and when I take him in my arms begin to feel a father's love and interest, hope and pride, enough to know what the feeling *will* be if not what it *is*. I think what is to be his future, his life. How strange a mystery this all is! This is to me the beginning of a new life. A happy one I believe. [*vol. 1, p. 456*]

Already the father of three sons, he received a telegram while fighting in the American Civil War, announcing the birth of a fourth.

Good! Very! I preferred a daughter, but in these times when women suffer so much I am not sure but we ought to rejoice that our girls are boys. [*vol. 2, p. 165*]

Enough is Enough

England, c.1632   Mary **Rich** *recalls her misgivings about her early fertility.*

When I was first married, and had my two children so fast, I feared much having so many, and was troubled when I found myself to be with child so soon; out of a proud conceit I had, that if I childed so thick it would spoil what my great vanity made me to fancy was tolerable (at least in my person); and out of a proud opinion too that I had, that if I had many to provide for they must be poor, because of my Lord's small estate; which my vanity made me not endure well to think of. And my husband too was, in some measure, guilty of the same fault; for though he was at as great a rate fond of his children he had as any father would be, yet when he had had two he would often say he feared he should have so many as would undo a younger brother. [*pp. 32–3*]

Mary lost her daughter in childhood and her son as a young adult; she had no more children.

England, 1667   Alice **Thornton**, *still not recovered after a long period of illness, is pregnant with her ninth child.*

And if it had been good in the eyes of my God I should much rather (because of that) not to have been in this condition. But it is not a Christian's part to choose anything of this nature, but what shall be the will of our Heavenly Father, be it never so contrary to our own desires. Therefore did I desire to submit in this dispensation, and depend upon his providence for the preservation of my life, Who had delivered me in all my extremities and afflictions. [*pp. 164–5*]

Scotland, c.1698   Margaret, Countess of Wemyss, to her daughter Anne. (The letter is in the **Melville** collection.)

I hear you have been taking a little physick, I hope it will do you good. I should have been sorry if you had so soon fallen with child before you recover some more strength. [*GD26/13/401/40*]

Scotland, 1778   James **Boswell** *writes about his wife Margaret after the birth of their fifth child. His wife had had an easier labour than during her last confinement.*

She however had suffered so severely that she told me she had now for the first time expressed a wish that she might have no more. I was satisfied to think she should not. [*vol. 13, p. 155*]

Margaret gave birth to their sixth child less than two years later.

*Molly **Tilghman** to her friend Polly Pearce. Henny (Henrietta) is her sister and Mrs McIlvaine her cousin.*

That reminds me of Henny, who I heard from last week, poor soul. She is decidedly *gone* to my great grief, and her own too. Only think of Mrs McIlvaine being the same way for her third time. It is really enough to distract her. [*p. 230*]

America, 1788

*Elizabeth **Drinker** writes about attending her daughter Sally during her sixth confinement. Sally is aged thirty-eight.*

She is in pain at times, forerunning pains of a lingering labour, a little low spirited . . . she told me with tears that this was her birth day, I endeavoured to talk her into better spirits, told her that, the time of her birth was over by some hours, she was now in her thirty-ninth year, and that this might possibly be the last trial of this sort, if she could suckle her baby for two years to come, as she had several times done heretofore. [*Drinker (b), p. 59*]

America, 1799

*Elizabeth **Wynne**, mother of five, confides to her diary.*

I have not been at all well for this week past, being most wretchedly sick and sleepy – c'est un mauvais signe! [*vol. 3, p. 155*]

Her sixth child was born eight months later.

England, 1805

*Mary **Walker**, mother of three children under the age of five, records.*

I find my children occupy much of the time; that if their maker could see fit to withhold from me any more till they require less of my time and attention, I think I should be reconciled to such allotment. [*p. 176*]

Her fourth child was born within two years.

America, 1842

*Edward **Stanley** writes to his wife, on hearing that she is pregnant for the tenth time.*

This your last misfortune is indeed most grievous and puts all others in the shade. What can you have been doing to account for so juvenile a proceeding, it comes very opportunely to disturb all your family arrangements and revives the nursery and Williams in full vigour. I only hope it is not the beginning of another flock for what to do with them I am sure I know not. I am afraid however it is too late to mend and you must make the best of it though bad is best.

England, 1847

Henrietta replies.

A hot bath, a tremendous walk and a great dose have succeeded but it is a warning.

Edward writes back.

I hope you are not going to do yourself any harm by your violent proceedings, for though it would be a great bore it is not worthwhile playing tricks to escape its consequences. If however you are none the worse the great result is all the better.

Henrietta responds.

I was sure you would feel the same horror I did at an increase of family but I am reassured for the future by the efficacy of the means. [*pp. 142–4*]

The means she employed were successful in the short term, though she did have another child in 1849.

England, 1859   *Queen **Victoria** writes to her daughter Vicky.*

You say 'how glad' Ada 'must be' at being again in that most charming situation, which you yourself frequently told me last year was so wretched. How can anyone, who has not been married above two years and three quarters, (like Ada) rejoice at being a third time in that condition? I positively think those ladies who are always enceinte quite disgusting; it is more like a rabbit or guinea-pig than anything else and really it is not very nice. There is Lady Kildare who has two a year one in January and one in December – and always is so, whenever one see her! And there is no end to the jokes about her. I know papa is shocked at that sort of thing. To be truly thankful for the blessing when one has a child and to be glad to have them leisurely (without which I can assure you, life is wretched I know this from the experience of the first four years of my marriage) and one becomes so worn out and one's nerves so miserable – I can understand (though I did not when I was younger). Let me repeat once more, dear, that it is very bad for any person to have them very fast – and that the poor children suffer for it, even more, not to speak of the ruin it is to the looks of a young woman – which she must not neglect for her husband's sake, particularly when she is a Princess and obliged to appear. [*Victoria (a), pp. 195–6*]

THAT NATURAL AND MOST NECESSARY EMPLOYMENT: CARING FOR AND BRINGING UP CHILDREN

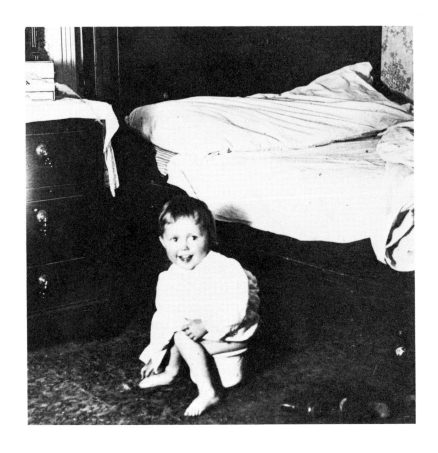

Introduction

It has been claimed that parents of the past paid scant attention to their infants. 'Having arrived,' maintain the historians Ivy Pinchbeck and Margaret Hewitt, 'the child's infant progress was deemed of too little interest or importance to his family to merit record'. The extracts quoted in 'Parental Affection, Pride and Exasperation' demonstrate quite the reverse, that children were clearly valued by their parents (see Frances Hatton, p. 56. and Rebecca Silliman, p. 58), their infantile progress watched over and commented upon. The pride and love experienced by those parents is unmistakable. Children, then as now, occupied a unique place in the home. Inevitably parenthood brought problems as well as pleasure: the crying, expense, noise and responsibility of children all caused parents moments of concern, irritation and fatigue. Some children were particularly difficult to contend with (John Todd, p. 60, and Elizabeth Prentiss, p. 60).

The feeding of babies was a worrisome business. Until the mid-eighteenth century, milk supplied by the mother or wet-nurse was the only viable method of feeding. Feeding vessels, particularly from 1700 onwards, were available but, because the principles of sterilization were not understood, it was considered a great achievement to rear a child by hand, even as late as the nineteenth century. The recourse to a wet-nurse has been put forward as evidence of the lack of care and affection shown to children. It has been argued that parents, especially mothers, were then freed from the trouble of tending their infants (perhaps entirely, since there was a high mortality rate for infants so nursed). The wet-nurse has been a much maligned figure, having been regarded as a mercenary harridan, purveyor of infant neglect. These claims must be put in perspective. First, the use of a wet-nurse was largely confined to the upper classes who could afford to pay for such services, and even here it was not universal. Secondly, there were several reasons why parents chose to employ a wet-nurse, over and above the inability of the mother to feed the child herself. It was believed that women who were feeding should abstain from sex, on the grounds that intercourse curdled the milk, and that if the mother became pregnant her milk supply would dry up. There may, therefore, have been pressure not to breastfeed from husbands, especially when a male heir was still to be produced, as in the case of Elizabeth Hatton (p. 64). Some women also felt that breastfeeding would age them and affect the shape of their breasts. Whatever the reason, wet-nurses were chosen with care, and the infants were visited regularly. There may indeed have been instances of neglect by individual nurses but in this situation steps were take to rectify the matter, as by Elizabeth Freke (p. 64) and Kate Russell (p. 71). We do not have accurate mortality figures for infants placed at nurse as yet, since no distinction was made between orphaned infants sent to a parish wet-nurse, who may have had several children under her care, and infants placed with a carefully chosen and supervised nurse. Research in this area currently being undertaken suggests that the mortality figures for the latter were lower than those for the former.

Our view of wet-nurses has been greatly influenced by the conditions in nineteenth-century baby farms and by the callous care given by some nurses to pauper infants. This behaviour should not be viewed as typical of the respectable wet-nurse, who took in infants to supplement her income and whose continued employment depended upon her looking after these infants carefully. Mothers could check the condition of the nurse's offspring before relinquishing any of their own to a nurse's care – as did Mary Verney (p. 63). As the quotation from Elizabeth Drinker's diary shows (p. 66), finding and keeping a suitable nurse was no simple matter, and could cause the mother more problems that breastfeeding the child herself. It is more likely that the great inertia of social custom decreed the continuance of the habit rather than wholesale indifference to the fate of infants.

Weaning was a notably anxious time for parents, both because there was a lack of foods for infants, and because the baby was now deprived of the immunity supplied by human milk and so became susceptible to disease (the Countess of Wemyss, p. 65). The reaction of the child to the event was also a matter of concern. Discovering what children were fed on in the past is not easy, since few references appear in the sources. It seems that bread and milk were the mainstays, eggs and simple cakes were added with discretion, and meats, except in broths or jellies, were regarded as unsuitable for young children (Elizabeth Gaskell, p. 81). The daily menu for foundlings at Christ's Hospital in 1678 was boiled beef, porridge, bread, water gruel with currants, cheese, milk porridge, pudding pies and milk. Plain food supplied at regular intervals was the advice given to parents and this seems to have been followed. What the advice books did not allow for was the dislike children had for certain foods. In some households meal times degenerated into a battle of wills (Elizabeth Grant, p. 78).

Until about the mid-eighteenth century, babies were swaddled – encased in a square of material around which long strips of cloth were tightly wrapped – for the first few months of life. It was believed that this was in the best interests of children since it kept their limbs straight, prevented them from going on all fours like animals, and helped to ward off rickets (the last idea was, of course, erroneous). This mode of clothing babies has also been seized upon by some historians to support the thesis of parental neglect and indifference. Swaddling, it is held, precluded interaction between mother and child. Furthermore, a child rendered immobile by this means could then be conveniently ignored. Swaddling, in actual fact, was a time-consuming, inconvenient process, but it did have the advantage of cocooning an infant in warmth and safety. The practice was coming under increasing attack in the eighteenth-century when it was felt that tight binding could be injurious to an infant's health (Sarah Pennington, p. 86). At about ten to twelve weeks of age, the child was short-coated – put into a long frock, just reaching to the feet. Both boys and girls were dressed in this fashion up to the age of six or seven when they adopted the appropriate adult styles of clothing. Boys were ceremoniously breeched – clad in doublet (later a coat and waistcoat), jerkin and hose like their father (Anne North, p. 82). By the eighteenth century they discarded their frocks at about the age of four. Girls assumed the dress of adult women: low-necked gown and leather or whalebone stays. Children's clothing became more informal in the late eighteenth century with the introduction of trousers and plain short jackets for boys and simple, straight dresses for girls. Opulent attire returned in the nineteenth century and clothing for girls in particular could be restrictive and uncomfortable (Catherine Carswell, p. 89).

Philippe Ariès asserted that because children were dressed as adults from about the age of seven on, they were therefore regarded as miniature adults: in other words, that there was no concept of childhood, as we know it; children jumped straight from infancy to adulthood. This places too much weight on the evidence. Children's clothes, like adult apparel, were subject to the whims of fashions. The age of seven, rather than being the age when adult status was achieved, may simply have been the age when gender differentiation was regarded as appropriate. Although the acquisition of adult clothing was seen by parents to mark a stage in growing up, it was only one of a series of such stages, and did not mark the end of childhood (Mather Byles, p. 88).

Parental Affection, Pride and Exasperation

England, 1630   *Hugh* **Cholmley** *on his son Richard.*

He died at the age of five years, yet had the courage and resolution of a man; for being to have an incision on a lump which arose in his arm, he would say, 'Father, would you have it done?' And I answered. 'Yes, sweet-heart; the doctor thinks it necessary.' Then would he say, 'Do it'; and held out his arm, without either shrinking or whining, though blood and corruption ran out. [*p. 50*]

England, 1647   *Mary* **Verney** *to her husband Ralph, describing their six-year-old son Jack. She and Ralph had been living in exile in France for three years while their son remained in England.*

I must give thee some account of our own babies here. For Jack his legs are most miserable, crooked as ever I saw any child's, and yet thank God he goes very strongly, and is very straight in his body as any child can be; and is a very fine child all but his legs, and truly I think would be much finer if we had him in ordering, for they let him eat anything that he hath a mind to, and he keeps a very ill diet; he hath an imperfection in his speech, and of all things he hates his book, truly 'tis time you had him with you for he learns nothing here. You would be much pleased with his company, for he is a very ready witted child and is very good company, and is so fond of his father and mother; he is always with me from the first hour that I came, and tells me that he would very fain go into France to his father; he sings prettily. [*(a) vol. 1, p. 379*]

England, 1662   *Adam* **Martindale** *on his two-year-old son John.*

He was a beautiful child, and very manly and courageous, for his age; of which this may pass for one specimen. We had a wanton tearing calf, that would run at children to bear them over. This calf he would encounter with a stick in his hand . . . stand his ground stoutly, beat it back, and triumph over it, crying *caw, caw,* meaning he had beaten the calf. I do not think one child of a hundred of his age durst do so much. [*p. 154*]

England, 1678   *Frances* **Hatton** *writes to her husband Christopher.*

I bless God all my dear children are well. My daughter Nanny is grown almost as tall as I, Susana breeds her teeth a pace. My affection is very equal to them all. Little Betty grows a very fine child, she is the most likely to make a handsomer woman than

Susana. She has the finest eyes and grows so quiet that as sure as ever I am up in a morning I spend my time among them. My daughter Nanny is a very good bedfellow and I would by no means part with her. [*Hatton (a), 4321*]

John **Churchill** *writes to his wife Sarah.*　　　　　　　*England, c.1687*

You cannot imagine how pleased I am with the children, for they having no body but their maid, they are so fond of me that when I am at home they will be always with me, kissing and hugging me . . . Miss is pulling me by the arm that she may write to her dear mamma, so that I will say no more. [*pp. 47–8*]

Rachel Cocke writes to Elizabeth **Jones** *describing the boisterous*　　*America, 1728* *behaviour of the latter's young son Tom*

[This] is enough to distract all about him except his papa and to him I believe all his noise is music. If he can't have and do everything he has a mind to he is ready to tear the house down, but if Nanny has opportunities, she will bring him to better order before you return. [*Jones (1), p. 49*]

Frances **Boscawen** *writes to her husband about their first child,*　　*England, 1747* *Edward, aged two and a half.*

I must have one observation in it that savours of vanity, but upon so true a foundation that it ought to excite your gratitude. The comparison of our children with your brother George's. I went directly from our boy to his girl. What a difference! In every circumstance, and in nothing more than behaviour. She would not come near me, and is as far from an agreeable child as she is from a pretty one. Ours is both, in the highest degree, and so everybody thinks. I wish you had seen him at his grandfather's yesterday and riding in the chair with mama. He stood, you may imagine, and was so delighted 'twould have entertained you. [*p. 28*]

Emily **Kildare** *writes about her children, Caroline aged eleven days,*　　*England, 1750* *George aged two and William aged one.*

You desire I will tell you something about my little girl. In the first place her name is Caroline Elizabeth Mabel . . . she is in the first place small, but fat and plump, has very fine dark *long* eyes, which I think a great beauty, don't you? and her nose and mouth like my mother's, with a peeked chin like me. As for her complexion, she is so full of the red gum that there is no judging of it, but what is best of all is that she is in perfect health and has been so ever since she was born.

But it's not fair to her brothers to entertain you only about her without mentioning them. So to begin with George. He is in the first place much improved as to his beauty, but the most entertaining, comical, arch little rogue that ever was, chatters incessantly, is immensely fond of me and coaxes me not a little, for he is cunning enough, very sweet-tempered and easily governed by gentle means; in short, if I was to set down and wish for a child, it would be just such a sort of boy as he is now. William is a sweet little child, too, in a different way. He is not so lively or active as George is by a good deal, but is forward enough both as to his walking and talking, for he says several words and walks quite alone. As for his little person it is fat, round and white, as he was when you saw him and does not improve as to that. He is the best-natured little creature than can be and excessively passionate already, but puts up his little mouth to kiss and be friends the very next minute. He is vastly fond of his nurse and does not care twopence for me; so, as you may imagine, I cannot for my life be as fond of him (though in reality I love him as well) as of George, who is always coaxing and kissing me, and does not care for any body else. [pp. 28–9]

America, 1779   Rebecca **Silliman** writes to her husband who is a prisoner of the British. Their two sons, Sellek and Benjamin, are aged two years and four months respectively.

I never made so good a nurse to any of my children as I do to the dear babe now in my lap. He is a fine little fat fellow, as good as possible at night, and so in the daytime too, if properly attended to. His little brother is very fond of him; they both sleep with me, and both awake before sunrise, when I get up and leave them to play together, – a sweet sight to a fond parent. Sellek and Bennie are my only constant companions, and sweet little sociable things they are. I long that you should see them. [vol. 1, p. 10]

England, 1789   William **Jones**, anxious that his income is not sufficient to maintain his family, frets.

As to myself, when I reflect on my present numerous family, and the large addition to it which I may in all probability expect, and think of the uncertainty of my employment, or the uncertainty of my own life, should I be ever so successful in my school, I seem oppressed with an insupportable load of cares and anxieties. [Jones (2), p. 97]

In 1797 he notes of his wife.

According to *her* estimate we shall not be able to support our dear family of nine children, even if we adopt a plan of the utmost prudence and economy. I thank heaven that one of my sons (William) is to all appearance well settled with Mr Lukyn, a stationer in St Paul's churchyard. Mr and Mrs Lukyn treat him very kindly and liberally. I have a little boy of theirs under my care for seven years in lieu of premium. [*Jones (2), p. 103*]

*John **Marshall** enthuses to his wife Polly about their children.*   *America, 1798*

Your sweet little Mary is one of the most fascinating little creatures I ever beheld. She has improved very much since I saw her and I cannot help agreeing that she is a substitute for her lovely sister. She talks in a way not easily to be understood though she comprehends very well everything that is said to her and is the most coquettish little prude and the most prudish little coquet I ever saw. I wish she were with you as I think she would entertain you more than all the rest of your children put together. Poor little John is cutting teeth and of course is sick. He appeared to know me as soon as he saw me. He would not come to me but he kept his eyes fixed on me as on a person he had some imperfect recollection of. I expect he has been taught to look at the picture and has some confused idea of a likeness. He is small and weakly but by no means an ugly child. If, as I hope, we have the happiness to raise him I trust he will do as well as the rest. Poor little fellow, the present hot weather is hard on him cutting teeth, but great care is taken of him and I hope he will do well. [*pp. 81–2*]

*Zilpah **Longfellow** to her brother on her children, Stephen aged two and Henry aged eight months.*   *America, 1807*

You would be delighted with my little Stephen. He is an engaging little fellow, now that he can talk and begins to have some ideas. He will ask a thousand questions in a minute, and can manage his playthings and draw about his horse, – 'Just like all children', you will say. No doubt of it; but it is the same to parents as if their child was the first in the world. I think you would like my little Henry Wadsworth. He is an active rogue, and wishes for nothing so much as singing and dancing. He would be very happy to have you raise him up to see the balls on the mirror. [*Longfellow (a), vol. 1, p. 6*]

*Elizabeth **Fry**, mother of six children, writes in her diary.*   *England, 1811*

Felt very low yesterday evening, rather unusually so for me partly from the children being naughty and trying. I also feel how poorly my duties are performed towards all. [*p. 143*]

I feel, at times, deeply pressed down, on account of my beloved
children. Their volatile minds try me; but, amidst my trials, I have
a secret hope concerning them, that all will end well; and a
blessing attend them, if they bow to the blessed yoke (for so I feel
it) in their youth. [*p. 145*]

England, 1812   *Anna **Braithwaite**, on holiday with her children, writes to her husband
Issac. Anne is aged three, Isaac two and Charles a few months.*

The dear children are well. Anna seems in better spirits than when
we left home, and is very fond of walking without taking hold.
Isaac is very sweet. He would laugh and talk from morning till
night if he might run about unrestrained. I never saw so good
tempered and merry a child. He is to be sure fond of mischief and
of paddling in all the puddles he can find. Dear Charles grows
sweeter every day. He takes so much notice, and can hold things
quite steadily in his hand. [*pp. 54–5*]

America, 1829   *John **Todd** on his daughter Mary, aged four months.*

Mary never has been well. She is a most lovely and playful and
perfectly amiable little girl, when free from pain, but this is but a
small part of the time. She cries more than any child that we ever
saw, sometimes there is not an hour in the night that we are not
disturbed, and do not have to get up to still her. We have asked the
advice of four different physicians, but nothing that we have ever
tried has done any good. We sometimes get quite discouraged,
and almost worn out with her. [*pp. 209–10*]

One year later.

Little Mary grows well, and learns to talk fast, and to *us* is
interesting; but oh, what a child! She never wants to sleep or to
rest. It seems as if we should never have a night's rest, or ever be
free from headache and fatigue. [*p. 213*]

America, 1832   *Robert **Lee** writes to his wife Molly while she and their son George,
aged fourteen months, are away on a visit.*

My sweet little boy what I would give to see him! The house is a
perfect desert without him and his mother and there is no comfort
in it. Take good care of him Molly and don't let him be spoiled,
direct him in *every* thing and leave *nothing* to the guidance of his
nurse. I am waking all night to hear his sweet little voice and if in
the morning I could only feel his little arms around my neck and
his dear little heart fluttering against my breast, I should be too
happy. [*Lee (2), p. 269*]

Elizabeth **Prentiss** *writes to Mrs Stearns about her second child*   America, 1849
Edward, who at four months is badly troubled with colic.

Dear little Eddy has found life altogether unkind thus far, and I
have had many hours of heartache on his account; but I hope he
may weather the storm and come out safely yet. The doctor
examined him all over yesterday, particularly his head, and said
he could not make him out a *sick* child, but that he thought his
want of flesh owing partly to his sufferings but more to the great
loss of sleep occasioned by his sufferings. Instead of sleeping
twelve hours out of the twenty-four, he sleeps but about seven and
that by means of laudanum. Isn't it a mercy that I have been able to
bear so well the fatigue and care and anxiety of these four hard
months? I feel that I have nothing to complain of, and a *great deal*
to be thankful for. [*p. 113*]

When Eddy was about eight months old, the doctor determined to
discontinue the use of opiates. He was now a fine, healthy baby,
bright-eyed and beautiful, and his colic was reducing itself to
certain seasons on each day, instead of occupying the whole day
and night as heretofore. We went through fire and water almost in
trying to procure for him natural sleep. We swung him in blankets,
wheeled him in little carts, walked the room with him by the hour,
etcetera, etcetera, but it was wonderful how little sleep he
obtained after all. He always looked wide awake and as if he did
not *need* sleep. His eyes had gradually become black, and when,
after a day of fatigue and care with him he would at last close
them, and we would flatter ourselves that now we too should
snatch a little rest, we would see them shining upon us in the most
amusing manner with a expression of content and even merri-
ment. [*p. 116*]

Rutherford **Hayes** *writes about his four-year-old son Birchard.*   America, 1857

Birch grows rapidly and now promises to be a large fleshy fellow
like his uncle Joe. He begins to *think*. He asked his mother who the
preacher talked to when he shut his eyes and looked up. She
replied, 'to God'. 'But where is God?' – 'In heaven where good
people are after they are dead.' – 'How do good people get up
there?' – 'God takes them.' 'How do God take them up?' His
mother hesitated 'Do he pull them up with a rope?'
   He saw a little boy doing something he did not approve of and
told his Uncle Joe: 'I would have whipped him but I did not know
how to *unbutton his pants*.' Oh, he grows. [*vol. 1, p. 521*]

Physical Development – Babyhood

England, 1608   *Anne, Countess of Arundel, writes to Mary **Talbot** about their grandson Frederick Henry, aged one month*

In truth the younger boy doth grieveth me and feareth me much with his extremity of crying, which is so vehement as I assure your ladyship there passeth not any day that his wind is not gone and in such sort black as I will not willingly be in the house again where a poor child shall be so long deferred from christening in such a case ... I know not good Madam what to wish for the disposing of the nurse, the child had very little of the red gum but doth all matters in good order and I am so fearful to change the nurse for fear of some distemper which I doubt would go fair with the child having these extreme fits, for I assure you once or twice the navel hath bled with his fits so that good madam I know not what to do. I hoped at the first he would have left it but as he groweth so they be longer. [MS3205, f. 145]

England, 1614   *Anne **Clifford** writes to her mother about her daughter Margaret, aged ten months.*

I have now returned from the Bath to my own house in the country, where I thank God I find my little one well, though I much feared it, for I have found your ladyship's words true about the nurse [I] had for her, for she hath been one of the most unhealthfullest women that I think I ever saw, and so extremely troubled with toothache and rheums and swelling in her face as could be, and one night she fell very ill, and was taken like an ague, so as she had but little milk left, and so I was enforced to send for the next woman that was by to give my child suck, whom hath continued with her ever since, and I thank God the child agrees so well with her milk as can be, so I mean not to change her any more. It is a miracle to me that the child should prosper so well, considering the change of her milk. She is but a little one, I confess, but a livelier and merrier thing was there never yet seen. [Clifford (b), p. 148]

England, 1631   *Simonds **D'Ewes** mourns the fatal result of wrong advice given to his wife.*

My dear wife [was] safely delivered of her first son, which brought to us, by its abortive end, much more sorrow than joy: and the rather because we feared it perished by the cursed ignorance or neglect of such as were employed about my child during her living-in, for it was a goodly sweet child born: but my wife having some resolution to be a nurse, it was fatally advised by such as were about her, that the child should not suck any other till her breasts were fully drawn and made fit for it, during which time it was so weakened, as it afterwards proved the cause of its ruin. [*vol. 2, pp. 44–5*]

In 1634, on the birth of his fourth son, the previous three having died as babies, he writes.

We had present affliction with him upon his birth, by the failing of two nurses, one after the other, within a fortnight after my wife had been delivered; so as being in a great strait, and fearing we might lose him as we had done our first, we were fain to pitch upon a poor woman who had been much misused and almost starved by a wicked husband. [*vol. 2, pp. 107–8*]

This son, too, died, at the age of nine months; Simonds blaming the nurse for neglecting the child.

Mary **Verney** *writes to her manservant Will. Her son Ralph, aged three weeks, is to be sent to the wet-nurse's home.*   England, 1647

Good Will, upon Tuesday next I intend to send my child to St Albans; the nurse is most extremely desirous to be at home, so if you can possible I would have you be there on Tuesday night and go to Tringe on Wednesday. The nurse sayeth her husband hath a very easy going horse, and she thinks it will be best for him to carry the child before him upon pillows, because she cannot ride between two panniers and hold the child. When you come there, you will quickly find which will be the best way to carry it; pray provide for both ways, and bring a footman to go by it. If her husband doth carry the child, she cannot ride behind him, so you must provide a horse for her; my sister Mary goes down with them, so you must bring up a pillion to carry her down behind you . . . Pray do you see that they take a great care of the child, and that they go very softly, for the weather is very hot; if he carries the child before him it must be tied about him with a garter, and truly I think it will be a very good way, for the child will not endure to be long out of one's arms. [*(a) vol. 1, p. 361*]

Six weeks later Mary has to change the wet-nurse, and, as she writes to her husband Ralph, the only suitable woman she could find is . . .

Raph Rodes' wife, and I fear they are but poor and she looks like a slattern but she sayeth if she takes the child she will have a mighty care of it, and truly she hath two as fine children of her own as ever I saw. [*(a) vol. 1, p. 380*]

England, c.1670   *Elizabeth* **Hatton** *writes to her daughter-in-law Cicelea about Cicelea's decision to breastfeed her own child. (Kit is Cicelea's husband Christopher.)*

[Lady Griffis will visit you since] she knows what 'tis to be a nurse, she was one her self a little while but could not go through with it. I know that Kit is too good natured since you are willing to give your self the trouble to suckle this a nights to be unwilling to it. I hope God will bless both you and him the better for it.

I am sensible that your being a nurse takes up most of your time that I write not so often to you as otherwise I should, and now I beg of your not so much to tire your self with nursing my little girl as to discourage you for nursing my little boy when that is born, I have against that come sent you the picture of a very pretty boy for a pattern that you may bring me one like it. [*Hatton (b), add. MSS 29571, ff. 1095*]

(Elizabeth probably means that she has sent Cicelea a picture of Christopher as a child in order to encourage the conception of a son.)

England, 1675   *Elizabeth* **Freke** *writes of the consequences of returning to her husband in Ireland and leaving her baby son with a nurse in England.*

My dear father sent for me over to England, my son being crippled by the carelessness of his nurse and about 14 of December broke his leg short in the hackle bone, which she kept private for near a quarter of a year till a jelly was grown between it; she keeping him in his cradle, and everybody believed he was breeding of his teeth, he having two at eighteen weeks old, and at that age could stand almost alone till this misfortune befell him. [*p. 25*]

The child was removed from this nurse and the bone in his leg re-set so that he suffered no permanent injury.

America, 1677   *Samuel* **Sewall** *writes about his son John, born on 1 April.*

The first woman the child sucked was Bridget Davenport . . . April 7, Saturday, first laboured to cause the child suck his mother, which he scarce did at all. In the afternoon my wife sat up, and he sucked the right breast bravely. [*vol. 5, p. 40*]

England, 1678   *Frances* **Hatton** *writes to her husband Christopher, three weeks after the birth of their daughter.*

There was but two things in the world that I set my heart upon. One the first was to suckle my poor child my self but my sore nipples would not give me leave I am so really discontented at it that I believe I shall never be cheerful again but I am resolved if ever I should have another I must try again. Everybody agreed it would do me good, I am so much troubled with rhume and my nurse keeper says that she knows several that has such fine kind of skins that the second time win their breast with pretty good ease. [*Hatton (a)*, 4322]

Margaret, Countess of Wemyss, advises her daughter Anne, Countess of Leven, on the hazards of eaning. (The letter is in the **Melville** *collection.)*   *Scotland, 1696*

I am very glad my dear that George was at first so easily weaned and made little noise but the brash and looseness comes a month or five weeks after. For God's sake advert to it and let his drink in the night be milk and boiled water with a bit of cinnamon in it for that agreed best with yourself, let me know if he likes broth and if he eats a little flesh sometimes. [*GD26/13/401/30*]

I am very sorry that George's looseness continues, it cannot but weaken him very much I think a biengreat [?] of diascordion dissolved in syrup of red poppies or gillyflowers or put into a little conserve of roses to cover the taste and then a little syrup about it will be very fit for him when he goes to bed. It did your brother much good when he almost a-died of a looseness. I think you should not slight it for it may prove very dangerous if it continue, and when the doctor is from you and cannot return for some days I would have you send for Mr Arthur to wait upon George for he has much experience of children . . . It is a great mercy that George has no more pain with his looseness. He must never taste ale now nor no kind of broth without rice. Let me know if he grow any worse for I will come to him. [*GD26/13/401/36*]

John **Stedman** *describes his misfortunes at the hands of wet-nurses.*   *England, 1744*

Four different wet-nurses were alternately turned out of doors on my account, and to the care of whom I had been entrusted, my poor mother being in too weak a condition to suckle me herself. The first of these bitches was turned off for having nearly suffocated me in bed; she having sleeped upon me till I was smothered and with skill and difficulty [I was] restored to life. The second had let me fall from her arms on the stones till my head was almost fractured, and I lay several hours in convulsions. The third carried me under a mouldered brick wall, which fell in a heap of rubbish just the moment we had passed by it, while the fourth proved to be a thief, and deprived me even of my very baby clothes. Thus was poor Johnny Stedman weaned some months before the usual time. [*p. 5*]

England, c.1760   *Sarah* **Pennington** *writes to Miss Louisa giving her directions on child care.*

Let us begin with food and rainment, the two first things necessary. The former I know you will, if possible, administer yourself in the manner nature has intended; where this happens, by some accident, to be impracticable, which is very rarely the case, cow's milk, diluted by water till it is brought to the same consistence of the mother's milk, unmixed either with flour, bread, biscuit or sugar, is by far the best substitute, and, as coming the nearest to what nature intended, will agree the best with *every* constitution; in hot weather the milk should be fresh drawn at least once in eight hours, and never given warmer than it comes from the cow. The finest children I ever saw were reared in this manner; without once tasting any thing else for the first twelve months, and in a single instance I knew it continued for eighteen months with equal success. This method is undoubtedly preferable to the bare hazard of imbibing ill-humour, or disease, from a woman whose temper and constitution must be very imperfectly known. [*vol. 3, pp. 123–5*]

All children will discover their desire of food by motions that plainly show them to be searching for something; these motions will be continued a considerable time without any cry, which is only the consequence of repeated disappointments in this search; such signs from them should always be waited for, carefully observed, and immediately answered; the offer of food when not wanted, being to the full as teasing to infants as the delay of it when required. If fed by hand it should be out of an vessel that will hold as much as they can take at once, nothing being more unnatural, and tormenting, than the feeding them with a spoon that must be taken every minute from their mouths to be replenished. I have often thought that a round flexible pipe might be contrived, for the feeding dry-nursed children, full of small holes at the end, within which pipe a piece of sponge might be placed to stop the liquor from flowing out, unless pressed or drawn by suction, and this pipe screwed to a spout on the vessel which contains the liquor; something of this kind would come much nearer to the method in which they receive the milk from the breast, and such a pipe might remain in their mouths 'till they dropped asleep, or took their heads from it, but whether an instrument of this sort could be made to answer I know not. [*vol. 4, pp. 12–14*]

America, 1781   *Elizabeth* **Drinker** *recounts the problems she encountered in finding a suitable wet-nurse for her son.*

Two days after the last memorandum my dear little Charles was born, on the 16th August towards evening; was favoured myself beyond expectation, but my poor baby was alive and that was all – did not expect he would survive many days; but he is now between ten and eleven weeks old, and appears to be thriving, which is wonderful, considering how unwell I was for near a month before his birth, and much falling away, the child little more than skin and bone – occasioned perhaps by a cold I caught. The first seven or eight months of my time, I was heartier and better than ever I had been in like situation – and am at present through mercy favourably recovered, so as to be able with the help of feeding to nurse my little one. Nurse Molly Morris was with me near two weeks, her Sister Sally Stanberry near four weeks, both good nurses. When the child was five days old he was taken with a sore mouth which prevented him from sucking for nine days: in which time my capacity for nursing him was much lessened – agreed with Rachel Bickerton a shoemaker's wife next door to come in four or five times a day to suckle him: which she did for four weeks – and with what little I could do in that way we made out for that time, having in the interim been disappointed of several Nurses; when Rachel was taken with the ague; and I left to nurse him myself, which (having gathered more strength and not getting a nurse to my mind) I was favoured to do much better than I could have expected. I had engaged one Nancy Pool a young widow who lived or had lived at Bristol, but she was prevented from coming by sickness. I then sent for Elizabeth Scott from Hadonfield, who was taken the next day she came with the chills and fever, she stayed with me in my chamber four days had two smart fits, and several after she left us. I then hired one Betty Larkey who stayed here but five or six days when I dismissed her as she by no means suited. It is a favour to be able to do that office oneself – as there is much trouble with nurses. [*Drinker (b), pp. 63–4*]

*Betty **Bishop** describes the reaction of her two-month-old daughter Betsy to weaning.*   *England, 1787*

Little dear Betsy brave and very quiet considering she has no breast. I began weaning of her yesterday morning on account of my nipples being so bad but very little milk. [*3/4/1787*]

*Molly **Tilghman** writes to Polly Pearce, telling her about her cousin's difficulties in breastfeeding.*   *America, 1789*

Poor Harriet has been so unlucky within the last fortnight, as to have a sore breast, which made us very uneasy. It gathered and broke in three days, and was as light as a thing of the kind could be but in my life I never saw a creature so terrified as she was. The idea of lancets, probes, and crooked scissors haunted her continually but happily none of them were necessary and her breast is now almost entirely well. [*pp. 232–3*]

England, 1798   Elizabeth **Wynne** *writes in her diary three days after the birth of her first child, Thomas.*

My little boy begins to suck very nicely and I am not at all troubled with my milk, he is a charming child and never cries. [*vol. 2, p. 203*]

England, 1835   Elizabeth **Gaskell** *relates in her diary how she deals with the crying bouts of her six-month-old daughter Marianne.*

Once or twice we have had grand cryings, which have been very distressing to me; but when I have convinced myself she is not in pain, is perfectly well and that she is only wanting to be taken up, I have been quite firm; though I have sometimes cried almost as much as she has . . . Crying has been a great difficulty with me. Books do so differ. One says 'Do not let them have anything they cry for,' another (Mme Necker de Saussure, 'Sur L'Education Progressive,' the nicest book I have read on the subject), says 'les larmes des enfants sont si amères, la calme parfaite de l'ame leur est si necessaire qu'il faut surtout épargner des larmes' ['Children's tears are so bitter, and complete calm of spirit so necessary, that one must at all costs spare them crying']. So I had to make a rule for myself, and though I am afraid I have not kept to it quite as I ought, I still think it a good one. We must consider that a cry is a child's only language for expressing its wants. It is its little way of saying 'I am hungry, I am very cold', and *so*, I don't think we should carry out the maxim of never letting a child have anything for crying. If it is to have the object for which it is crying I would give it *directly*, giving up any little occupation or purpose of my own, rather than try its patience *unnecessarily*. But if it is improper for it to obtain the object, I think it right to withhold it steadily, however much the little creature may cry. I think, after one or two attempts to conquer by crying, the child would become aware that *one* cry or indication of a want was sufficient, and I think the habit of crying would be broken. I am almost sure even my partial adherence to this plan has prevented many crying fits with Marianne. [*pp. 7–9*]

*Lucy **Lovell** has misgivings about the way she chose to wean her fourteen-month-old daughter Laura. Lucy remained downstairs in the house while her sister stayed upstairs with Laura.*   *America, 1840*

Towards night I went up and took her. She asked to nurse but did not cry much and soon got down on the floor and began to play. She was easily weaned, seeming to understand that she could not nurse again, but from that time for more than a month she would always cry if I left her a moment when she was awake. I could not even get up to go across the room, when she was playing on the floor, without her crying. I attributed this to my leaving her all day when I weaned her, and should never advise any mother to do so. [*p. 56*]

*Mary **Walker** recalls that she was unable to nurse her first-born, Cyrus.*   *America, 1843*

Have very little hopes of being able to nurse much. Sometimes am tempted to murmur, but then I reflect how many other blessings I enjoy. [*p. 114*]

I was very anxious about my babe and extremely reluctant to relinquish the idea of nursing him but I had experienced so much torture that I was at last glad when no alternative was left me. [*p. 257*]

Cyrus was fed partly by bottle and partly by an Indian wet-nurse.

*John **Russell** relates the difficulties his wife Kate encountered when she attempted to breastfeed. (Lady Stanley is Kate's mother and Merriman her doctor.)*   *England, 1865*

Sunday 13 (one day after the birth).
Baby would not suck, and had to be fed by Mrs Potts, whose child is four months old.

Monday 14.
Though perfectly well Kate had much trouble today from baby not sucking. He would not or could not do it. Another baby took a little but Kate still suffered much pain in her breasts. In the evening bed time I sucked a little thinking it might do good, but I could not get much. Since I had to apply all my sucking power to get any milk it is no wonder the infant found it too hard for him. The milk was not nasty, but much too sweet to be pleasant; like the sweetest syrup. It seems very badly managed by nature that little babies should not always find it as easy to suck as little puppies; but if this is one of the arrangements that was made in consequence of Original Sin of course we must not complain of it.

Tuesday 15.

Baby still refuses to suck. Kate was not very happy or comfortable today having had a bad night and suffering much from headache. I was annoyed at the nursing not being successful and did not feel so happy as the first day. However Lady Stanley says she is sure to nurse with perseverance.

Monday 21.

Lady Stanley appears to be dispirited about Kate, says she is too weak, and that baby is not flourishing as he does not get enough. Kate cannot bear the notion of a wet-nurse and I dislike it nearly as much but there seems no hope of her nursing now.

Tuesday 22.

Papa, Mama, the boys and Agatha came today; Mama admired the baby and thought him very fine. I thought he looked pale, and am afraid we must get him a wet-nurse if he is to thrive. However, all who saw him seemed to be pleased with him. Dear Kate struggled hard against wet-nurse, but in the evening declared her readiness to give up nursing if the child's health would be better with another woman. A terrible disappointment to her, for we both care very much about ladies nursing, but I doubt not her strong sense of duty will overcome the reluctance to relinquish this harassing attempt to feed her baby when nature does not provide the means of doing so.

Friday 25.

Lady Stanley has found a woman (married three months, confined three weeks) who she thinks will do for a wet-nurse.

Saturday 26.

Merriman came today and finally decided that Kate must give up nursing. She was of course dreadfully unhappy but bore it very well. Indeed she has been wonderfully good and patient in all her trials. The wet-nurse was examined and approved. She came this evening. [*vol. 1, pp. 403–5*]

Two months later Kate writes of another problem involving her baby's dry-nurse.

The *good trusted clever* Davies is gone for good – and such a good riddance I never knew of. I have been deceived and with the very highest recommendations she had, it is too horrid.
    My wet-nurse (Lizzy) told me that Davies was very unkind to

the child. The poor woman had lost her own baby and in her grief she could not help telling me all Davies did to mine feeling for a mother being ignorant of such things. I hardly could have believed it but all the other servants had been disgusted by it and told me the same – so I wrote to consult Mama and she said 'Send her away at once' which I did at three hours notice yesterday, as had she stayed she would have worried Lizzy's milk away with her fury. These are one or two of her horrid ways. It makes my blood boil for my precious little darling, to think what he has had to bear. I am too furious. When he cried she used to shake him – when she washed him she used to stuff the sponge in his little mouth – push her finger (beast!) in his little throat – say she hated the child, wished he were dead – used to let him lie on the floor screaming while she sat quietly by and said screams did not annoy her, it was good for his lungs, besides she liked me to hear him scream as she thought otherwise I should think she had nothing to do and as soon as I came into the room she would take him into her arms and cant over him as if she loved him dearly. She hated being at Alderley because Mama and Madame used always to be coming into the room and to Mama she used to lie and when asked if Baby had been out say yes, when she had never stirred from the room. She thought she could manage me as she liked and that I would never find out or find fault with her, and no more I think I should as I trusted her so implicitly. She would not let the wet-nurse suckle him before he came to me, that he might scream and that I might know what a trouble he was – she sat in her room most of the day I find reading novels and never nursed the baby or spoke to it.

She said she meant to leave me in March anyhow as she hated the child and did not think the place grand enough. She said she had been accustomed to double her wages (£25) by the baby's clothes she got. She always put on it wet diapers though the nurse asked her to let her air them and so it often had a stomach ache, then she gave it an empty bottle in its cot to suck the tube and keep it quiet so making it suck in only wind. No wonder it cried and was so unhappy. I am so angry with her. Lizzie has had a child before and she quite understands the care of one and as this one is very strong and very well she will do till I can get a nurse and is far better than that wretch of a woman. I shall not get another in a hurry and without great investigation but shall feel afraid for Davies was so praised and so sensible and nice spoken to me. Of course I will never recommend her.

Karl complained to me also of her behaviour to Baby. Sweet little lamb I do so love it, and have it so much with me now and superintend its washing and dressing but Lizzy is so nice and loves it nearly like her own. [*vol. 1, p. 415*]

Physical Development – Infancy

England, 1607   *Anne, Countess of Arundel, writes to Mary **Talbot** about their grandson James, Lord Maltravers, aged about seven months.*

Our little Jamie hath been very evil but I thank our lord he is much better but his cough is not yet gone. He was sometimes at the first distemper of heat and would groan so in his sleep as if I had not remembered his father's hard breeding of teeth I should have been more grieved, but my good daughter I did find to shed tears though she made the best show before me that she could. [*MS3202, f. 473*]

Three months later.

Our little jewel hath had three fits of an ague three nights together but I thank our Lord he hath now escaped it two or three nights; but no more teeth, yet broken flesh though we hope that to be the cause. I beseech you good sister let me know whether you think it fit now he is thus old to let him sometimes suck of a little bone for hitherto I have not suffered the nurse to use him to any flesh. [*MS3205, f. 141*]

England, 1615   *Anne **Clifford** writes to her mother about her daughter Margaret, aged thirteen months.*

On the 29th of the last month I was sent for to Bollbroke in all haste for the poor child was extremely ill with her teeth, and so I carried Dr Barker down with me, who gave the nurse and her some things that he carried down with him, and I thank God she is so well amended as I could wish, or desire and begins to prattle and go. [*Clifford (b), p. 151*]

Seven months later.

We perceived the child had two great teeth come out so that in all she had now eighteen.

When Margaret was almost two, Anne writes.

Upon the 1st I cut the child's strings off from her coats and made her use togs alone, so as she had two or three falls at first but had no hurt with them. [*Clifford (a), pp. 57, 66*]

Nathaniel Bacon writes to his wife, Jane **Cornwallis***, about their*   *England, c.1625*
children, Nicholas aged three and Jane aged eighteen months.

Our children are well; and little Nick hath cast his coat, and seemeth metamorphosed into a grasshopper. Jane is a very modest maiden, and is wholly taken up with travelling by her self which she performeth very handsomely and will be ready to run at your command when you return. [*p. 84*]

The following year he writes to his wife.

For little Jane in particular, I should have been glad to have understood some of her new language. [*p. 140*]

Eliza **Cornwallis** *to her mother-in-law, Jane, on her daughter Harriet*   *England, 1639*
and her son Fred.

I am sorry silly Harriet is still so great a waggler, for now I shall fear her not out growing it but God's will be done; and for Fred, I think the best is your opinion of not letting him use them [his legs] till it shall please God to give him more strength. [*p. 291*]

Frances **Hatton***, pregnant with her second child, writes to her husband*   *England, 1677*
Christopher about their infant daughter.

Poor little Susana is very ill about her teeth. I hope in God they will not be long before they be cut, she bears it with a great deal of patience.
    My brother Hatton will tell you what a fine girl Susana is. She will be called by no name but little Lady Hatton, she talks extreme plain and I hope her teeth will come at last but I am afraid she may be inclined to the rickets. Oh my Lord if I should die, show particular kindness to that child for if I have ten thousand sons I can not love them so well. [*Hatton (b), add MSS 29571, ff. 380, 459*]

Samuel **Sewall** *on his son Hull, aged nineteen months.*   *America, 1686*

Little Hull speaks 'apple' plainly in the hearing of his Grandmother and Eliza Lane; this is the first word. [*vol. 5, p. 122*]

Catherine **Verney** *writes to her husband concerning their son Jack,*   *England, 1715*
aged four.

Pray desire cousin Peg to buy me a pair of leading strings for Jack. There is stuff made on purpose that is very strong, for he is so heavy I dare not venture him with common ribbon. [*(a) vol. 2, p. 131*]

America, 1728   *Thomas* **Jones** *to his wife Elizabeth on their son Thomas, aged two.*

[There is] great alteration in the use of his feet in so short a time, and I believe [he] is as forward in that as most children of two years old . . . when he falls I order him not to be taken up by which means he takes it patiently, unless he hurts himself pretty much . . . he is very backward with his tongue, I use him to Pa-pa; and Ma-ma, and in a morning he say (not Tea) but Tee, and sometimes mo' which is all the improvement he has made that way; he grows tall and is fine Boy. [*Jones (1), p. 46*]

America, 1785   *Mary Badger to her mother Mary Harrad. (The letter is in the* **Saltonstall** *collection.)*

My little George is out at [nurse?] yet and as fine a Little fellow as ever you saw. You would be diverted to see him at eight month old tied in his chair at table eating fat pork and Indian cake for his dinner. I expect to take him home in April next and I flatter myself he will run about the house by that time. He has already a number of teeth and I hope will get the rest soon. [*vol. 1, p. 534*]

England, 1785   *Charlotte* **Papendiek** *takes her eighteen-month-old daughter to see Queen Charlotte.*

Her Majesty recommended leading strings – a band round the waist, with a loop on each side, of a length to hold, so as to support the child in case she should stumble, and I immediately attended to this advice. [*vol. 1, p. 229*]

England, 1785   *John* **Stedman** *writes in his journal about his son George, aged sixteen months.*

I buy leading strings for little George.

Three months later.

I buy a bottle of *Godfrey's Cordial* for making children sleep, since Geordy keeps all the house awake, also almost kills his poor mother. [*pp. 262, 269*]

England, 1796   *Fanny* **Burney** *writes about her son Alexander, aged two. (Fanny's husband was French.)*

[He] has made no further advance but that of calling out, as he saw our two watches hung on two opposite hooks over the chamber chimney-piece, 'Watch papa, – watch, mama,' so, though his first speech is English, the idiom is French.

Three months later, Alexander's speech has improved markedly.

He has repeated readily whatever we have desired; and yesterday, while he was eating his dry toast, perceiving the cat, he threw her a bit, calling out, 'Eat it, Buff!' Just now, taking the string that fastens his gown round the neck, he said, 'Ett's tie it on, mama'. [*vol. 6, pp. 79, 91*]

*Thomas **Moore** records the progress of his offspring. (Bessy is his wife.)*   *England, 1813*

On Barbara, aged ten months.

Our little Barbara is growing very amusing. She (what they call) *started* yesterday in walking; that is, got up off the ground by herself, and walked alone to a great distance, without any one near her. Bessy's heart was almost flying out of her mouth all the while with fright, but I held her away, and would not let her assist the young adventurer. [*vol. 1, p. 329*]

On Russell, aged nine months.

Our dear little Russell, who becomes prettier every day, has at length cut two teeth, which mama insists upon my recording in this journal. [*vol. 4, p. 160*]

*Ellen **Weeton** delights in the development of her eleven-month-old   *England, 1816*
daughter Mary, who has just been taken for her first walk.*

I have been much diverted with Mary today. I took her by the hand, and she walked all the way from hence as far as our late house in Chapel-lane. She had so many things to look at, that I thought we should scarcely ever arrive. She stopped at every open door, to look into the houses. There were many groups of little children in the street, and she would walk up to them, and shout at them; she set her foot upon the step of a door where there happened to be a cake-shop, so I bought her a cake; and then she wanted to stand still in street whilst she ate it. [*vol. 2, pp. 143–4*]

*Elizabeth **Gaskell** charts the progress of her six-month-old daughter   *England, 1835*
Marianne.*

She has two teeth cut with very little trouble; but I believe the worst are to come. She is very strong in her limbs, though, because she is so fat, we do not let her use her ankles at all, and I hope she will be rather late in walking that her little legs may be very firm. I shall find it difficult to damp the energies of the servants in this respect, but I intend that she shall teach herself to walk and receive no assistance from hands, etcetera. She lies down on the floor a good deal, and kicks about; a practice I began very early, and which has done her a great deal of good. She goes to bed *awake;* another practice I began early, and which is so comfortable I wonder it is not more generally adopted . . . I never leave her till she is asleep (except in extreme cases), and as she is put to bed at a regular time (six o'clock) she generally gets very sleepy while being undressed. While the undressing is going on, I never like her to be talked to, played with, or excited; yet sometimes she is so playful when she ought to be put down, that a turn or two up and down the room is required to soothe her, still putting her down awake. Sometimes she will cry a little, and when I turn her over in her cot she fancies she is going to be taken up and is still in a moment, making the peculiar little triumphing noise she always does when she is pleased. [pp. 7–9]

America, 1840 *Lucy* **Lovell** *on her daughter Laura, aged eighteen months.*

In the course of the summer I got Laura so that she would go to sleep in her little crib. Sometimes I had some difficulty with her, but generally when she saw that I was decided, she would go quietly to sleep. She usually took a book in her hand when she went into her crib, and held it fast, till she was asleep, and she looked so lovely to the eye of a parent as she lay with her little limbs curled up and her book in her hand. [*pp. 57–8*]

Laura started walking at this age, helped by her elder sister Caroline.

This was a time of interest to us all. Caroline took great delight in enticing her to come to her. She was very fearful to take a step at first, and for several days would fall two or three times in going from one side of the room to the other, but soon became accustomed to it, and would laugh heartily whenever she fell, and jump up and continue her tottering walk. By degrees her limbs gained strength and she ventured to get out at the door and walk on the ground. She would frequently get her little sun bonnet, and putting it on with the front behind, and cape before, would be out and walking off towards the barn before we missed her from her play in the house. [*p. 58*]

America, 1845 *Fanny* **Longfellow** *describes her son Charles, aged nine months, to her sister-in-law Mary.*

The infant Hercules has developed a tooth at last and has been promoted into shoes and short petticoats, so that he creeps about the room like a spider and is beginning to stand up alone with the help of a chair. His physique flourishes with ever increasing vigor, and he is hard at work upon something from dawn till dusk. I rejoice to see him so well, but sometimes sigh for a little more sentiment and repose in his nature! [*Longfellow (b), pp. 118–19*]

Food and Drink

*Nathaniel Bacon writes to his wife Jane **Cornwallis** about their son Nicholas aged about five*

England, 1624

Nick sends you word of a brood of young chickens, and a disaster he escaped at my being with him; for he ate so much milk porridge at supper that he cried out, (O Lord!) I think I have almost broke mine gut; and I was fain to walk him a turn or two about the chamber to digest it. [*p. 99*]

*Thomas **Tryon** advises on the feeding of children.*
England, c.1680

Let their food be temperate, both as to quality and quantity; the simpler it is the more healthful . . .

The most convenient times for children to eat, for those from two to six years old, are at eight, twelve and four o'clock. For all people above six years old, are eight or nine in the morning, and three or four afternoon. Let your children's food be as simple as you can, spoon-meats principally; let each have his mess distinct from the other, nor let them have more than one sort at a meal; let them not murmur or show any dislike to their food, but oblige them to a strict silence during all the time, teaching them with great awfulness and consideration to praise their creator before and after each meal. [*pp. 114, 119–20*]

*John **Byrom** writes to his wife, giving his views on the best way of caring for their children.*
England, 1729

Do not children go too bare about the neck for coughs and cold weather? I am sure that herbs, roots and fruits in season, good house-bread, water porridge, milk fresh, etcetera, are the properest food for them, and for drink, water and milk, and wine, ale, beer, posset, or any liquor that is in its natural or artificial purity, whenever they have the least occasion for it. [*vol. 34, p. 389*]

*Sarah **Pennington** advises Miss Louisa on what food to give children.*
England, c.1750

With regard to diet, I know not that any particular regimen, after children are past the state of infancy, is absolutely necessary; the most plain and simple kinds are certainly best, if for no other reason than because they will not be tempted to eat too much, which, in every period of life, is the baneful source of innumerable dieseases; to regulate the quantity is, I believe, much more material than the quality, of their food; it will contibute much to their health to bring them early to three or four regular meals in a day, without giving them any thing to eat in the intermediate space, because, by continually throwing in new matter, the regular course of digestion is interrupted, the tone of the stomach weakened, and a bad chill produced. Water is the best liquor, and in all the little complaints they are incident to, water-gruel and abstinence are generally better remedies than medicine. Worms they will escape being troubled with, if they have but a small quantity of fruit, and that perfectly ripe; under which restrictions, they may very safely be permitted to have some of every kind in its season. [*vol. 3, pp. 131–2*]

America, 1786   *Theodosia* **Burr** *writes to her husband Aaron about their ailing daughter Sally, aged two.*

I have just determined to take a room at aunt Clarke's till Sally recovers her appetite; by the advice of the physician, we have changed her food from vegetable to animal. A change of air may be equally beneficial.

He replies.

Why are you so cautiously silent as to our little Sally? You do not say that she is better or worse; from which I conclude she is worse. I am not wholly pleased with your plan of meat diet. It is recommended upon the idea that she has no disorder but a general debility. All the disorders of this season as apt to be attended with fevers, in which case animal diet is unfriendly. I beg you to watch the effects of this whim with great attention. So essential a change will have certainly visible effects. Remember, I do not absolutely condemn, because I do not know the principles, but am fearful. [*vol. 1, pp. 275–6*]

Scotland, 1806   *In her memoirs Elizabeth* **Grant** *recalls with horror childhood battles over food. She was about nine years old at the time of the following extract.*

The milk rebellion was crushed immediately; in his dressing-gown, with his whip in his hand, he attended our breakfast . . . that disgusting milk! He began with me; my beseeching look was answered by a sharp cut, followed by as many more as were necessary to empty the basin; Jane obeyed at once, and William after one good hint. They suffered less than I did; William cared less, he did not enjoy his breakfast, but he could take it; Jane always got rid of it [by vomiting], she had therefore only hunger to endure; I, whose stomach was either weaker or stronger, had to bear an aching head, a heavy, sick painful feeling which spoilt my whole morning, and prevented any appetite for dinner, where again we constantly met with sorrow. Whatever was on the table we were each to eat, no choice was allowed us. The dinners were very good, one dish of meat with vegetables, one tart or pudding. On broth or fish days no pudding, these days were therefore not in favour; but our *maigre* days, two in the week during summer, we delighted in, fruit and eggs being our favourite dishes. How happy our dinner hour was when aunt Lissy was with us! a scene of distress often afterwards. My mother never had such an idea as that of entering her nursery, when she wanted her children or her maids she rang for them; aunt Mary, of course, had no business there; the cook was pretty sure of this, the broth got greasy, the vegetables heavy with water, the puddings were seldom brown. Mrs Millar allowed no orts, our shoulders of mutton – we ate all the shoulders – were to be cut fair, fat and lean, and to be eaten fair, a hard task for Jane and me. The stomachs which rejected milk could not easily manage fat except when we were under the lash, then indeed the fat and the tears were swallowed together; but my father could not always be found to act overseer, and we had sometimes a good fight for it with our upright nurse, a fight ending in victory as regarded the fat, though we suffered in another way the pains of defeat, as on these occasions we were deprived of pudding; then, if I were saucy, or Jane in a sulky fit, the scene often ended in the dark closet, where we cried for an hour or more, while William and little Mary finished the pudding.

This barbarity lasted only a short time, owing to my ingenious manufacture of small paper bags which we concealed in our laps under the table, and took opportunities of filling with our bits of fat, these we afterwards warily disposed of, at Twyford through the yew hedge into the river, in town elsewhere.

Another serious grief we had connected with our food. We could refuse nothing that was prepared for us; if we did we not only got nothing else, but the dish declined was put by to appear at the next meal, and be disposed of before we were permitted to have what else there was. Jane greatly disliked green vegetables, spinach or cabbage in particular; it was nature speaking (poor nature!, so unheeded in those times) for these plants disagreed with her, yet she must eat them. I have known a plate of spinach kept for her from dinner one day to supper the next, offered at each meal and refused, and not even a bit of bread substituted all those long hours, till sheer hunger got the better of her dislike, and she gave herself a night of sickness by swallowing the mess. Fancy a young child kept thirty hours without food and then given poison! The dungeons of feudal times were in their degree not more iniquitous than these proceedings. [*Grant (2), pp. 56, 57–9*]

England, c.1830   *Mary **Haldane** recalls the preventative measures taken during a cholera outbreak.*

We children were given port wine daily to strengthen our systems against an attack, a treatment to which we did not object. In those days children were always given a mug of ale at dinner time. [*p. 53*]

England, 1835   *Elizabeth **Gaskell** on her daughter Marianne, aged one.*

She suffered a good deal from the changes of weather we have had, and I have found it necessary to leave off milk as an article of diet at present. She lives on broth thickened with arrowroot, and I think this food strengthens her; but she is still a delicate child, and backward in walking. [*p. 12*]

When Marianne was two.

A few weeks ago she got a habit of refusing her food, saying 'bye-bye', etcetera, when a spoonful was offered to her which she did not quite approve. I found the best plan was to take her at her word, and quietly send the plate away, which at first produced sad fits of crying, and throwing herself back; but after once or twice she became less saucy and takes her food very pleasantly now. [*p. 25*]

Marianne was not given meat to eat until the age of three and a half.

England, 1887   *Thomas **Cobden-Sanderson** on his son Richard, aged two. The whole family were vegetarians.*

Breakfast soon after eight o'clock – feed Dickie porridge and bread and butter and jam, milk and water. He is very fond of water, and drinks a good deal at breakfast.

At eleven o'clock he goes to bed, and sleeps till 12.30. Lunch soon after one o'clock. I feed Dickie with Dickie's help, or perhaps, vice versa, he feeds himself with my help – potatoes, stewed pears, and rice pudding – no meat ever. After lunch go upstairs and all play together for a while. [*vol. 1, pp. 253–4*]

Clothing

*Anne **Clifford** on the clothing of her daughter Margaret, aged two*   England, 1617
years and nine months.

April.
The 28th was the first time the child put on a pair of whalebone
bodice

May.
The 2nd: the child put on her first coat that was laced with lace,
being of red baize.
   The 15th: the child put on her white coats and left off many
things from her head, the weather growing extreme hot.

January 1619.
This day the child did put on her crimson velvet coat laced with
silver lace, which was the first velvet coat she ever had. [*Clifford
(a), pp. 66, 67, 83*]

*Henry **Slingsby** notes in his diary.*   England, 1641

In 1641 I sent from London against Easter a suit of clothes for my
son Thomas, being the first breeches and doublet that he ever had,
and made by my tailor Mr Miller; it was too soon for him to wear
them being but five years old, but that his mother had a desire to
see him in them, how proper a man he would be. [*pp. 71–2*]

*Elizabeth **Hatton** writes to her daughter-in-law Cicelea. (Lady Thanet*   England, c.1670
is Cicelea's mother.)

I am very glad to hear that Miss thrives so well though you tell me
she is not so fair as my grand-niece, yet I doubt not but when she
grows a woman she will vie beauty with her. I desired Kit to tell
you that I coated all mine about ten or eleven weeks old but I never
put them into bodies till two or three years of age, only little
double fustian bodies that were sewed to their under coat and if
the weather were very cold when they were coated I continued a
little roller about them the longer, but I am sure you will be better
directed by my Lady Thanet than by any thing from me. [*Hatton
(b), add. MSS 29571, f. 105*]

*George **Gordon-Cummings**, a merchant's apprentice, writes to his*   Scotland, 1674
father Ludovic, lamenting his lack of clothing.

Sir my hat is now very ill worn and hath much need of being
supplied, my linens are in worse case because they were but old
when I got them which is now two years ago. I have here sent an

account of all for your more satisfactions. I stand in need of nothing more than I can at this time remember but one pair of britches for to wear with my last summer suit because that stuff did not at all last in the britches but did instantly cut . . .

I brought with me of linings as in the following compt.

5 pair of lining sleeves, 2 pair whereof may be as yet worn, the other 3 will scarcely stick together

5 cravats none whereof can be worn but in extreme pieces

5 shirts, 2 whereof were almost wholly worn when I was sick, the other 3 must be mended

4 napkins, 2 whereof were lost when I was sick the other 2 I have yet.

I brought with me two coats, one whereof being the whitish grey stuff lasted me three months with much ado. The other I made up and have yet but cannot wear it because it is too short. I also brought with me two pair of britches, one whereof were Ludovic's old [? MS torn] ones and were all gone ere I came to town with the riding, the other I wore nine months and now are not sticking together. The two just coats cannot be worn any of them being more that two years old. The summer last being so straitened I took of (truly I must confess without your order which shall not again happen) some summer clothes, the britches whereof (as above) are all gone. The coat would put by a good part of this summer if I had britches conform to it. [*dep. 175/1348*]

England, 1679   Anne **North** *writes to her son Francis informing him of his son's change of dress. Her grandson Francis was aged six.*

You cannot believe the great concern that was in the whole family here last Wednesday, it being the day that the tailor was to help to dress little Frank in his breeches in order to [fit him for] an everyday suit. Never had any bride that was to be dressed upon her wedding night more hands about her, some the legs and some the arms, the tailor buttoning and others putting on the sword, and so many lookers on that had I not had a finger amongst them I could not have seen him. When he was quite dressed he acted his part as well as any of them, for he desired he might go down to inquire for the little gentleman that was there the day before in a black coat, and speak to the men to tell the gentleman when he came from school that there was a gallant with very fine clothes and a sword to have waited upon him, and would come again upon Sunday next. But this was not all for there was great contrivings while he was dressing who should have the first salute, but he said if old Lane had been here she should, but he gave it me to quiet them all. They are very fit, everything, and he looks taller and prettier than in his coats. Little Charles rejoiced as much as he did, for he jumped all the while about him and took notice of everything. I went to Bury and bought everything for another suit, which will be finished upon Saturday, so the coats are to be quite left off upon Sunday. I consider it is not yet term time and since you could not have the pleasure of the first sight I have resolved you should have a full relation . . . When he was dressed he asked Buckle whether muffs were out of fashion because they had not sent him one. [*vol. 3, p. 215*]

Items of clothing taken by eleven-year-old John **Livingston** *to school.*   *America, 1690*

Eleven new shirts: four pair laced sleeves; eight plain cravats; four stript waistcoats with black buttons; one flowered waistcoat; four new osinbrig britches; one grey hat with a black ribbon; one grey hat with a blue ribbon; one dozen black buttons; one dozen coloured buttons; three pair gold buttons; three pair silver buttons; two pair fine blue stockings; one pair fine red stockings; four white handkerchiefs; three pair gloves; one stuff coat with black buttons; one cloth coat; one pair blue plush britches; one pair serge britches; two combs; one pair new shoes; silk and thread to mend his clothes. [*p. 37*]

Lydia **Coleman** *complains that her grandson Richard, whom she looks*   *America, c.1720*
after while he attends school in Boston, does not take care of his clothes.

As for Richard, since I told him I would write to his Father he is more orderly, and he is very hungry, and has grown so much that all his clothes is too little for him . . . He is a brisk child and grows very cute and won't wear his new silk coat that was made for him. He won't wear it every day so that I don't know what to do with it. It won't make him a jacket. I would have him a good husbander but he is but a child. For shoes, gloves, hankers, and stockings, they ask very dear, eight shillings for a pair and Richard takes no care of them. Richard wears out nigh twelve pairs of shoes a year. He brought twelve hankers with him and they have all been lost long ago; and I have bought him three or four more at a time. His way is to tie knotties at one end and beat the boys with them and then to lose them and he cares not a bit what I will say to him. [*pp. 292–3*]

Frances **Boscawen** *writes to her husband about their son Edward, aged*   *England, 1747*
almost three. His friend Charles was three.

The two Marsham boys have been to see him. They are fine children and the best behaved I ever saw, doing everything at a word – and, indeed, a look – of their father's. Charles makes a much better figure in breeches that I could have imagined, for he is considerably shorter than our boy, and my Lord scolds me vastly for keeping him in petticoats. [*p. 56*]

Dr Mamma

I have been very well since
I came here except that I had a Cold and but
now it is quite away since been in a great want
for Cloaths all this time — Colonel Campbell came &
has two weeks ago & has exchanged ... Mr Lesly for ...
Brother or not I want to ... that I told Mr Lesly for since
Letters or not I have never got an account ...
him. So I beg that I have ... a note from ... Jenkins
... from Edinburg him at a great ... of them ... & ...
... have now one but the Favr of them ... I ...
that brought to those either you or Papa and quick
to Colonel Campbells. I wish your Health may meet Peel
I am

Dr Mr Lesly
went again to With the greatest Respect
Colonel Campbells Your Most Gratefull Son
I told him that I
could want Cloaths
no longer and Colonel   Murray Fletcher
Campbell said that
he did not remember of
Papas speaking of getting
me Cloaths

respect your Letter
to be found at St Pauls
School

Pleas Send up My Stockings that I did not
take with me with Captin Steal who I believe
will Sail first for London.

P.S. Offer my humble Duety to all
my Sisters and Brothers.

Letter from Henry Fletcher, 1739

Dr Mamma

I have been very well since I came here except that I had a litel
could but now it is quite away. I have been in a great want for
cloaths all this time. Colonel Campbell came to toun two
weeks ago & has never yet sent or inqueird whither or not I
wanted cloaths. I told Mr Leslie to tell him & he did so, but I
have never got an account yet about them. likewise I am at a
great want for stockings for I have not one but the pair of blew
ons & a pair that I bought. So I hope either you or Pappa will
write to Colonel Campbell. I wait your answer nixt post.
I am

Dr Mamma
with the greates(t) respect
your most deutifull son
Henry Fletcher

dereek your litter to be found at St Pauls school

PS Mr Leslie went again to Colonel Campbells & told him that
I could want cloaths no longer and Colonel Campbell said that
he did not remember of Pappa's speaking of gitting me
cloaths

Please send up my stockings that I did not take with me with
Captin Steal who I belive will sail first for London.

PS Offer my humble deuty to all my Sisters and Brothers

National Library of Scotland, Ms 16510/236

England, c.1760   Sarah **Pennington** *instructs Miss Louisa on the appropriate method of dressing infants.*

Many prudent alterations have of late years been made in the first dress of infants, but many more are yet wanting; the barbarous custom of swathing is not yet universally exploded, and others little less injurious too generally retained; particularly that of dividing their garments into a multiplicity of pieces, which not only prolong the uneasy sensation which to them always accompanies dressing, but by the unequal pressure of different bandages their shape is often injured, and even their health impaired; the whole of a child's first habit need consist of no more than three pieces, viz. a shirt, a robe, and a cap; the two last should be quilted of a proper thickness to be sufficiently warm. The cap should be fastened by a band of soft linen under the chin, sewed to one side of it and buttoned on the other; if a knot is thought necessary for girls, that should first be sewed on the cap; the robe and shirt should be made open before; the sleeves put into each other, that both may be put on together; they must be wide enough in the back to prevent any difficulty in getting the last arm through. The robe should lap over on the breast, and be fastened by flat buttons, placed at different distances, to make it more or less tight, which is preferable to strings as being the quickest. By this method the whole business of dressing (which is evidently a most disagreeable operation to infants, and with which it has been customary to torment them for two hours at a time) may be dispatched in two minutes, and in a manner so easy to themselves as scarcely to occasion a cry; which is a matter of much greater consequence than it is generally thought. When they are coated that may be managed as expeditiously, and with as much ease by tacking the petticoats and robe to the stays, which instead of lacing should be buttoned on; loose plaits might hang from the top of the robe and fall over these buttons in such a manner as to make a much prettier dress than that now used, and this continued for the first three or four years would not only contribute much to the regularity of their growth, but also to the sweetness of their temper, which early teasing is too apt to sour. [*vol. 3, pp. 126–30*]

America, 1772   Anna **Winslow**, *aged twelve, has been sent to school in Boston and finds the fashions there very different from her rural home. She writes to her mother.*

The black hat I gratefully receive as your present, but if Captain Jarvise had arrived here with it about the time he sailed from his place for Cumberland it would have been of more service to me, for I have obliged to borrow . . . I hope aunt won't let me wear the black hat with the red dominie . . . Dear mamma, you don't know the fashion here – I beg to look like other folk. [*p. 7*]

She eventually acquires a new outfit in Boston.

I was dressed in my yellow coat, my black bib and apron, my pompadour shoes, the cap my aunt Storer sometime since presented me (with blue ribbons on it) and a very handsome locket in the shape of a heart she gave me – the paste pin my Honoured Papa presented me with in my new cap. My new cloak and bonnet on, my pompadour gloves etcetera, etcetera. And I would tell you, that *for the first time, they all liked my dress very much.* My cloak and bonnet are really very handsome, and so they had need to be. For they cost an amazing sight of money, not quite $45 though Aunt Suky said that she supposed Aunt Deming would be frightened out of her wits at the money it cost. I have got *one* covering, by the cost, that is genteel and I like it much myself. [*pp. 13-14*]

*Thomas **Jefferson** to his daughter Martha, aged eleven.*   *America, 1783*

I do not wish you to be gaily clothed at this time of life, but that your wear should be fine of its kind. But above all things and at all times let your clothes be neat, whole, and properly put on. Do not fancy you must wear them till the dirt is visible to the eye. You will be the last one who is sensible of this. Some ladies think they may, under the privilege of deshabillé, be loose and negligent of their dress in the morning. But be you, from the moment you rise till you go to bed, as cleanly and properly dressed as at the hours of dinner or tea. A lady who has been seen as a sloven or a slut in the morning, will never efface the impression she has made, with all the dress and pageantry she can afterwards involve herself in. Nothing is so disgusting to our sex as a want of cleanliness and delicacy in yours. I hope, therefore, the moment you rise from bed, your first work will be to dress yourself in such style, as that you may be seen by any gentleman without his being able to discover a pin amiss, or any other circumstance of neatness wanting. [*p. 71*]

*Charlotte **Papendiek** on the clothing of her eleven-month-old Charlotte.*   *England, 1783*

Dr Khone had poor baby weaned, but she did not mind it, and at this time we put her into short coats. We made her four white frocks and two coloured ones, with the skirts full and three tucks and a hem; the bodies plain, cut cross-ways, and the sleeves plain, with a cuff turned up. These, with converting of underclothing, nurse, I, and a workwoman finished off in a week. The rest of her attire was, long cotton or thread mitts, without fingers, tied round the arm high above the elbow, a double muslin handkerchief crossed and tied behind in a bow, or if cold a silk pelerine, with the same coloured bonnet, close front, high caul, with a bow in front. Baby's was blue, and very pretty did she look. [*vol. 1, pp. 220-21*]

America, 1786   *Reverend Mather **Byles** to his sisters, relating the breeching ceremony of his son Belchar.*

Belchar finishing his sixth year, makes his first appearance in jacket and trousers: and I assure you he strutts, and swells, and puffs, and looks as important as a Boston Committeeman. It was an affecting and interesting sight, when with calmness, delibera-tion, and solemnity, he collected, of his own accord, all his tunics, petticoats, and linen, folded them up very carefully in the exactest order, and presented them to Louisa for doll-rags. He next proceeded into the kitchen, took up the cat, whom he is to hug no longer, and gave her the last affectionate embrace. He then went up stairs, stripped himself of the clothes he had on, assumed his new garb, returned with his eyes sparkling, and very politely paid his compliments to the family. In short, the whole scene was vastly pathetic and sentimental. [*p. 285*]

America, 1797   *Leverett **Saltonstall**, a law student, writes to his father.*

Honored father, – I feel necessitated to inform you, what you cannot be surprised to hear, that I am in great want of a new suit of clothes. My coat, which was a year old last May, is very much rusty and threadbare and my pantaloons are old and much worn. I have delayed this request as long as I could, out of a consideration of your great and necessary expenses. But situated as I am, my dress ought to be such that I may look and *feel*, if I expect to *appear* like a gentleman. Much depends on external appearance, indeed the world is governed by appearances; and we shall all find if we look into our own breasts, that we are considerably influenced by the dress of a stranger. I should like either black or blue. Would it not be best to buy the cloth at Haverhill and send it to me? Or shall I buy it with the assistance of Mrs T.'s advice? [*vol. 2, p. 159*]

Dear son, – In your last letter to me you mentioned the want of clothes – as I wish you to appear decent, but not extravagant, I consent to your request, at the same time reminding you of economy. If you could get an opportunity to come home for a few days, without any expense, you can have your clothes made here by Kent equal to any one, and have a good choice of cloths. Perhaps you can appear decently till your visit at Thanksgiving which will probably be in six or seven weeks? Or shall the cloth be forwarded to you? Will no other colour suit but black or blue? In this query I have no choice, suit yourself. [*vol. 2, p. 165*]

Nathaniel Saltonstall junior writes to his elder brother Leverett.

I have written to Par about a pair of boots. You know the fashion I suppose, and I'll thank you to attend to them for if they suit me they will wear much longer than if they don't. I want them made long and considerably higher before than behind. I will enclose a pattern. The string enclosed is the rise of my leg and the length of my foot to the knee. If Mulakin makes them tell him to make the foot part, one size larger than my last shoes and I want the legs cut very large so that they will go on and off without any difficulty and be sure to get the best leather.

I want what you call two thirds. I suppose you will call me an old maid but I don't care. [*vol. 2, p. 123*]

*Mary **Haldane** writes in her autobiography about the way in which she was dressed as child.*   *England, 1830s*

We were dressed in white cambric frocks in the morning with low necks and short sleeves and had broad blue or pink sashes tied behind. When we went out of doors we wore white spencers of cambric muslin with frills round the waist and long sleeves and collars and cuffs, the sashes being dispensed with. Drawn silk bonnets were worn with net caps covering the head and bordered with tiny roses or baby ribbon. The latter was very becoming, and net caps were thought essential for cleanliness. In winter we donned pelisses and beaver bonnets for out-of-doors, and in the house dresses of fine crimson merino. It was the fashion then to have the drawers long, showing the double-worked frills below the hem of the dress. When King George IV died in 1830 I remember the pride we had in our black and white gingham frocks which we wore in mourning. [*pp. 50–51*]

*Caroline **Richards**, aged ten, and her sister Anna, aged seven, wanted to wear the latest fashion.*   *America, 1852*

We asked Grandmother if we could have some hoop skirts like the seminary girls and she said no, we were not old enough. When we were downtown Anna bought a reed for 10 cents and ran it into the hem of her underskirt and says she is going to wear it to school tomorrow. I think Grandmother will laugh out loud for once, when she sees it, but I don't think Anna will wear it to school or anywhere else. She wouldn't want to if she knew how terrible it looked. [*p. 26*]

*Catherine **Carswell** recalls the clothes she wore as a child.*   *Scotland, 1880s*

We wore in winter heavy woollen combinations and over that a substantial long cloth chemise stretching from neck to knee and with prickly Swiss trimming round neck and armholes; then a

wadded stay-belt with buttons at intervals to which other garments had to be attached. Long, thick stockings of black cashmere
were joined to the stays by elastic: white long-cloth knickers (also
trimmed Swiss) were buttoned to it. Over them a scalloped white
flannel bodiced petticoat, and last of all a complicated high necked
dress – and for school a holland apron over the dress. On Sunday
for some reason, the dress was made far more complicated and
abounding in discomforts. In one of these – it was patterned with
lozenges, the shape of which has ever since made me feel slightly
ill – I suffered so acutely and continuously that I had bilious
attacks. It was a misery which increased when a coat was added
and I had to sit still for nearly two hours in church without having
the coat removed. By the time we emerged, unless I had mercifully
fallen asleep, I was like a fish on land gasping for air at every pore.
Yet all this was as nothing compared to what we wore when we
became young ladies and put up our hair.

When we were verging on our teens, my sister and I, in scorn of
young ladies vowed to each other (1) that we would never wear
'real stays with bones in them' and (2) that we should never carry a
parasol. We did not keep our vows. At eighteen I wore the same
garments as at eight – except that they were longer and the top
petticoat was a divided affair, white camisole above and frilled silk
or stout mohair as to skirt. The straight padded band of our stays
became confining and stiff with steel fronts. The neckbands of
dresses were fortified with whalebones and the lined bodices also.
The skirt, also lined, and reaching to the ground in front and at the
back, had braid all round inside the hem which came constantly
unstitched as it caught in the wearer's heel. Our hair was rolled up
over a pad on top, to which pad a hat was precariously pinned and
a veil adjusted. Gloves were a necessity, and usually an umbrella
or parasol. With one hand, while out walking, the back of the skirt
had to be held clear of the pavement in such a manner as just to
show an edge of petticoat but no stocking or ankle. This involved
many backward and downward glances. The other hand was
usually occupied in grasping the hat brim and frantically adjusting
veil – both subject to the least breath of wind. The umbrella or
parasol being on the hat arm it was hard to assume an uncon-
cerned smile. [*vol. 1. pp. 31112*]

England, 1882   *Mary* **Brabazon** *recalls the day when her son Normy, aged thirteen,
discarded his childish clothing.*

Sunday 18th June, was a very sad one to me, as Normy for the first
time put on manly attire, and it made me realise how time had
passed, and that I must very soon bid him farewell. It is sad to feel
his childhood is passing away. [*p. 56*]

CHILDREN ARE HORRIBLY INSECURE; THE LIFE OF A PARENT IS THE LIFE OF A GAMBLER:
CHILDHOOD ACCIDENTS, ILLNESS AND DEATH

Introduction

The path of growing up was strewn with pitfalls. At home there were the hazards of open fires and pots on the stove, the dangerous attractions of pins and guns; and outside there was the risky allure of rivers and horses to resist (Alice Thornton, p. 96, and Fanny Longfellow, p. 99). There was also illness. Children's health was a matter of grave concern to their parents. Children were considered to be soft, weak beings who needed to be strengthened by cold water bathing and fresh (particularly sea) air (Elizabeth Gaskell, p. 106). This regime was designed to harden them and to ward off ailments such as rickets and fevers. By the nineteenth century cold baths were adopted not so much as a health measure but as a part of a routine of austerity for children, aimed at instilling moral character (Mary Haldane, p. 106). For Elizabeth Grant (p. 105) it was a very unpleasant experience.

The main childhood diseases of the seventeenth century were worms, fevers of various sorts, smallpox, diphtheria, whooping cough, rickets and measles. By the eighteenth century, smallpox and rickets were at their height, and in the nineteenth century tuberculosis, diphtheria, and typhus were on the increase and cholera made its first appearance. The main remedies employed were issues, cupping, leeches, blisters, splints, swathing, purging, ass's milk and sea bathing (Mary Lovett, p. 111. Landon Carter, p. 112 and Arthur Young, p. 115).

Many doctors felt unable to deal with childhood illness; it was difficult to diagnose, and children possessed a disquieting tendency to succumb to whatever disease afflicted them. Parents, however, were well-versed in medical skills and were prepared to treat their offspring themselves, even in defiance of the doctors' advice, as in the case of Anne, Countess of Arundel (p. 107). Medical books were available for consultation, and there were tried and tested family remedies noted down in recipe books and handed on through the generations (Fletcher family book, p. 101, and Brooke family book, p. 102).

Smallpox was very much a disease of childhood – 87 per cent of all deaths from it occurred among those under the age of sixteen – and one of the major advances in children's health care was the introduction of inoculation against it. In 1721 Lady Mary Wortley Montagu decided to put into practice a procedure she had observed on her trips to Turkey and arranged to have her daughter inoculated. Smallpox inoculation was part of Asiatic folk tradition and had been carried out prior to this, but her decision drew attention to the measure. The first publicized inoculations were carried out in America at the same time. Inoculation involved the injection of the smallpox virus taken from a pustule on someone suffering from the disease. The person injected then experienced pustular eruptions around the body, a mild form of smallpox, was infectious to unprotected people and developed the antibodies which prevented him or her from catching a severe case of the disease. Vaccination, the injection of the virus taken from a cow suffering from cowpox, was introduced by Edward Jenner in 1796. It resulted in a local eruption at the site of the injection only, so that the person was not infectious. The inoculation procedure often involved a lengthy preparatory regime. Smallpox was thought to be inflamed by animal foods but reduced by purging, bleeding and vegetarian diet. Therefore, for about ten days the patient underwent purgings and bleedings to ensure that he or she would be free from all physical ills (Frances Boscawen, p. 102, and Elizabeth Drinker, p. 103). The inoculation itself was a relatively simple matter, though it could prove fatal or ineffective. Smallpox inoculation was not universal; parents were concerned about its hazards, about giving their child a disease, and some had religious objections to the procedure.

Tuberculosis reached peak levels from the late eighteenth century well into the twentieth. The bovine form, affecting children, was generally contracted from drinking contaminated milk. It could cause death, but its victims were more likely to survive and be protected from more serious forms of tuberculosis in later life. The introduction of the pasteurization of milk ensured the control of bovine tuberculosis, but at the expense of leaving more of the population unprotected against intestinal or respiratory forms. These usually affected young adults and were often fatal. Until the vaccine was produced in 1921, there were no effective means of treatment. The sufferer was almost invariably condemned to endure a distressing, slow decline (Emily Shore, p. 119).

Parental anxiety at the sickness of their offspring was exacerbated by the fact that any illness could lead to death. The higher infant and child mortality rates of the past have led some historians to claim that because so many children died their deaths were not seriously mourned. Parents, it has been argued, maintained an emotional detachment from their children. The infant and child mortality rate, however, has been exaggerated. From 1600 to 1900, the mortality rate for children under the age of one varied between 13 and 15 per cent and was at its highest in the first half of the eighteenth century and again in the early nineteenth century. The death rate for children aged up to nine varied between 22 and 28 per cent, peaking in the nineteenth century. As the selection given here illustrates, children could pull through serious illnesses (Nancy Shippen, p. 114, and William Macready, p. 118). Perhaps the level of childhood morbidity was more influential in determining parental reaction than the level of childhood mortality.

The extracts cited in this chapter emphasize the grief felt by parents when their children did die. Familiarity with death did not induce indifference. Many were consoled by their Christian faith, which counselled resignation to God's will, and by their belief that children were on loan from God, who could recall them whenever he wished. In addition, some comforted themselves with the thought that the child was in a 'better place' (Ann Grant, p. 129). In practice it could be difficult for a mother or father to reconcile their religious belief with the searing sense of loss which assaulted them after the death of one of their children (Nehemiah Wallington, p. 123, and Mary Timms, p. 129). Some parents even considered that God was punishing them for loving their child too much (Ebenezer Erskine, p. 125, and Arthur Young, p. 127). A difference in the extent of grief experienced at the death of a child was noted by some parents through the centuries – for instance, Simonds D'Ewes (p.123) and James Parker (p.126). An older child was felt to be a greater loss since the parent not only grieved for what the child would one day become, but also for what the child was to them at the moment of death.

Accidents and Mishaps

England, 1660

*Alice **Thornton** on her children, Katy, aged four, and Alice (Naly), aged six.*

My dear Katy was playing under the table with her sister, (being about three years old, but a very brave, strong child, and full of mettle . . . always continued very healthful and strong, and full of tricks, and indeed apt to fall into dangers), as she was playing with pins, and putting them into her mouth, her sister see her, and cried out for fear she should do herself hurt. But she would not be counselled with her, and at last she got a pin cross her throat. By God's pleasure I was just near her, and catched her up in my arms, and put my fingers immediately into her throat, and the pin was cross, and I had much to do to get it out, but with all the force I had, it pleased God to strengthen me to do it. [*pp. 129-130*]

America, 1688

*Samuel **Sewall** describes in his diary an accident which happened to his eight-year-old daughter Hannah.*

Little Hannah going to school in the morn, being entered a little within the Schoolhouse Lane, is rid over by David Lopes, [she] fell on her back, but I hope [is] little hurt, save that her teeth bled a little, [and she] was much frighted; but went to school. [*vol. 5, p. 231*]

Four years later he notes the mishap which befell his son Joseph, aged four.

Joseph put his Grandmother and Mother in great fear by swallowing a bullet which for a while stuck in his throat. He had quite got it down, before I knew what the matter was . . . when I come home from the funeral, my wife shows me the bullet Joseph swallowed, which he voided in the orchard. The Lord help us to praise Him for his distinguishing favour. [*vol. 5, p. 374*]

Scotland, 1699

*George **Turnbull** on his son William, aged almost three.*

My son William met with a very merciful providence, being in the chamber alone at the fire his clothes took low, and were all burnt, his hair, and very eyelids scorched, and yet his face and whole body untouched . . . a mercy not to be forgotten. [*pp. 380–81*]

America, 1780

*Elizabeth **Drinker** on her son Henry, aged ten.*

Little Henry fell into the river this afternoon, and after remaining a quarter of an hour in his wet clothes, came home very cold and coughing. We stripped him, and after rubbing him well with a coarse towel, put on warm dry clothes, gave hime some rum and water to drink and made him jump a rope till he sweated. He is bravely this evening. [*Drinker (a), p. 127*]

Elizabeth **Drinker** *describes the trials endured by her grandchild, Eliza Downing, aged three, who had pushed a piece of nutshell up her nose.* America, 1792

Our dear little Eliza on seventh day night last, put a piece of a nutshell up her nose, which continues there yet. The Doctor has made an attempt to take it out, with an instrument but without success, they bound her eyes, and held her fast down, she cried so, that nothing could be done.

March 16.

The Doctor has ordered Sally Downing to syringe the child's nose with warm water – and afterwards to put oil in it. She is terrified at the sight of the Doctor and will not suffer him to examine it.

March 18.

Doctor Shippen who Kuhn called in, tried with an instrument to take the nutshell out of the poor dear child's nose, but could not effect it.

March 20.

The Doctor made another vain attempt to extract the nutshell.

March 21.

Eliza is cheerful, though I believe feels a constant uneasy sensation. Doctor Kuhn called this afternoon says he hopes it will rot away, advises syringing with warm water and using oil, to keep it sweet and to prevent a polypus from forming.

March 22.

Our little Eliza here this morning, I could plainly discover when she kissed me, that her nose was offensive. I went home with her before dinner, stayed dinner there. After dinner her Father made an attempt with the silver hook, to no purpose but to make her nose bleed, she screaming violently all the time. It being a case of so much consequence he was loath to give out, and with three to hold her fast down, tried again and was favour'd to relieve the dear child. He brought away with the hook half of a ground nut-shell which had been there near two weeks, – it has taken one burden off my mind, had it continued, the consequence might have been distressing indeed. [(b), pp. 15–16]

England, 1784   *Faith **Gray** on her two-year-old daughter Margaret.*

Margaret Gray was scalded with boiling starch on her head, and face and was very ill and delirious at times for the first four or five days. [p. 72]

America, 1836   *Caroline **Phelps** describes the accident which befell her daughter Emily, aged almost three. Her son Thomas was four.*

The last of August my little girl got badly burned with powder. My oldest boy emptied a pound of powder on the floor in an empty room and got some fire and threw on the powder, it did not flash. He told his sister to blow on the fire, which she did, and the blaze all went up in her face and burned her hair off back to her crown, one ear and both eyes, her chin was not burned but her nose was very badly burned. I ran as soon as I heard her scream and a squaw had got to her first and was holding her in her arms. My child was so black I hardly knew her. I took her in the other room and gave her thirty drops of laundanum and put sweet oil on her and then fanned her all night. The next morning she got to sleep for a little while. I sent thirty miles for a doctor, but he was gone from home . . . We put all kinds of medicine on that we thought was good, but her face was so swollen the fifth day that she did not look like [a] human being. I did not think she could live long in this situation. We did everything we could for her, but nothing seemed to do much good. We concluded to send for an Indian doctor – he came and stayed with us several days, her burns healed all right – right away, but I thought she never could see any more, but I tried to hire her to open her eyes but she would not try. The thirtieth day I told her to open her eyes and see what a lovely bonnet she had, but she refused. I was determined to make her try to open her eyes, so I said, Oh just see that snake. She jumped up and opened her eyes, but she was so glad to see me and her brother she forgot the snake. She clapped her little hands and laughed out. I was so overjoyed I had to cry, to think she could see again. We kept the room darkened for two weeks more, when her eyes got stronger we let her go out. The marks showed for a long time but no scar is to be seen. [pp. 225–6]

*Fanny **Longfellow** writes to her sister-in-law Mary after Fanny's eleven-year-old son Charles has destroyed his thumb in a shooting accident.*   America, 1856

I have not had a moment's time to write you or you should not have been left in ignorance of all the particulars of Charley's sad accident. His father was obliged to watch with him all night, for more than a week, and I was needed all day, whenever baby could spare me, so that we have been much absorbed since it happened. It has been a sore trial to us, completely unnerving us for the time, and the thought of our boy's maimed hand has been before our eyes and hearts through all the sleepless nights and anxious days. But all has gone on as well as possible, and we begin to feel more resigned, and to be grateful it was not his face, nor right hand, that suffered. He has helped us by the astonishing bravery with which he has borne all the horror and suffering, walking home more than a mile, 'without crying once', as his companion said (who had the presence of mind to bind up his hand with a handkerchief and tie it tight with the cord of the powder-flask), and as soon as his hand was dressed, with the blessed help of ether, he begged us not to worry saying, 'Ah, Doctor, ether is much better than gunpowder', on which text, you know, I could preach a sermon. The doctor is in daily admiration of his courage, for this daily dressing gets to be very trying to the nerves, as well as painful, but he is cheerful and hardly winces, and is now allowed to go out freely to recover his strength. It will be a fresh blow to me when his hand is well enough to be uncovered, but 'sufficient for the day', etcetera. I trust he will never feel it as we do, and that it may have a lasting beneficial effect on his character. The gun burst, either from being overloaded, or from being worthless, we do not know which. We feel very grateful to the older boy, who brought him so well home, without allowing him to yield to faintness, etcetera. Think what a walk for the poor fellow! He was at Fresh Pond. He bought the gun with money he had saved up, but Henry had told him only to use percussion-caps with it, but the temptation was too great – he yielded and was severely punished. [*Longfellow (b), pp. 203–4*]

Health Care Regimes, Preventative Measures and Suggested Remedies

England, 1623

*Endymion **Porter** writes to his wife Olive about their two-year-old son George.*

I would have you cut George his hair somewhat short, and not to beat him overmuch. I hope you let him go bareheaded, for otherwise he will be so tender that upon every occasion you will have him sick. [*p. 68*]

England, 1638

*Medicinal recipes for children contained in Ann **Brockman**'s medical book.*

For all kinds of impostures and ague that breedeth in children, for worms that are in children this is a precious oil.

Take a great handful of wormwood, as much as of featherfew, as much of tansy, as much of sotherwood, as much of rue. Beat all these together, with a pound of barroms grease till they be fine beaten, then take the stuff and pull it into pound balls, then put it into a vessel and set it into a low cellar eight days till it be hore. Then take it and break it into a frying pan, and put to it the gall of an eye and seethe it on the fire with hot embers, and so let it be on the fire an hour together, and ever be stirring of it, and at the hour's end, set it to cool, and then strain it into a clean vessel and keep it for a precious ointment. [*add. MSS 45197, f. 2*]

England, 1660

*Dr M. Xoucheret writes to Frances Cavendish, sending advice and pills for the purging of her young children. (The letter is in the **Portland** collection.)*

According to your Honour's commands I send by this bearer in a basket three sets of purging pills: one for my Lady Elizabeth, one for my Lady Frances, and one other for my Lady Margaret. You must have a care that they be not changed from pot to pot for each of them are of different strength. They are to be taken by each Lady four at a time, taking them in a spoonful of syrup or violets or by themselves about three or four of the clock in the night or very late when they go to bed, keeping their chamber the next day . . . I desire you will be pleased not to purge them so often as usually in this hot weather nor at any other time except upon urgent necessity or else you shall destroy their strength. I send you also a bottle of lawdirte[?] purging infusion such a[s] I did purge them with when I was at Wallingoe. It shall not treat them so much as the pills and it is not unpleasant to take. When you please to have them use it, my Lady Elizabeth shall take five ounces of it, my Lady Frances four, and my Lady Margaret, four ounces also, my Lord Mansfield shall take four ounces also and for my little Lady Catherine let her take an ounce in the night and if by the morning it should not work, let her drink an ounce about six or seven of the clock in the morning. I hope these will be physicking sufficient to them this spring and summer. [PW1/30]

Remedies contained in the **Fletcher** *family medical book.*

*Scotland,
17th century*

For the rickets:

1. In the morning when the child arises, anoint the region of his liver and spleen with the liniment made of liverwort and fresh butter. At that same time after gentle friction of his legs and thighs, they are to be anointed with one ointment made thus; take sage, red mint, St John's wort and dainwort (or Walwort) of each two large handful, stamp them well in a mortar with one handful of fresh tallow, then put all together in a close[d] bottle or glass, and when it is well stopped, cover it all over with the best clay that can be had, set it in an oven, and let it stand with the bread until it be baked then draw it out, and break the glass. In the midst of it you shall find a green ointment. A very little thereof will serve to anoint the legs and thighs of the child any morning. Then put on his clothes and give him a draught of his mare's milk.

2. But the rest of the day he must drink only of the ale following, and in the night also; take a gallon of wort, boil among it of polypody roots, of sarsaparilla roots, of each an ounce. Of hinds-tongue, maidenhair and liverwort, of each an handful. Of the middle rind of tamarisk, and of the ash tree, of each half an ounce. Of maces and yellow lentils, of each an quarter of an ounce. Of great raisins, half a pound. They must be boiled until the third part of the wort be spent, then strain it, and work it with barm as you do ordinarily, and keep it for your use.

3. Every night, or (if the child be weak) every other night bathe him with this water, rubbing his legs and thighs with the herbs softly. Take ground ivy, and catmint, of each six handfuls. Of fox gloves, two handfuls. Boil them well in half a gallon of water and mix it with more, then you are to use it. If the child be strong he may be dipped in the water, but if you find him weak, it will be better to foment his body with woollen cloths dipped in the water only.

These things may be done until his breath or vital spirits begin to fail. [MS17851/223]

England, early 18th century

*Remedies for childhood diseases in the **Brooke** family recipe book.*

An outward application for the whooping cough:

Mix an equal quantity of spirit of hawthorne and oil of amber not exceeding half an ounce at a time because in often opening it decays. With this anoint the palms of the hands, pit of the stomach and soles of the feet for a month together and let no water come nigh any of the parts anointed. The fingers and backs of the hands may be wiped with a wet cloth.

For the whooping cough:

Six cloves of garlic peeled and boiled in a pint of spring water, with two ounces of brown sugar candy, till it is reduced to half. Take a teaspoonful whenever the cough is troublesome. [B (O) v. 14, ff. 1. .]

England, 1755

*Frances **Boscawen** describes to her husband the procedure for the inoculation of her son Billy, aged three, against smallpox.*

I must beg you not to be uneasy about the child. He is in the most desirable state for inoculation that can be. Mr Hawkins felt his pulse said he wanted no bleeding, no purging, but a little rhubarb, and he assures me that in all his practice he never remarked a more favourable run of inoculated patients, not one having yet had it full . . .

I have been summoned upstairs to assist at the solemnity of poor Billy's rhubarb, for the pretty cur was asleep when Burges sent it. I have not been able to get it all down – he reached [retched] so. However, as 'tis prescribed, I shall attempt the remainder tomorrow morning, but now the sweet soul was so sleepy and tired, and tried so honestly to do his best to oblige 'May', the little stomach heaving all the while, that I must have had have a heart of flint to torment him any more.

Three days later.

Pray Papa! Pray to God to bless us, for we are inoculated. This day exactly at noon it was done; no fuss, no rout, no assistance. Nobody with me but the servants. I held the child myself and so effectually employed his eyes and attentions (by a bit of gold lace which I was putting into forms to lace his waistcoat) that he never was sensible of the first arm. For the second, he pretended to wince a little, but I had a sugar plum ready which stopped the whimper before it was well formed. And he is now . . . tattling here by my bureau with some cards and papers, etcetera; for the weather is so very hot that I reckon that the chief service I can do him is to provide him such amusements as will keep him still and quiet. So that, instead of waggons, carts and post-chaises, we shall deal altogether in mills, pictures, dolls, London cries, and such sedentary amusements. [*pp. 167, 168, 170*]

Six weeks after this Billy had completely recovered.

A letter of advice on how to treat rickets sent to Joseph **Perry**.   *America, 1769*

In the rickets the best corrective I have ever found is a syrup made of black cherries. Thus. Take of cherries (dried ones are as good as any) and put them into a vessel with water. Set the vessel near the fire and let the water be scalding hot. Then take the cherries into a thin cloth and squeeze them into the vessel, and sweeten the liquor with molasses. Give two spoonfuls of this two or three times in a day. If you dip your child, do it in this manner: viz: naked, in the morning, head foremost in cold water, don't dress it immediately, but let it be made warm in the cradle and sweat at least half an hour moderately. Do this three mornings going and if one or both feet are cold while other parts sweat (which is sometimes the case) let a little blood be taken out of the feet the second morning and it will cause them to sweat afterwards. Before the dips of the child give it some snakeroot and saffron steeped in rum and water, give this immediately before dipping and after you have dipped the child three mornings give it several times a day the following syrup made of comfrey, hartshorn, red roses, hog-brake roots, knot-grass, petty-moral roots, sweeten the syrup with molasses. Physicians are generally fearful about dipping when the fever is hard, but oftentimes all attempts to lower it without dipping are in vain. Experience has taught me that these fears are groundless, that many have about dipping in rickety fevers; I have found in a multitude of instances of dipping [it] is [a] most effectual means to break a rickety fever. These directions are agreeable to what I have practised for many years. [*p. 8*]

Elizabeth **Drinker** *records in her diary the inoculation of her three-*   *America, 1773*
year-old son Henry.

18 February.

Henry Drinker junior took a pill, fifth day, in order to prepare him for inoculation; it made him very sick and vomited him several times.

21 February.

First day he took the second pill, which also made him very sick.

24 February.

Took another pill, which likewise made him very sick.

27 February.

The child took a dose of jollop, which vomited him several times but did not purge him.

28 February.

First day, our little Henry was inoculated by Doctor Redman, between twelve and one o'clock. He took a pill this evening, which did not make him sick as the others has done.

2 March.

He took a pill; but a little sick with it.

3 March.

He took the sixth and last pill.

5 March.

He took a dose of jollop, it vomited him as the other had done but did not purge him. In the evening he was feverish and unwell.

6 March.

Continued the same though at times cheerful. He has not had a stool for three days past.

7 March.

First day; the child continues feverish; Molly Moore gave him a glister, in order to open his bowels, which had the desired effect; some appearances of smallpox this evening.

8 March.

Eight or ten come out; he had been taken in the yard and to J. Howels today and has drank water from the pump, several times.

9 March.

Several more have appeared, he continues feverish.

10 March.

Seems bravely, but very cross . . .

12 and 13 March.

The smallpox begins to turn, he has about forty or fifty and is through mercy bravely.

15 March.

He took a dose of jollop, which did not work.

18 March.

He took another dose of jollop which vomited him once, but did not purge. His arm is not quite as well as could be wished.

15 April.

The child's arm appears to be healed. It has been a long time sore, though not very bad. [*Drinker (b), pp. 96–7*]

The entire experience had lasted two months.

*Thomas Fremantle writes to his wife Elizabeth **Wynne**. They have four children: Thomas aged five; Emma aged four; Charles aged three and Henry aged one.*   *England, 1803*

If there is any subject on which I feel diffident, it is that your kindness and affection for the children will lead you to take *too much care* of them, believe me nothing tends more to health than exercise and air, and that the more they are out of the house the better ... consider what your boys must undergo before they arrive even at manhood, and I am sure you will agree with me that it is not wise to bring them up too tenderly. [*vol. 3, p. 96*]

*Elizabeth **Grant** graphically relates the misery of cold-water bathing in winter. (Mrs Millar is her nurse.)*   *Scotland, c.1807*

In town, a large, long tub, stood in the kitchen court, the ice on the top of which had often to be broken before our horrid plunge into it; we were brought down from the very top of the house, four pairs of stairs, with only a cotton cloak over our night-gowns, just to chill us completely before the dreadful shock. How I screamed, begged, prayed, entreated to be saved, half the tender-hearted maids in tears besides me: all no use, Millar had her orders (so had dear Betty, but did she always obey them?). Nearly senseless I have been taken to the housekeeper's room, which was always warm, to be dried; there we dressed, without any flannel, and in cotton frocks with short sleeves and low necks. Revived by the fire, we were enabled to endure the next bit of martyrdom, an hour upon the low sofa, so many yards from the nursery hearth, our books in our hands, while our cold breakfast was preparing. [*Grant (2), pp. 56–7*]

America, 1828 John **Todd** *writes of his six-week-old daughter Mary.*

Little Mary seems pretty well, except that I am obliged to give her physic often. Last Wednesday evening I gave her more than an even teaspoonful of salts. She has needed nothing since. When she does, I think I shall give her an emetic. P.S. Yesterday Doctor Cutter was here, and advised us to give Mary a dose of calomel and jalap. [*p. 206*]

England, 1830s Mary **Haldane** *recollects the austere regime of her childhood. (Miss Taylor is her governess.)*

While with Miss Taylor our feet were placed in the stocks during lesson time, and we held a back board behind our backs, being seated on narrow seats that only just held us. The day commenced by our being wakened by our nurses, taken by the two, and plunged over head in a deep bath of cold water. Our cribs were made for us by the joiner engaged on the house, and they were of pinewood without springs, and had cross-bars on which we rested on mattresses of straw . . . The rule of life was Spartan, but I do not regret it. [*pp. 45–6*]

England, 1836 Elizabeth **Gaskell** *writes about her daughter Marianne, aged about twenty months. Marianne was a delicate child and the doctor prescribed sea-bathing to strengthen her.*

It was necessary for her to bathe, and I dreaded it for her. Luckily, her Aunt Anne, a capital bather, was with us, and undertook the charge of her, which was so much better than being frightened by being given over to a strange woman in an uncouth dress. We made the period of suspense as short as possible, undressing her directly, and giving her plunges immediately. I stood on the rocks with a shawl ready to receive her and give her a biscuit; and though she often said while being undressed, 'Baby not bathe, Mama', we never had any crying or screaming. She has lately had occasion to take one or two doses of Epsom salts, and I have always told her beforehand they were bad, bad, but were to do her good, and she has taken them directly, looking, however, strongly inclined to cry when the cup is taken from her lips; but a biscuit as a reward soon puts a stop to this. [*p. 26*]

Illness

*Anne, Countess of Arundel, writes to Gilbert **Talbot** about their grandson Frederick Henry, aged one month.*   *England, 1606*

[He] grew much out of temper and sweat so much and on Sunday so sick and burnt so much and groaned so pitifully as I had Doctor Foster to look on the child but I durst not to do any thing that he named but with carduus water and cordials divers times, blessed be our Lord he found amendment. [MS3205, f. 149]

*John, Earl of **Lauderdale** writes to John, Earl of Tweedale, about his grandson Charles, aged fifteen months. Lauderdale's wife is ill in bed and his daughter has just given birth, so the burden of nursing the sick falls on him. ('Nostre fils' is Lauderdale's son-in-law and 'nostre fille' his daughter.)*   *Scotland, 1668*

And for a new and sharp affliction to me, our dear little man Charles grew sick on Tuesday, but the causes are so apparent that neither the physicians nor I were any thing apprehensive of it, for he hath four great teeth broken the flesh, and his gums for his eye-teeth [are] much swelled, and [he keeps] his finger continually in his mouth. His frowardness and great heat made me conclude him sick, but I apprehended nothing till Tuesday about six o'clock at night when I was talking with the physician about my wife; a sudden alarm comes in that my dear baby Charles had taken a convulsion. The physicians and I run in to his chamber and found him stiff with his arms out and his eyes staring. Never did I see a convulsion before (for never child of mine had it) and it was a dreadful sight. By God's providence the physicians were present; they presently undressed him, made him be rubbed and went to write their prescriptions. The women said he was out of the fit, but the doctors said No, or if he was it was another. Always, before their prescription was written he was clearly out of it. So whether it was two fits or one the convulsions lasted not half a quarter of an hour. They made all the directions, especially forbidding him his nurse's breast, which was obeyed. He was well watched all night; sure I slept little. When the doctors and I talked together, they said they liked it the better that it came by the pain of so many teeth, but if it had come by the beginning of smallpox or measles, they would not be so apprehensive. He slept ill all night, was most impatient for the breast, and was in a cruel heat. When the physicians came yesterday morning they found him in a great fever, but within an hour they did see apparent signs of the smallpox. They were pleased with it, appointed him to suck again, which strangely recovered the child's humour. All this while the mother and grandmother knew nothing, for the physicians positively forbade it. My first care was to remove the other child and nurse with maids to another side of the house, where they are very well. My babe Charles grew much better, his smallpox struck out handsomely, and in the afternoon and towards the evening he plays as merrily as ever. He slept well and sucked well all night and the most part of this day, only he is more froward than when in health, but his fever is much abated and the smallpox strike out finely and seem not to be many, I cannot see twenty or thirty in his face. We have now told my wife of the smallpox, but not a word of the convulsion; my daughter knows nothing of neither. My wife being still kept in bed, I have chosen to shut my self up here, so does *nostre fils* at nights, but he goes abroad in the afternoons, though not to Court. I sent my excuse to the King, and that I would not presume to wait on him, the smallpox being in my house and I compelled by my wife's sickness and my daughter's lying in to stay here.

Two days later.

Our dear little man Charles looks hopefully for his condition. He hath little or no fever, his pox come on finely and are of a good colour, his eye is very sharp and well though his pain is great which makes his froward often. Yet he is at fits and often as merry as ever. Last night I was playing with him, and called him pockie rogue; presently he pointed to his pox with his little finger distinctly one by one. This he did repeat again before the doctors this day, and I wondered to see him understand that word. The Doctors give him nothing, only they appoint his nurse to drink a posset constantly with hartshorn and marigold flowers and other things of that nature in it. In a word by God's great mercy he is yet in a hopeful condition. *Nostre fille* mends well and knows nothing of all this. The little one is very well. Never was I so free of business and yet never so unwilling to write. Here I am in a troublesome government going to and again from one sick one to another and attending doctors, surgeon apothecaries and nurses; a government I was never shaped for and of which I am most heartily weary. [*pp. 183-4, 185-6*]

Five days after this Charles was quite well again.

*George, Earl of **Sutherland**, to his wife, Jean, on their new baby.*

Dearest heart, – Mine to you was not well away when I reflected on my neglect of what doctor Cunningham advised anent the child and nurse; he does not allow you to give him the syrup of peal roses for he says although it may loose him for a time yet he will be the more constipated thereafter. He allows that you give him the syrup of violets or sugar candy and to eat the oil of sweet almonds and he says that he would have you taking some good fresh butter and rending it with honey and putting some of that in an oil bevrie to the child and giving him it. He hopes for the blessing of God that this may open his belly and as for defluxion and rest he says that few new born babies escape it but ordinarily it wears away and by the Lord's blessing on the syrup of violet and oil of sweet almonds it will give him ease. However, it is our duty to submit to Him. Let us not repine at the Lord's dispensations but however He shall be pleased to dispose of the child or us that we may say good is the will of the Lord, and let us not sin away the last great mercy and deliverance you have gotten by our too great anxiety for the child, for anxiety may add to our trouble but it cannot help us. As for the nurse, the doctor ordains her flesh but seldom and when she gets any that it may be a piece of roasted mutton or a leg of fowl and she may get barley broth, shaps or bevrie and that she may get only small beer to drink. [*dep. 313/501*]

*Increase **Mather** on his sons Nathaniel and Samuel.*

5 February.

My Nathaniel taken ill with vomiting and gripings, worms etc.

6 February.

Sat up all night with Nathaniel who continued to be ill. Towards morning God rebated the fever and the pains which were upon him. A.M., studied sermon. Nathaniel continuing ill, much hindered in my studies.

7 February.

Interrupted in studies by Nat's illness. Sic P.M., little do children think, what affection is in the heart of a father. Let the Lord do with me and mine what seemeth him good. I desire to trust in his power and mercy.

8 February.

Nathaniel something better . . . This day Nathaniel somewhat revived.

9 February.

In the night my Samuel was taken very ill, and in a fever this morning and Nathaniel seemingly iller today than yesterday. There hath been much health in my family for a long time; and God has spared the lives of all my children, but I have not been thankful and humble as I should have been, and therefore God is righteous in afflicting me. I have nothing to say but to lie down abased before him, and let him do with me and mine as seemeth him good, only I can not but trust in him that he will be gracious, for his own Name's sake. In prayer not altogether without hope. Could do little at my study because of children's illness.

10 February.

Samuel mended (after I had wept and prayed for his life) upon using salad oil and a clyster. This day I fasted and prayed in my study, begging for the lives of my two sick children Nathaniel and Samuel. [*Mather (a), pp. 341–2*]

By 21st February both boys had pulled through their illness.

America, 1694 *Cotton **Mather** was upset at the sickness of his four-year-old daughter Katherine.*

My little and my only, Katherine, was taken so dangerously sick, that small hope of her life was left unto us. In my distress, when I saw the Lord thus *quenching the coal that was left* unto me, and rending him out of my bosom one that had lived so long with me, as to steal a *room* there, and a *lamb* that was indeed unto me *as a daughter*, I cast myself at the feet of his holy Sovereignty. [*Mather (b), vol. 7, p. 179*]

Katherine was well again in a few days.

Scotland, 1703 *George **Turnbull** records in his diary the last illness of his six-year-old son William, who had succumbed to a fever.*

My son William's fever increased; he much troubled with a gross defluxion both at his eyes, nose, and mouth, and that night grew worse. On Tuesday morning very early I sent for provost Edgar apothecary in Hadington, and Mr Brown minister of Spot, both persons of known skill. About ten of the clock they came. After they had seen the child, and considered his case, doves [?] were applied to his soles, and a blistering plaster applied to his neck, and a cordial julep now and then, it being the fifth day of his sickness. About midday he passed some urine, which being kept did not appear ill, and about two in the afternoon he got passage of his belly, and came out of the bed himself to do it: but in the evening all grew worse upon him, and next day, Wednesday 24 of February 1703, it pleased a holy and wise God to remove him from this life to a better in the seventh year of his age, being born April 16, 1696. He was indeed a child pleasant and desirable, of a sweet natural disposition, grave and wise above his years, and seriously religious, a reprover of sin in his comrades, and frequent in his private devotions as he was capable: and I am confident is now in eternal glory. [*pp. 427–8*]

*Claver **Morris** treats his ten-year-old son, William.*   *England, 1719*

My son being ill, and supposing it would come to the measles, I gave him a gentle purge just as I saw immediately some breaking out on the skin. The purge made him very sick, and worked with him three or four times. About five in the afternoon five spoonfuls of his cordial mixture were given. [*p. 67*]

William was seriously ill, but he survived the attack.

*Mary **Lovett** writes to her brother John Verney about her sick son Verney.*   *England 1723*

My poor child is in his bed and alive, which is wonderful; for three days we all thought he was dying, my sister sat up with him a Thursday night to see his last, and several more, but he tugged hard and I hope has got the better for this time. For though he is extreme weak and worn to nothing, the doctor says he is but patched up for his lungs are certainly decaying and he fears he is in a consumption. He must go into a milk diet and drink asses' milk if I can get it, and be blooded every month this six months, as for the milk diet I am sure he'll never go into it, so he must have but a short life the Doctor says, for if this ever comes upon him again he is gone. He has spit a deal of blood and has been three times blooded this week, and the Doctor fetched in the night to him. [*(b) v. 2, p. 218*]

The doctor's fears for Verney Lovett were unfounded and he did not succumb to tuberculosis.

*John **Byrom** writes to his wife about their baby daughter Ellen.*   *England, 1729*

I am sorry to hear of Nelly's being so ill and weakly, but am not able to add anything to the care which you take of her by any physic of mine, the diet of children is the only thing to look after; I do not admire vomits for them, or blisters, or any thing else, hardly; I like of your going into the country with her. [*vol. 34, p. 356*]

Ellen died six months later.

England, 1748   Frances **Boscawen** *writes to her husband about their three children: Edward, aged three; Fanny, aged twenty-two months and Bess, aged nine months.*

All three children have been ill at once. The two girls had coughs and fevers occasioned by teeth, which were lanced immediately. The boy had a violent and never-ceasing cough, which I am inclined to believe he caught from his sister's breath. It totally deprived him of rest, so that, by the third night, he too was in a fever. By this time, you may imagine, we had decreed them for the measles; all three coughs, all three fevers, resembled it too much. You can imagine the state I was in. For poor Fanny I trembled, her breath and lungs being already so oppressed that 'twas pain to hear her, and the slut would not drink anything, though she was dying of thirst. There was no sort of liquor I did not try her with. Tea I made in her sight; water with a roast apple; mingled with a drop of wine in warm water; milk; jelly. No, nothing would do, and she still persisted to cry, 'No, no, no, can't.' This she had occasion to repeat twenty times a day, sometimes when nobody asked. As to the medicines, the few we gave her we thre down by force, but you know it must be a trifle that could be obtained that way of drink.

As to the dear boy, he would at all times take anything I brought him; but then I dreaded a bleeding, which would have been necessary in the measles. I did not doubt my being able to persuade him to it. I had even got his promise. But I distrusted myself. I doubted my being able to stay in the room, and the least signs of fear in me would have inspired and justified his.

In short, my dearest husband, I have endured a great deal, and can never be enough thankful to the gracious providence that has comforted me and cured them. The boy and the little one now come down stairs. Frances keeps chamber still; but they have been purged, and tomorrow the two eldest begin asses' milk. Bess, as you know, has provision of that sort nearer at hand. [*pp. 74–5*]

America, 1757   Landon **Carter** *on the trouble of treating sick children; his daughter Judy was aged ten.*

It is necessary that man should be acquainted with affliction and 'tis certainly nothing short of it to be confined a whole year in tending one's sick children. Mine are now never well. Indeed I may believe there are many reasons for it besides the constitution of the air which has been very bad. I have none but negros to tend my children nor can I get anyone and they use their own children to such loads of gross food that they are not judges when a child, not so used to be exposed to different weathers and not so inured to exercise, comes to eat. They let them press their appetites as their own children did and thus they are constantly sick. Judy Carter, who has been as well for many weeks as ever child was, by being suffered after her dinner to some of her sister's barley broth yesterday took in such a load as could not be contained in her stomach and this day she was seized with a natural vomiting. I found nothing but food coming up and therefore ordered a small dose of ipecacuanha to help to clear the over-burdened stomach. The medicine I gave produced a while good effects by bringing off a good deal of filth and bile but it had too powerful an effect on her weak stomach for she vomited six times yellow bile, and whether an ague intervened I don't know but she lost her pulse for two hours and quite dead coldness and hardly alive with nervous catchings in her hands and jaws so that I fancied her death near. However I gave her pulvis cartian five grains, salt tartar five grains, pulvis castor two grains in a weak julep of rum, water and mint and in about two and a half hours her pulse beat and after a good sleep nature seemed to recover and a small fever ensued which wore away by night gradually and the child mended, grew cheerful and had an appetite to eat which I sparingly indulged but she lost all her bloom off her face this morning. [*Carter (a), vol. 1, p. 194*]

Anna **Winslow**, *at school in Boston, describes her ailments to her mother.* *America, 1772*

My honored Mamma will be so good as to excuse my using the pen of an old friend just here, because I am disabled by a whitlow on my fourth finger and something like one on my middle finger, from using my own pen; but although my right hand is in bondage, my left is free . . . My fingers are not the only part of me that has suffered with sores this fortnight, for I have had an ugly great boil upon my right hip and about a dozen small ones – I am at present swathed hip and thigh as Samson smote Philistines, but my soreness is near over. My aunt thought it highly proper to give me some cooling physic, so last Tuesday I took 1-2 ounce of Globe salt (a disagreeable potion) and kept chamber. Since which, there has been no new eruption, and a great alteration for the better in those I had before. [*pp. 20–21*]

Charlotte **Papendiek** *recalls the treatment she received when she was ill at the age of nine.* *England, 1774*

I was attacked with inflammation of the eyes, which increased in an alarming degree. Everything usual was tried, all to no effect. Leeches were then resorted to, three on each temple, which, being applied in the morning continued to bleed profusely for twelve hours. To stop it at bedtime, a cobweb was recommended . . . I then went on a visit to Streatham . . . At first I revived a little, but in a few days the inflammation came on again, and my father fetched me back. An issue in the left arm was then resorted to, but was of no avail, and lastly the seaside was proposed and determined on . . . Medical advice was that I should take sea water on the beach every alternate day, beginning with less than half a pint, before breakfast; and bathing, as I was not alarmed at it and even liked it, was to be used three times in seven days. I remained six weeks, when my father fetched me back, finding me quite recovered. [*vol. 1, pp. 65–8*]

Scotland, 1776   *Harriet* **Leith** *on the illness of her son John, aged about fifteen.*

In spite of the cold changeable weather, I think John is considerable better within these last six or seven days. The heats upon his skin which gave him much uneasiness has I believe been chiefly carried off by a moisture upon his skin Thursday and Friday last, and a very profuse sweat 'twixt Saturday and Sunday. These complaints, (although, from what has happened since agreeable, which I impute in a great measure to them) alarmed me dreadfully at the time upon many accounts, and had they continued must have been very weakening, as well as increased his aptness to catch cold. But their having gone off without any remedy, but a mattress put above his bed, in place of under it, is a very agreeable circumstance . . . I've yet been able to hear of no milk ass, nearer than Aberdeen but the new calved cow's milk and conserve of roses agrees with John to a wonder. He was likewise advised to try an issue in his arm which he ha[s had?]. [*GD30/32/15*]

Two months after this, John was spitting blood and was advised to refrain from drinking goat's milk; he died four months later.

America, 1783   *Nancy* **Shippen** *on the illness of her seventeen-month-old daughter Margaret.*

28 May.

I was waked this morning at five o'clock with the cries of my baby. It seemed to be at a distance. I jumped up – frightened half to death – run to mamma's room where the child was, and found it almost in fits with pain. I screamed as loud as the child – to see her in such agonies. Papa was obliged to take me out of the room or I should have fainted. I never in all my life felt as I did then. She continued in that situation almost an hour, and then slept two. In that time the maid told me that the child woke as usual at daybreak – that she being very sleepy she forgot to take care of her – and left the dear creature all alone – that she give *her* her snuff box to play with – and then went to sleep. In the meantime the child opened the box and the snuff flew into her eyes, nose, and mouth – and very near strangled her. I never will permit her to be taken up again when she wakes. Her dear eyes are always open at daybreak – therefore she is generally taken up out of my bed softly and carried downstairs without waking me. For the future I will take her up myself. After her nap she seemed pretty well – and ate hearty. About ten she went to sleep again and woke with a high fever. I was very much alarmed and called Papa – he thought her ill – she continued to grow worse. He ordered balm tea and lime juice and sugar. I gave it her – then he gave her a dose of nitre. In the afternoon a little better – I never left her all day except to eat a little dinner and then I stayed but five minutes. This evening her fever grew worse – I was almost distracted. I believe I sent for Papa near a hundred times. He gave her a dose this evening that has done her good – she sleeps sweetly, her fever is abated. It is near twelve o'clock – every creature in the house sleeps but me – I have no inclination. I will watch my dear baby all night – I feel pleasure in doing her this service. I begin to be alarmed – she has slept without stirring for four hours – I will call my father. The watchman calls one o'clock – I went to Papa and told him my fears – he relieved them by telling me the longer she sleeps the better – she may he thinks sleep off her disorder.

1 June.

My baby thank God is much recovered. These six days past she has been so ill her life has been despaired of. I nursed her attentively – I never left her more than an hour altogether. O! what I have suffered! For several hours I thought she was dying – what I felt then it is impossible to describe. I have been ill too myself with fatigue and want of sleep. [pp. 150–52]

*In his autobiography, Arthur **Young** recalls the serious illness of his* *England, 1797*
fourteen-year-old daughter Martha-Ann (Bobbin). In January 1797 she had been sent to school in London, and rapidly became sick. Bobbin was given steel, asses' ilk and red wine to strengthen her, but by June she was gravely ill.

Dr Wollaston, the eminent physician at Bury, has been consulted; he gives little hopes, but advises a milk and vegetable diet, and said that sea air and a humid mild climate would be good. I next wrote to Dr Thornton, who recommended an egg and meat diet; and Mr Martyn, in a letter, desired me to try the inhaling of ether, in fact, all has been done that the urgency of the case required, but, alas! She is past the assistance of all human power. [p. 277]

Bobbin died in July (see p. 127).

Address to dear Isabella on this Author

a recovery

O Isa I'm did visit me

Arrived the last extremity

How often did I think of you

Sure had your graceful form to view

So dear's your own my weak embrace

Indeed I thought I'd run my race

Good care I'm ever was of me taken

But indeed I was much shaken

At last I saw my strength did pain

And but last away went pain

At length the doctor thought I might

Stay in the Parlour till the night

I now continue so to do

Farewell to Nancy and to you. [signature]

Poem by Marjory Fleming, 1811

Address to dear Isabella on the authors recovery

O Isa pain did visit me
I was at the last extremity
How often did I think of you
I wished your graceful form to view
To clasp you in my weak embrace
Indeed I thought Id run my race
Good care Im sure was of me taken
But indeed I was much shaken
At last I daily strength did gain
And O at last away went pain
At length the docter thought I might
Stay in the parlour till the night
I now continue so to do
Farewell to Nancy and to you
wrote by M F

National Library of Scotland, Ms 1100

England, 1802

*Sydney **Smith** writes to Mrs Beach about his method of treating his six-month-old daughter.*

My little girl is perfectly recovered from a severe attack of the croup. By the bye, it may be worth while to inform you that she was saved from this fatal and rapid disease by taking two grains of calomel every hour till the symptoms subsided, and then gradually lessening the doses; so that she took in twenty-four hours thirty-two grains, besides bleeding and blistering and emetics; and she is not yet six months old. [*vol. 1, p. 71*]

One year later he writes of his son Noel, aged three.

Noel has this evening coughed up a good deal of clotted blood which has alarmed me a good deal and my wife much more. The child however does not appear ill.

On Tuesday he had two fits, and on Thursday night eight; last night he escaped; today is much better, and I think is almost out of danger . . .

My little boy is thank God recovered. I sat up with him for two nights, expecting every moment to be his last. [*vol. 1. pp. 87, 88, 90*]

Noel died six weeks later.

Children are horribly insecure; the life of a parent is the life of a gambler. [*vol. 1, p. 92*]

America, 1832

*John **Todd** describes his emotions when his daughter Martha, aged sixteen months, was seriously ill.*

I go to her bedside and gaze, and hear her short groans, as long as I can stay, and then go away to weep. Wonderful skill! in creating and planting in the human heart that wonderful passion which we call *parental*! As I go about the house (and oh, this feeling is to increase to *agony*!) I see her little chair, her clothes, her things; here she sat, there she sung, there she gave me her sweet looks; every spot is associated with the past, and with fear. Her little swing, her place at the table, are empty.

I know we ought not to refuse to give this dear one, this sweet child, back to her Maker and Father: she must be better off than with us; but oh, the agony of breaking the heart-strings! [*p. 241*]

Martha recovered and a month later she was able to walk a few steps.

England, 1833

*William **Macready** receives word that his two-year-old son William is ill.*

The news quite struck me down, making me quite faint and sick. If it be the will of Almighty God to try my spirits by the illness of these dear babes, may he give me power of mind and body to support it; at present I am helpless under the idea. [*vol. 1, pp. 24–5*]

In 1840 his son Henry, aged twenty months, is very ill.

September.

My darling boy, Henry, very unwell; he seems wasting and sinking away – my heart fell down within me as I looked at the thin face of the dear, dear child.

November.

Very much fatigued by the wakeful night I had through the dear, dear little Henry, who seems falling back.

When I went into the next room to look at my dear suffering boy I was shocked and cut to the very heart to see the little wasted, emaciated child, lying in a state of exhaustion on the nurse's lap. This is what was once my lovely boy – the dear, dear blessed child!

December.

Darling Henry better. Oh thank God! Whilst trying to divert the dear boy he smiled twice. No sunshine was ever brighter or more cheering to the earth than those dear smiles to my heart. [*vol. 2, pp. 85, 96, 97, 112*]

Henry died in 1857.

Emily **Shore**, *aged eighteen, records in her diary how she coped with the knowledge she was dying of tuberculosis.*   *England, 1837–9*

December 1837.

Well it is no use to go on always struggling with weakness and incapability of exertion. I cannot hold out for ever; and now I begin to feel thoroughly ill. I am afraid I must relax. [*p. 231*]

July 1838.

I have been addicted of late to growing faint after breakfast. I do not mind it myself, only that it alarms papa and mama. Poor papa is so anxious about me, that one would think every cough I utter is my death-knell . . . I suppose I am never to be strong again. It is nearly three months since I walked into the Forest, and now I am always left behind when others go out. This evening I could almost have cried when I saw mamma, Aunt Charlotte, Cousin Susan, and the four children set forth joyously to ramble in some of the loveliest glades, and poor I was obliged to content myself with the dull drawing-room. [*p. 256*]

July 1838.

Here is a query, which I shall be able to answer decidedly at the end of this volume, most likely before. What is indicated by all these symptoms – this constant shortness of breath, now tinged with blood, this quick pulse, this painfully craving appetite, which a very little satisfies even to disgust, these restless, feverish nights, continual palpitations of the heart, and deep, circumscribed flushes? Is it consumption really come at last, after so many threatenings? I am not taken by surprise, for I have had it steadily, almost daily, in view for two years, and have always known that my lungs were delicate. I feel no uneasiness on the subject, even if my ideas (I cannot call them fears) prove right. It must be my business to prepare for another world; may God give me grace to do so. [p. 264]

July 1838.

What share the weakness of my bodily health has in it I cannot exactly say, but I feel myself sinking into a gloom and melancholy I cannot describe. I have a sort of hermit-like misanthropic feeling. I am quite pining for entire quiet. I have more constant depression of spirits that I have ever known before, and seem to have lost all interest in my occupations. I feel almost as if I shall soon have done with this world, as if my studying days were quite over, and as if I had no longer any interest in the busy scenes of life. [p. 267]

In the autumn of 1838 Emily went to Madeira to live for the benefit of her health. The move, however, was in vain.

April 1839.

On the 4th of April I broke a blood-vessel, and am now dying of consumption, in great suffering, and may not live many weeks. God be merciful to me a sinner. [p. 350]

She died two months later at the age of nineteen.

England, 1849 *Henrietta **Stanley** writes to her husband, Edward, about their three-week-old baby daughter, Mary. Henrietta is all the more distressed because she had not wanted more children (see Chapter 1, pp. 49–50).*

I am so fretted about dear baby I must write to you. Yesterday afternoon the little thing was uncomfortable and when the nurse came she could not suck from wind. She has continued poorly all night and today I was quite shocked when I came upstairs at the change which had taken place in the baby, so thin and its little hands cold and shrivelled. Dr Locock ordered her castor oil and sal volatile which Williams had given. . . .

Eleven o'clock. I have just sent for Dr Locock I am so uneasy about dear Baby.

Seven o'clock Monday morning. Baby no better, pinched and blue. Locock ordered brandy in her milk, it is the nurse's milk put down her throat in spoonfuls.

Six o'clock. I think Baby is better. I have more hope.

12 o'clock. I am more and more anxious. Poor dear little lamb it looks so worn and piteous. When Locock comes again he is to decide about her being baptized. I shall be so wretched to lose her she is such a darling and I feel it quite a punishment for having said I did not wish for a child. I did not know how fast love grows for babies but as I sit by its cradle and hear its faint moans it goes through my heart. I feel very poorly, quite knocked up. I am sure you will feel for the little soft thing you have watched the last fortnight as well as for me. She sleeps continuously and when she is roused to take food her eyes look quite dead.

Two o'clock. It has been a cholera attack without pain, and now she is exhausted. She has no disease. [pp. 205-7]

The child died the next day.

Elizabeth **Prentiss** *describes her feelings during the illness of her eighteen-month-old daughter.* America, 1856

1 February.

I have had no heart to make a record of what has befallen us since I last wrote. And yet I may, sometime, want to recall this experience, painful as it is. Dear little baby had been improving in health, and on Wednesday we went to dine at Mrs Wainwright's. We went at four. About eight, word came that she was ill. When I got home I found her insensible, with her eyes wide open, her breathing terrific, and her condition in every respect very alarming. Just as Dr Buck was coming in, she roused a little, but soon relapsed into the same state. He told us she was dying. I felt like a stone. *In a moment* I seemed to give up my hold on her. She appeared no longer mine but God's. It is always so in such great emergencies. *Then*, my will that struggles so about trifles, makes no effort. But as we sat up hour after hour watching the alterations of color in her purple face and listening to that terrible gasping, rattling sound, I said to myself 'A few more nights like this, and I do believe my body and soul would yield to such anguish.' Oh, why should I try to tell myself what a night it was. God knows, God only! How he has smitten me by means of this child, He well knows. Twelve hours of martyrdom to me such as I never had known. Then to our unspeakable amazement she roused up, nursed, and then fell into a sweet sleep of some hours.

3 February.

The stupor, or whatever it is, in which that dreadful night has left me, is on me still. I have no more sense of feeling than a stone. I kneel down before God and do not say a word. I take up a book and read, but get hold of nothing. At church I felt afraid I should fall upon the people and tear them. I could wish no one to pity me or even know that I am smitten. It does seem to me that those who can sit down and cry, know nothing of misery . . .

6 February.

She still lives. I know not what to think. One moment I think one thing and the next another. It is harder to submit to this suspense than to a real, decided blow. But I desire to leave it to my God. He knows all her history and all mine. He orders all these aggravating circumstances and I would not change them. My darling has not lived in vain. For eighteen months she has been the little rod used by my Father for my chastisement and not, I think, quite in vain. Oh my God! stay not Thy hand till Thou hast perfected that which concerneth me. Send anything rather than unsanctified prosperity. [*pp. 144–5*]

Her daughter lived.

Death

Nehemiah **Wallington** *recalls his feelings at the death of his daughter Elizabeth, aged four.*

The grief for this child was so great that I forgot myself so much that I did offend God in it; for I broke all my purposes, promises, and covenants with my God, for I was much distracted in my mind, and could not be comforted, although my friends speak comfortably unto me. [*Wallington (a), p. xix*]

In 1627 his only son died and his wife reproved him for his excessive grief.

Husband, say we should put our child forth to nurse and when we see time fit we send for our child and if the nurse should deny us our child and should think much at us that we fetch it home again, we should then be very angry with her. Even so stands the case for us for God gave us this child to nurse for him for a while and now he requires it of us again, therefore let us give it to him willingly. [*Wallington (b), f. 422*]

Simonds **D'Ewes** *on the death of his son Clopton, aged nearly two.*

We both found the sorrow for the loss of this child, on whom we had bestowed so much care and affection, and whose delicate favour and bright grey eye was so deeply imprinted in our hearts, far to surpass our grief for the decease of his three elder brothers, who, dying almost as soon as they were born, were not so endeared to us as this was. [*vol. 2, pp. 146–7*]

Alice **Thornton** *lost her baby son William. She had been delighted with the birth of a son.*

But it so pleased God to shorten this joy, least I should be too much transported, that I was visited with another trial; for on the Friday sennight after, he began to be very angry and froward, after his dressing in the morning; so that I perceived him not to be well, upon which I gave him gasgoine powder and cordial, least it should be the red gum in children, usual at that time, to strike it out of his heart at morning after his dressing. And having had three hour's sleep, his face when he awaked was full of red round spots like the smallpox, being of the compass of a half penny, and all wheeled white over, these continuing in his face till night, and being in a slumber in my arms on my knee he would sweetly lift up his eyes to heaven and smile, as if the old saying was true in this sweet infant, that he saw angels in heaven. But then, whether through cold upon his dressing then, or what else was the cause, the Lord knoweth, the spots struck in, and [he] grew very sick all night, and about nine o'clock on Saturday morning he sweetly departed this life, to the great discomfort of his weak mother, whose only comfort is that the Lord, I hope, has received him to that place of rest in heaven where little children beholds the face of their heavenly Father, to his God and my God. [*pp. 124–5*]

England, 1672   *Charles* **Hatton** *writes to his brother Christopher on the death of his son Robin.*

I now write to your Lordship in a very great disorder and affliction for the loss of my dear and only child whom God hath taken from me and thereby rendered his poor mother and my self two disconsolable creatures. My sister Hatton's token to him was bestowed in laying him in the ground with his sisters. I beseech God reward it to her and God grant that neither she nor your lordship may know what the loss of a child is. [*Hatton (b), add. MSS29571, f. 181*]

England, 1697   *Matthew* **Henry** *writes to his sister.*

We received the tidings of the death of your dear little one. He that gives may not only take, because what we hold is by lease but take as soon as he pleased because what we hold is by lease *at will*. The child is dead but not extinct, not lost. We must not say *it is not* for it is where it is best to be, and where we hope to be. You said you gave it up freely to be the Lord's, and may He not do what He will with His own, especially since it is His own by our consent, I hope the Lord will support you under the affliction and sanctify it to you, [*Eng. letters E. 29, f. 122*]

America, 1710   *William* **Byrd** *writes in his diary about the death of his son Parke, aged six months.*

I rose at six o'clock and as soon as I came out news was brought that the child was very ill. We went out and found him just ready to die and he died about eight o'clock in the morning. God gives and God takes away; blessed be the name of God. Mrs Harrison and Mr Anderson and his wife and some other company came to see us in our affliction. My wife was much afflicted but I submitted to His judgement better, notwithstanding I was very sensible of my loss; but God's will be done.

The next day.

My wife had several fits of tears for our dear son but kept within the bounds of submission.

Three days after this.

My wife continued to be exceedingly afflicted for the loss of her child, notwithstanding I comforted her as well as I could. [*Byrd (a)*, pp. 186, 187, 188]

*Cotton **Mather** on the death of his daughter Jerusha, aged two years.*   *America, 1711*

I am again called unto the sacrifice of my dear, dear daughter Jerusha. I begged, I begged, that such a bitter cup, as the death of that lovely child, might pass from me. *Nevertheless* – My glorious Lord, brought me to glorify Him, with the most submissive resignation.

The following day.

Betwixt nine and ten at night, my lovely Jerusha expired. She was two years, and about seven months, old. Just before she died, she asked me to pray with her; which I did, with a distressed, but resigning soul; and I gave her up unto the Lord. The minute that she died, she said, *That she would go to Jesus Christ.* She had lain speechless many hours, but in her last moments, her speech returned to her. Lord I am oppressed; undertake for me! [*Mather (b), vol. 8, p. 261*]

*Ebenezer **Erskine**'s three sons, Ralph aged two, Henry aged nine and*   *England, 1713*
Alexander aged five, all died from smallpox and measles within a few months of one another.

April.

My dear, sweet, and pleasant child, Ralph, died on Thursday, last week, about a quarter after seven in the morning. His death was very grievous and affecting to my wife and me; but good is the will of the Lord ... After his breath was gone and his body swathed, the company having taken a little refreshment, I was called to return thanks, which I did but towards the end, when I came to take notice of the present providence, that God had plucked one of the sweet flowers of my family, my heart burst out into tears, so that I was able to go no further. [*Erskine (1), p. 266*]

Henry, his eldest son, aged eight, died on 8 June and on 20 June Alexander died.

Upon the 20th Day of June, being Saturday, about four in the morning, the Lord was pleased to take away from me another pleasant pledge, a child of five years of age, his name Alexander. My affections were exceedingly knit to him, and I was comforting myself in having him, after his brother Henry's death; but it seems the Lord will not allow me to settle my affections on any thing here below. I cannot express the grief of my heart for the loss of this child, the other two strokes being so late . . . I hope to be gathered unto Christ with my little ones ere long. I have had a sore parting; but they and I, I hope, shall have a joyful meeting. [*Erskine (1), pp. 269–70*]

England, 1737　　*John **Verney** writes to his sister Mrs Stone after the death of his son John.*

Dear Sister, – Your repeated concern for my dear child ought always to be remembered, and no one was more sensible of it than he was while living, but he left us yesterday morning, about nine o'clock, and we can never see him more in this world, but I trust in God we shall all meet in Heaven, where I daresay he now is in perfect happiness, which I can never more enjoy here for want of him. I know how you share with us in this affliction, and entreat you to moderate it since it is God's will. [*(b) p. 146*]

America, 1769　　*William Ronald writes to James **Parker** on the death of the latter's son. Although commiserating, Ronald offers consolation in the fact that the younger and not the older boy died.*

However tender the heart may be, and whatever the attachment a parent may have to his offspring, the heart can be but a little affected with their loss in comparison with what we feel when deprived of those whose infant prattle and dawning reason . . . has deeply impressed their image in our breasts, and fancy long after paints to us what the little innocent would have been in their riper years had not death untimely cut them off. [*Parker (2), p. 74*]

England, 1774　　*John **Stedman**'s son John died at the age of seventeen while serving his apprenticeship at sea. John composed an elegy for him.*

O agonising pain! pain never felt before,
My manly boy, my John, my sailor, is no more
Still let me mourn with hope, – and God adore,
With hope to see my sailor once again,
Floating on seas of bliss, – thro' the azure main,
Till then, a short farewell, my lovely boy
Thy shipmates' darling, and thy father's joy.

[*p. 376*]

*Arthur **Young** recalls his grief at the death of his fourteen-year-old* *England, 1797*
daughter Martha-Ann (Bobbin).

My poor dear child breathed her last at twelve minutes past one o'clock on Friday morning, the 14th. I was on my knees at her bedside in great agony of mind. She looked at me and said, *'Pray for me!'* I answered her that I did. She replied, *'Do it now, papa'*, on which I poured forth aloud ejaculations to the Almighty, that He would have compassion and heal the affliction of my child. She clasped her hands together in the attitude of praying, and when I had done said, 'amen' – her last words. Thank God of His infinite mercy she expired without a groan, or her face being the least agitated; her inspirations were gradually changed from being very distressing, till they became lost in gentleness, and at the last she went off like a bird.

Thus fled one of the sweetest tempers and, for her years, one of the best understandings that I ever met with. She was a companion for mature years, for there was in her none of the childish stuff of most girls. And there fled the first hope of my life, the child on whom I wished to rest in the afflictions of my age, should I reach such a period. But the Almighty's will be done, and may I turn the event to the benefit of my soul, and in such a manner as to trust through the mediation of my Redeemer to become worthy to join her in a better world. [*pp. 279–80*]

Three days after her death, Arthur returns home.

On going into the library the window looks into the little garden in which I have so many times seen her happy. O gracious and merciful God! Pardon me for allowing any earthly object thus to engross my feelings and overpower my whole soul! But what were they not on seeing and weeping over the roses, variegated sage, and other plants she had set there and cultivated with her dear hands. But every room, every spot is full of her, and it sinks my very heart to see them. Tuesday evening, the 18th, her remains arrived, and at mid-night her brother read the service over her in a most impressive manner. I buried her in my pew, fixing the coffin so that when I kneel it will be between her head and her dear heart. This I did as a means of preserving the grief I feel, and hope to feel while breath is in my body. It turns all my views to an hereafter, and fills my mind with earnest wishes, that when the great author of my existence may please to take me I may join my child in a better world. [*p. 281*]

He never recovered from Bobbin's death.

Scotland, 1812 *Lady **Fleming** writes to her niece Isabella after the death of her nine-year-old daughter Marjory.*

The constant confinement to the room where my child suffered and died is adverse to the recovery of my spirits, but I am gaining a little strength and hope I shall soon be able to change the scene by going into the parlour. Yet where can I go that I shall not be reminded of my last darling. Every object is so associated with her idea that to forget her is impossible. You more than any one else can imagine and sympathise in the blank I feel, yet even you can hardly conceive it. Her constant good humour gave a cheerfulness to our domestic circle which made us feel no want of society. Her poor father unceasingly deplores his loss. I fear he idolized her so much and was too vain of her talents, besides death was a scene altogether new to him and oh how striking was her death. How often did I wish you had seen her cold remains. Most justly may I say with Young 'Lovely in death the beauteous ruin lay' for never did I behold so beautiful an object. [*Fleming (a), MS1100, f. 13*]

England, 1815 *Maria **Capel** writes to her grandmother, the Dowager Countess of Uxbridge, about the death of her baby sister, aged seven weeks.*

The painful task has devolved upon me, my dearest Grand Mama, to acquaint you with the death of our dear little Baby. I have now a letter before me which I had written to you last Saturday to tell you that she had been ill a week but was then much better and considered out of danger. Sunday morning at about six she was taken suddenly worse – Mama was immediately alarmed by the fixed and glassy look of her beautiful eyes – and Mr Doratt, who was sent for, said she could not outlive the day. Mama insisted upon holding her in her arms – everything which could be thought of was tried – but without effect, and the little angel expired with her face on Mama's breast, at a little past eleven, but so peaceably that we did not perceive it till several minutes had passed. Dearest Mama gave her Baby one kiss – and Papa supported her, while we removed the child, and laid it out, washed and dressed it ourselves. Since that, Mama has never left its side – and behaves like a perfect angel. I sat up with it last night for I loved it so much, and held its little cold hand all the time. Oh! my dearest Grand Mama, you can have no idea of any thing so lovely as she looks. Mama's resignation is admirable, I never can forget it. But she was *such* a treasure, *so* angelic *so* beautiful, she was the admiration of the town – and we were so proud of her. We have had her picture taken. [*pp. 140-3*]

Lady Caroline also writes.

I go with a heavy heart, but I have got the picture of my baby to gaze upon and so remind me of the foolish pride I took in her beauty and the blind security I felt in her flourishing health and strength. Oh Mama, how dare we boast of any thing! . . .

From the window of the rampart room I can see at a distance the wall of the place where she lies, and extraordinary as it may appear I feel a sense of comfort in knowing I can see it when I please, and a dread of deserting it, that there may be folly in, but that I cannot conquer. [*pp. 144, 147–8*]

Anne **Grant** *sympathizes with Mrs Frederick Grant after the loss of the latter's son.*   *Scotland, 1826*

I did not hear at the time it happened of your loss, which you well know to be your sensible, engaging Frederick's gain. Our mental sight, which pursues these objects of our tenderest affection beyond the reach of sense, is dim and clouded at best; but the sense of suffering, in having any thing entwined with our heart-strings torn from us, is present, acute, and mingles with every feeling. I still feel a pang at the recollection of what it cost me to part with a wonderful premature boy of four years old. It was my first affliction; and consolation was distressing to me, because I knew how little any one but a suffering parent can enter into that distress where a child, too young to interest any but those about him, is taken away from the evil to come. [*Grant (1) (b) vol. 2, p. 106*]

Mary **Timms** *records her reaction to the death of her two-year-old daughter Mary Anne in her diary.*   *England, 1836*

How transient are all things here below! How soon are our hopes and prospects blasted! My babe, my dear Mary Anne is taken from me, to bloom in paradise. Ah! I fondly hoped she would have been spared to us; but God has seen good to separate us, perhaps but for a little while. O how painful to nature! my heart bleeds. I am jealous of the worms; I do not like to give my Mary Anne to them; but the mandate is, 'dust thou art, and unto dust shalt thou return'. This consoles me, *it is the will of my heavenly Father*. I know it is my duty to submit to be resigned. Perhaps she is taken from some impending storm. Happy voyager! no sooner launched, than safely landed. Thy mourning days are over. Thou has gained fair Canaan's coast before me. Sweet babe! thou hast passed the bounds of time, and perhaps – O delightful thought! – thou art permitted to be thy mother's guardian angel, and wilt be the first to meet her on yon blest shore. [*pp. 87–8*]

England, 1840 *Sara **Coleridge** writes to Mrs Stanger after the death of her eleven-day-old daughter Bertha.*

Our loss indeed has been a great disappointment, and even a sorrow; for, strange as it may seem, these little speechless creatures, with their wandering, unspeaking eyes, do twine themselves around a parent's heart from the hour of their birth. Henry suffered more than I could have imagined, and I was sorry to see him watch the poor babe so closely, when it was plain that the little darling was not for this world, and that all our visions of a 'dark-eyed Bertha', a third joy and comfort of the remainder of our own pilgrimage, must be exchanged for better hopes, and thoughts more entirely accordant with such a religious frame of mind as it is our best interest to attain. I had great pleasure in anticipating the added interest that you would take in her as your godchild. But this is among the dreams to be relinquished. Her remains are at Hampstead, besides those of my little frail and delicate twins. [*vol. 1, pp. 243–4*]

America, 1848 *Fanny **Longfellow** relates the death of her eighteen-month-old daughter Fanny.*

29 August.

Poor baby drooping today, and at night very feverish with symptoms of dysentery. Dr Hoffendahl wrapped her in wet bandages about the abdomen, also one on her head. I watched her all night and the fever yielded to these good measures.

30 August.

Very hot. Darling baby very feeble though without fever. She is as quiet and patient as possible, uttering no complaint. Very restless and wakeful all night.

1 September.

Baby confined to her bed and lying there so sadly patient, with her poor pale face and hollow eyes – such a contrast to her usual exuberant life, I can hardly bear it. Thank God the disease is no worse however.

2 September.

The Doctor thinks baby decidedly better today, and my heart is lightened a little. But she is so thin and feeble, and lies upon her pillow almost without consciousness. Kept up the wet bandages on the abdomen.

6 September.

A very anxious heavy day. Poor baby seemed to have much trouble in her head, and the doctor feared congestion of the brain. She was quieter after a wet towel on the head, and had a tranquil night. Nursey Blake watching her, who had come, much to my comfort.

7 September.

Doctor thinks baby decidedly better today. The bad symptoms in her head have gone away, but she is very very weak, so that she can hardly bear being moved and does not seem to know me, which is very hard to bear.

8 September.

Baby no worse, though needing a little mercury. The doctor does not venture to check the disease at once on account of her teeth. Poor darling lies perfectly passive, with her large hollow eyes looking up so pathetically, but never a smile or a word. My courage is almost broken . . .

9 September.

Baby showed some pain today, which went through all my nerves. Pretty good day on the whole. She looks to me like mother, her sharpened features given her a much older look.

10 September.

A day of agony unutterable. The doctor evidently shocked at baby's state, and hope almost dies within me. Another physician watched with us through the long, long night, giving no sign of cheer.

11 September.

Sinking, sinking away from us. Felt a terrible desire to seize her in my arms and warm her to life again at my breast. Oh for one look of love, one word or smile! Mary was with us all day. Painlessly, in a deep trance, she breathed. Held her hand and heard the breathing shorten, then cease, without a flutter. A most holy, beautiful thing she lay and at night of look angelic and so happy.

12 September.

Cut a few locks from her holy head, placed her in the library. With unopened roses about her, one in her hand, that little hand which always grasped them so lovingly. Dr Francis spoke over her, and she was carried to Mr Auburn. Struggled almost in vain with the terrible hunger of the heart to hold her once more. Every room, every object recalls her, and the house is desolation.

13 September.

Cannot keep from despairing now of the other children, and thinking how they will look when dead. Their gleeful voices agonize me. Charley told Nurse Blake, 'Sissy was up in the sky,' and when I told him yesterday, he said, 'Oh, I want to go too.' When death first enters a house, he throws so long a shadow – it seems to touch every one.

14 September.

A cold, dark day in sympathy with our gloom . . . She is every-where. In the garden I see only her merry steps and little hands grasping the flowers with glee and shouting 'Pretty', and then I see her with them in her cold hands. But she is playing with the flowers of Paradise, I fondly trust.

16 September.

How dear is 'every little plot of ground. Paced by those blessed feet around'. The little white bonnet is at my side out of doors and at night. I fancy a cry in the nursery and listen thinking she must be there. But I thank God all tears are wiped from her eyes and that she can never know such grief as mine.

14 October.

Very weary and wretched. I seem to have lost interest in the future and can enjoy my children only from hour to hour. I feel as if my lost darling were drawing me to her – as I controlled her before birth so does she me now. [*Longfellow (b), pp. 140–42, 144*]

America, 1852   *Elizabeth **Prentiss** lost her three-year-old son Edward on 16 January; in May her month-old baby daughter Elizabeth died from erysipelas.*

Here I sit with empty hands. I have had the little coffin in my arms, but my baby's face could not be seen, so rudely had death marred it. Empty hands, empty hands, a worn-out exhausted body, and unutterable longings to flee from a world that has had for me so many sharp experiences. God help me, my baby, my baby! God help me, my little lost Eddy! [*p. 137*]

Introduction

We know from sources such as pictures, artefacts and contemporary social commentaries that children both possessed toys and played as far back as we can probe. Unfortunately, it has proved very difficult to obtain evidence on these topics from literary sources, particularly from pre-1800 texts. This chapter is thus weighted to the nineteenth century, and I have been unable to locate any information on the organization of a child's day prior to 1700.

The material available on the day-to-day routine of children indicates a packed timetable, with little free time (Maria Carter, p. 139, and John Todd, p. 140). Kate Russell (p. 142) was very unusual in her desire to have her offspring spend a large part of the day unsupervised. Other children were much more regimented with almost every minute of their time allocated to a specific activity.

Great progress was made in the manufacture and sale of toys during the sixteenth and seventeenth centuries. Iconographic evidence for the early modern period reveals the existence of such toys as soldiers, horses, puppets, bowls, balls, rattles, dolls, stilts, skittles, tops, swings, crossbows and equipment for games like tennis, trap ball and hockey. The early dolls – known as 'babies' till the eighteenth century – were made of wood and leather stuffed with bran or cloth. Dolls imported from Germany had the added attraction of movable arms and legs. Until the late nineteenth century, when baby dolls were introduced, they resembled adults in miniature. Some of the beautifully dressed dolls which survive from the nineteenth century were in fact fashion models, used by dressmakers to display their skills and designs. Dolls were not mass produced until the Edwardian era.

During the eighteenth century toys began to be designed exclusively for children, and books were written specifically for them. Cheap toys in tin and lead (ensuring that nearly all children could own some kind of plaything) as well as clockwork toys, houses, prams and cradles for dolls, kites and hoops all appeared on the market, to be sold in the new toyshops. The first jigsaw was invented by a schoolteacher at Harrow in 1760, who used it as a device to teach his class geography. During the nineteenth century enormous steps were taken in the toy trade to satisfy the huge demand, accompanied by as large an advance in toy inventions. Complicated mechanical toys, magic lanterns, trains and scientific toys all became available for purchase.

'If a present-day school child was wafted back to any previous century he would probably find himself more at home with the games being played than with any other social custom', conclude

Iona and Peter Opie in *Children's Games in Street and Playground*. Many of the activities described in the quotations do bear a striking similarity to child's play today (Thomas Boston, p. 147, and Catherine Carswell, p. 152). A large component of children's play, in the past as now, lay in the imitation of the rituals and customs seen round about (Nicholas Blundell, p. 148, and Caroline Head, p. 152). Running through the material especially for the early selections is a belief that play is something for young children which should be dispensed with when they begin their education (Henry Slingsby, p.147, and Lord Chesterfield, p. 149). It was a distraction from the more serious matter of learning and thus, though condoned for young children, it was frowned upon as an excessive lapse into childishness for older offspring. Not until the nineteenth century was play considered to have an educative value in itself (Sara Coleridge, p. 151). Little girls in particular were to be kept from an over-indulgence in recreation in case they grew up too fond of idleness (John Harrower, p. 150, and Annie de Rothschild, p. 158). In the early nineteenth century it was strongly felt that play should teach children, notably female children, the habits of industry and application (Susan Huntington, p. 150). As Mary Sewell observes (p. 151), 'perfect play is the anticipation of perfect work'. There is evidence, too, of the cloistering of some girls from the amusements of the outside world (Mary Haldane, p. 157, and Mary Hughes, p. 158). Whereas their brothers were encouraged to sample a variety of recreational pastimes, girls, it appears, were not to be seduced from the pursuit of domesticity and the acquisition of housekeeping skills.

Daily Activities

*Grisell **Baillie** gives instructions to the governess of her nine-year-old*   Scotland, 1705
daughter Grisell.

Directions for Grisie given [to] May Menzies.

To rise by seven o'clock and go about her duty of reading,
etcetera etcetera, and be dressed to come to breakfast at nine, to
play on the spinnet till eleven, from eleven till twelve to write and
read French. At two o'clock sew her seam till four, at four learn
arithmetic, after that dance and play on the spinnet again till six
and play herself till supper and to bed at nine. [*p. xlvii*]

*Maria **Carter**, aged about fourteen, depicts a normal day to her cousin.*   America, 1756

Well then first begin, I am awakened out of a sound sleep with
some croaking voice either Patty's, Milly's, or some other of our
domestics with 'Miss Polly Miss Polly' get up, 'tis time to rise, Mr
Price is downstairs, and though I hear them I lie quite snug till my
Grandmama uses her Voice, then up I get, huddle on my clothes
and down to book, then to breakfast, then to school again, and
maybe I have an hour to myself before dinner, then the same story
over again till twilight, and then a small portion of time before I go
to rest. [*Carter (c), p. 14*]

*Richard **Cumberland**, aged nineteen, writes to his brother George from*   England, 1772
Magdalene College, Cambridge.

About seven o'clock in the morning the bedmaker comes in, lights
the fires, puts on the kettle, and sets the room to rights; at half past
seven the bell begins to ring, when we immediately get up, dress
ourselves and go to Chapel; the prayers usually take up half an
hour; on our return we find everything ready for breakfast and we
send to the butler for whatever we choose, at nine o'clock we go to
Mr Deighton who gives us a lecture on Euclid which lasts till ten or
sometimes longer; at eleven, Mr Purkis reads us a lecture on
morality for about an hour or an hour and a half, and between that
and dinner we usually spend in dressing, the dinner bell rings at
one o'clock . . . We seldom stay longer in the hall, than two o'clock,
when it is customary to invite one another to drink wine in our
rooms; but as this is a fashion not at all agreeable to me, for several
reasons, I avoid it as much as I can, and for this reason generally
engage some one to walk after dinner; the afternoon is at our own
disposal not having any particular business to do unless it is to
prepare for lectures the next day. At four o'clock the bedmaker
comes to know if we drink tea at home and what we choose to eat,
we generally form parties for tea, either among ourselves, or from
other colleges. [*p. 31*]

Most Deare Mother:,

my petition to you is: that you will be pleased to Deliuer this
Inclosed to my father: I haue made bold to send him a
Regester: wherby hee may see my loue: and allso you:
how I haue spent my tyme: not that I haue been all this while
About it: but attynueing to it: I am Entring upon two: or three:
gume flowers: and A little fruit(if you please) for the basket
it is bespoken: but not yet made: I am allso Entring upon the
vyall: the which: together with my Dansing: and Sume other
necessary things take of my tyme from my worke: but all:
Considered: I shall Indeauour to Improue my tyme for
the best: my humble Dutey to your selfe: my Respects
to my sisters: my Joyfull wishes Atending my Sister wood,
my thanks for her fauour: all being done: I beseech you
to beleiue mee:.
                          Your most Affectionate: and
                          Obedient Daughter:
                          Kathrine Oxinden:,

My most humble
Seruice presented:
      M: F: .

Letter from Katherine Oxinden, 1655

Most Deare Mother,
my petitione to you is: that you will be pleased to Deliver this
Inclosed to my father: I have made bold to send him a
regester: whereby hee may see my love and allso you: how I
have spent my tyme: not that I have been all this while About
it: but attayneing to it: I am entring upon two: or three: gume
flowers: and a little fruit (if you please) for the basket it is
bespoken: but not yet made: I am allso entring upon the vyall:
the which together with my Dansing: and Sume other
nesescary things take of my tyme from my worke: but all
Considered: I shall Indeavour to improve my tyme for the
best; my humble dutey to your selfe: my respects to my
sisters: my joyfull wishes atending my sister wood: my
thanks for her favour: all being done: I beseech you to beleive
mee:
Your most afectionate and
obedient daughter
Kathirine Oxinden

British Library, add mss 28004 f 11

Scotland, 1806   *Elizabeth* **Grant**, *having related the strict discipline she and her siblings were subjected to, turns to happier themes.*

This is the dark side of the picture; we had very happy hours as well; despotically as we were ruled in some respects, we were left in other ways to our own devices. We disposed of our time very much according to our own fancies, subject to certain rules. We were always to appear at the breakfast table of our father and mother some time between ten and eleven o'clock; the last of the three regular ringings of my father's dressing-room bell was our signal for leaving our plays; we ran off to brush our hair, wash our hands, and seize our books, with which we repaired to the breakfast room, where our duties were to run messages; in summer to amuse ourselves quietly till called upon to stir; in winter to make the toast. Breakfast over, we said our few lessons to my mother, and read in turns. I was supposed to have practised the pianoforte early. It we were wanted again during the day we were sent for, though frequently we spent the whole morning in the drawing-room, where we employed ourselves as we liked, provided we made no noise . . . In the hot summer days aunt Mary often read to us fairy tales, or bits from the Elegant Extracts, latterly Pope's Homer, which with her explanations we enjoyed extremely, all but the shield of Achilles, the long description of which I feared was never to end. When my father was away my mother dined with us early, and in the evenings we took long drives in the open landau and four. When he was at home, and the late dinner proceeded in full form – and what a tedious ceremony it was! – we all appeared at the dessert, or rather the second course, in full dress like the footmen. We sat in a row – we four, little Mary and all, on four chairs placed against the wall – trained to perfect quiet; we were to see and to smell, but to taste nothing, to hear and not to speak; but on the dessert appearing we were released, called forward to receive a little wine, a little fruit, and a biscuit, and then to have our game at romps. [*Grant (2), pp. 60–61*]

America, 1817   *John* **Todd**, *aged seventeen, writes to his elder brother relating his daily timetable.*

I rise at six in the morning, make fires, etcetera; saw wood till eight o'clock (in which time I can saw enough to last three fires during the twenty-four hours); breakfast; get to school at half-past eight; recite a Greek lesson at nine o'clock; a Latin lesson at half-past ten; at eleven the school is dismissed; get home at half-past eleven; go on errands, etcetera till one; dine at half-past one; get to school at two; recite a Latin lesson at half-past two; a grammar lesson at three; another Latin lesson at four; school dismissed at half-past four; return home; drink tea; write for Mr

Evans till nine; attend family prayers at half-past nine; get my Greek lesson for the next morning; retire to bed at eleven. [*p. 57*]

John would devote only half an hour a week to idleness and recreation.

*Henry **Alford**, aged twelve, writes to his aunt from his school.* *England, 1822*

I will tell you in what manner we spend the day. At eight o'clock the bell rings to get up, but we generally get up before to skate and slide etcetera. At nine the bell rings for prayers, when we all assemble in the hall and Lord Calthorpe expounds a chapter and prays, which generally takes up till ten, when we go to breakfast; after breakfast we separate, and go out or do what we like till two, when the bell rings for luncheon, which takes up but very little time. After luncheon we separate as before till five o'clock, when the first bell rings to dress for dinner; at half-past five the bell rings again to go into the dining-room for dinner, which takes us up altogether till half-past seven, when we retire into the drawing-room, where tea and coffee are immediately brought in; we remain there till the bell rings for prayers, which are the same as in the morning, only no expounding; after prayers we some of us go to bed, others stay longer. [*p. 13*]

*Laura **Spears**, with her mother and three-year-old brother Prescott, accompanied her father on a whaling voyage round Cape Horn. The trip commenced when Laura was six and lasted three years. She kept a journal of the journey, from which a selection of extracts is quoted.* *America, 1869*

1869.

The wind blows very hard. We had ducks for dinner. I study my lessons every day. Mama has given me some worsted and I am making a toilet cushion.

Uncle Nathan came on board and spent the forenoon. He gave us some sweet potatoes and some limejuice and some coconuts and a few pumpkins.

Papa opened one of the coconuts. It is soft inside. Prescott loves them. There is a fly on my finger. He has flew off now.

It is a calm day and very pleasant. Papa has made two boat sails. PS I have made eight babies.

Mama is reading a book. Prescott is swinging. Prescott is sitting in the chair. It is very pleasant. I have a green pencil and some paper. And a little knife. Prescott is out on deck.

1870.

It is quite pleasant today, the hens have laid fifty eggs. Papa came home last night and brought lots of papers and books. Mrs Dexter sent Prescott and I some candy. Papa has a trap and has caught six mice. We caught one last night. The first one we caught was quite a large one. It is quite smooth today. Prescott is up on deck playing. I am going up now to swing. Papa is fixing the water closet. Prescott is eating eggs. He loves them. So do I. We have piecoe [?] for dinner. We are going aboard of the ship Emily Morgan to see some dogs. I think I shall have a good time. I went on board the Emily Morgan and had a nice time. Mrs Dexter gave me some cards to play with, and a bottle of hair oil and she gave me a little dog but we forgot him.

It is a pleasant day, it is quite smooth today. The men are boiling out the blubber in the try pots. The pots are real large. When the men are going to boil out the blubber, two men get in the pots and squeeze out the blubber and are way up their knees of oil. When the men at the mast head say there she blows, Papa gives them fifty pounds of tobacco. Prescott is up on deck, and Mama too. I am going up too. It is most supper time. I have been up on deck. I can't think of much to write. I went to bed last night and got up this morning. We had baked potatoes for supper and biscuit. Would you like to hear some news? Well I don't know of any. [*pp. 131–8*]

England, 1871 Katherine **Russell** *writes to a prospective governess about her two children, Frank aged six and Rachel aged three.*

[Frank] is intensely active minded and will learn whenever he can. The girl is three and rather backward; she only knows her letters but talks German as well as English and cares for singing and she would have to be taught. Both could learn French.

Both are strong and healthy children and are never ailing hitherto. The boy sleeps in my room. The girl would sleep with you. Both get up at half-past six and are with me from seven to eight. At eight breakfast with me, at quarter to nine go out till twelve or one, part of the time on a pony that they ride in turn and part of the time alone. I like them to be much alone and unwatched. At 1.30 they dine with us and often go out with us after. At five have tea with us and stay with their father till near six. At seven go to bed.

I want someone to dress and undress them, see to their clothes, etcetera. They seldom change during the day except in London.

They make their own beds, fold up their own things at night and on coming home, and I like and care for them to learn to be *useful and independent* as much as anything else. *Work* of all sorts is to be taught them as necessary and desirable. [*vol. 2, p. 415*]

Toys

*Endymion **Porter** sends a gift to his son George, aged three.*   *England, 1623*

I sent you by Sir John Epsley six little glass bottles with silver chains for little George, and I make no doubt but he will keep a terrible stir with them. [*p. 68*]

*Jean Wemyss, Countess of **Sutherland**, entered into her account book purchases of gifts for her small children James, Margaret and Archibald.*   *Scotland, 1652*

1652	£	s	d
[For Margaret] a rattle to the child	0	4	0
[For James] for a drum to him	0	14	0
for a baby to my daughter Meg	0	13	4

1653			
¼lb sugar candy for the bairns	1	0	0
a bust of sugar almonds which I bought for the bairns in Shirishall	0	15	0
4 golf balls to James	0	16	0
[For James] 4 arrows to his bows	0	16	0
bow string to him	0	2	0
sugar candy and licorice to my daughter	1	4	0
a rattle for Archibald	0	2	0
new testament and catechism to Lord James	2	14	0

[*dep. 313/502*]

*Penelope **Mordaunt** writes to her husband about a misfortune which befell their young daughter Penelope.*   *England, 1699*

I write this at my brother's where I this day dined and Pen. It's the first time I have been out; but dinner not coming so soon as Pen wanted it, to quiet her Mrs Richardson would lend her a wax baby in swaddles which she was very fond of; but at last down came the baby and broke to pieces. Your daughter did fall a stowing and squealing that the baby was broke; that you would have laughed to have seen her, but her uncle asking her who she was angry at she was quiet, but would not endure to see the baby; and there was to have been a great christening of it and Pen was to have been the godmother but the life was very short. [*CR1368, vol. 1, f. 21*]

England, 1723   *John* **Verney**, *aged twelve, writes to his father Ralph from school.*

Dear papa, – George brought me some gingerbread which you was so kind as to send me, as also a couple of handkerchiefs, but we have found the other again in one of my coat pockets. I beg the favour of you, if it will not be troublesome, that you will desire my dear Mama to send me a little tea and sugar, as also a pair of battledores and shuttlecocks. [(b) v. 2, p. 134]

America, 1787   *Tommy* **Shippen** *writes to his sister Nancy about a doll to be given to her five-year-old daughter Margaret.*

Before I take leave of them entirely I must speak of *the doll*, because Mrs Hunter has become a party concerned. This doll then which has been matter of so great expectation, which has so often been promised and so long neglected, which is to be ever memorable when finished and to unite all the taste and graces of a fashionable lady, having been purchased in embryo by your brother, is now at the house of Mrs Hunter, and from all I can learn engages great part of the attention of the whole family. The hair dresser is making for it a wig or chevelure, the whalebone man a pair of stays, the milliner a full dress, and the shifts-petticoat and handkerchief divide the cares of the ladies. In short no pains are sparing to send the lady in question complete and perfect into the world, where very few can boast as much at going out of it. But every picture that is justly drawn has its black as well as its fair side, and so must also the picture of the doll. By some ill-fated misadventure the toy woman in Bond Street, perceiving perhaps that I looked at the beauty of her face more eagerly than at that of the toy I was purchasing, gave me O! wicked mischief! a face with a crooked mouth. [*pp. 254–5*]

Despite the splendours of this doll, Margaret preferred her dog.

England, 1792   *Mary* **Hamilton** *writes to her five-year-old daughter Louisa. (Morrison is the maid.)*

Lady Cremorne, one of *your friends*, has sent you a fine undressed doll which is gone by the coach to day, it is directed to Mr Suttersfield so you must ask Grandpapa to be so good as to send for it, and on Tuesday or Wednesday you will receive from me of a pretty thing to drink out of, and Morrison, who dearly loves you, has sent you a present also, you must not spoil nor lose it . . .

You must work very hard for dolly, for poor thing she is quite naked, and take care of her fine hair. [*pp. 300–301*]

*Fanny **Burney** took her three-year-old son Alexander to visit the royal family. At first he was shy.*   *England, 1798*

Princess Elizabeth then entered, attended by a page, who was loaded with playthings, which she had been sending for. You may suppose him caught now! He seized upon dogs, horses, chaise, a cobbler, a watchman, and all he could grasp; but would not give his little person or his cheeks, to my great confusion, for any of them. [*vol. 6, p. 152*]

It was with great difficulty I could part my little love from his grand collection of new playthings, all of which he had dragged into the painting-room, and wanted now to pull them downstairs to the Queen's apartment. I persuaded him, however, to relinquish the design without a quarrel, by promising we would return for them . . .

The Queen . . . had a Noah's ark ready displayed upon the table for him . . . he was now soon in raptures; and, as the various animals were produced, looked with a delight that danced in all his features; he capered with joy; such as, 'O! a tow [cow]!' But, at the dog, he clapped his little hands, and running close to her Majesty, leant upon her lap, exclaiming. 'O; it's bow wow!' 'And do you know this, little man?' said the Queen, showing him a cat.

'Yes,' cried he, again jumping as he leant upon her, 'its name is talled pussey!' And, at the appearance of Noah, in a green mantle, and leaning on a stick, he said, 'At's the shepherd's boy!'. [*vol. 6, pp. 153–7*]

*Mary **Sewell** recalls the time when she and her sister purchased a toy despite lacking sufficient funds to do so.*   *England, c.1805*

I am sure my sister Elizabeth and I shall never forget our secretly getting into debt. We were taken to Norwich with our father and mother. Not far from the inn where my father put up was a small shop where children's toys were sold. These were the high times of our baby-house, and in the shop-window we saw some little tin and lead plates, the very things for our baby house kitchen. We ventured into the shop to inquire the price; they came to more than we had by a penny or half-penny, I forget which. Temptation was very strong, and we asked if the man could trust us till we came again and paid him. He evidently saw that we were not thieves, and consented, and we went off with our prize. We very seldom went to Norwich, and we were unwilling to trust any one with our disgraceful secret, and this penny hung about our necks for weeks, attended with the most anxious fear lest the man should see father and tell him of it. I forget the particulars of the repayment, but I know in some way our consciences obtained peace. [*pp. 26–7*]

America, 1852 *Caroline* **Richards**, *aged ten, and her sister Anna, aged eight, were brought up by their grandmother after their mother's death. Caroline records the visits of their father in her diary.*

Father and Uncle Edward Richards came to see us yesterday and took us down to Mr Corson's store and told us we could have anything we wanted. So we asked for several kinds of candy, stick candy and lemon drops and bulls' eyes, and then they got us two rubber balls and two jumping ropes with handles and two hoops and sticks to roll them with and two red carnelian rings and two bracelets. We enjoyed getting them very much, and expect to have lots of fun. [*p. 25*]

America, 1856 *Rutherford* **Hayes** *describes the Christmas presents of his son Birchard, aged three.*

What a triumphant day for him Christmas was! He found in his stockings a picture-book and knick-knacks. His good friends, Mr and Mrs Warren, brought him a barking monkey and a box out of which sprung when opened a queer, terrible looking little old man which made his eyes start out with mingled fright and joy. He is a little timid about such horrors, but soon mastered his fears and enjoyed it boisterously. I took him to Judge James's room in the morning of Christmas day and enjoyed his happiness in gazing at toys in the show-windows. His constant question was 'What is all-that?' He catches all our phrases which sound queerly in his little mouth. Speaking of the figure in his surprise box he says, 'It is a terrible thing.' [*vol. 1, p. 507*]

Scotland, c.1870 *David* **Cairns** *remembers the toys he and his siblings owned.*

We had few toys but got on pretty well without them. Willie was a great pole-jumper and used to go about with an eight-foot pole charging dykes and gates, and we had parallel bars in the garden on which we worked off our energy. I think we had one home-made bat and a cricket ball, Jessie had a doll or two. I had also, first and last, two pairs of skates and three fishing-rods and tackle, of which more later. For indoor games we had draughts and chess and darts which we made ourselves, as we did our bows and arrows. Of real playing-cards we had none, but we had card games of an educational as well as recreational type, 'Quartettes', 'History Cards' and so on . . . And, of course, for school, we had marbles, or 'bools', as the simple pottery articles were named . . . We had also 'peeries' or tops. I think that is nearly a complete inventory of our play apparatus. [*pp. 53–4*]

Play

*Lucy **Hutchinson** describes her preference, as a child, for academic learning rather than recreational pursuits.*   *England c.1627*

As for music and dancing I profited very little in them, and would never practise my lute or harpsichords but when my masters were with me; and for my needle I absolutely hated it; play among other children I despised, and when I was forced to entertain such as came to visit me, I tired them with more grave instructions than their mothers, and plucked all their babies to pieces, and kept the children in such awe, that they were glad when I entertained myself with elder company. [*vol. 1. p. 26*]

*Adam **Martindale** recalls his godmother presenting him with a horn-book when he was six.*   *England, 1629*

A gift in itself exceedingly small and contemptible, but in respect of the design and event, worth more than its weight in gold. For till that time I was all for childish play, and never thought of learning. [*p. 5*]

*Walter **Pringle** recollects his childhood.*   *Scotland, c.1630*

In my childhood, though I was much indulged by my parents, and greatly given to playing, yet now and then I had some far off looks towards God. [*p. 3*]

*Henry **Slingsby** ponders upon the cause of the slow progress made by his four-year-old son Thomas.*   *England, 1630*

I find him duller to learn this year then the last, which would discourage one, but that I think the cause to be his too much minding play, which takes off his mind from his book; therefore they do ill that do foment and cherish that humour in a child, and by inventing new sports increase his desire to play, which causeth a great aversion to their book; and their mind being at first seasoned with vanity, will not easily lose the relish of it. [*pp. 53–4*]

*Thomas **Boston** recalls the games he used to play at grammar school between the ages of eleven and thirteen.*   *Scotland, 1687*

By means of my education, and natural disposition, I was of a sober and harmless deportment, preserved from the common vices of children in towns. I was at no time what they call a vicious or a roguish boy; neither was I so addicted to play as to forget my business; though I was a dextrous player at such games as required art and nimbleness. And towards the latter end of this period, having had frequent occasion to see soldiers exercised, I had a peculiar faculty at mustering and exercising my school-fellows accordingly, by the several words and motions of the exercise of the musket; they being formed into a body, under a captain. The which exercise I have managed, to as much weariness and pain of my breast, as sometimes I have preached. [*p. 4*]

England, 1696 *Dr Thomas Knipe, master of Westminster School, writes to Lord* **Herbert**, *complaining that the latter's son Henry prefers play to study.*

I was several times sending him home to your Lordship as hopeless, as indeed I have sometimes threatened him; but that I imputed his carelessness to his childishness, which, though it has remained longer with him than others of his age, I expected would go off by degrees; and then I knew his parts, which I don't at all find fault with, joined with the continuation of my care, would make amends for neglect of his childhood, and please both your Lordship and himself at last; for learning is to children as tobacco is to some people, it makes them sick at first, and when they have got the trick of it, they will never leave it. But hitherto he has been so much a child, that when he has been called from his play to his studies, he has stood in the yard, crying, and blubbering, and roaring, as your own servants have sometimes heard him, because he might not play longer; when other children have gone immediately to their studies, laughing all the way to see him such a child. If this infirmity of his leaves him, I don't doubt but, upon his continuance with me, to finish him. [*vol. 1, p. 164*]

America, 1705 *Cotton* **Mather** *does not wish his children to be too fond of playing.*

I am not fond of proposing *play* to them, as a reward of any diligent application to learn what is good; lest they should think diversion to be a better and nobler thing than diligence. [*Mather (b), vol. 7, p. 536*]

England, 1712 *Nicholas* **Blundell** *on his daughters Margaret, aged seven, and Frances, aged five.*

My daughters buried one of their dolls with a great deal of formality, they had a garland of flowers carried before it and at least twenty of their playfellows and others that they invited were at the burial.

Two years later Blundell made a toy for his children.

I made a shuttlecock for my children but they could not play with it. [*Blundell (a), vol. 112, pp. 29, 115*]

Mr Butterfield writes to Ralph **Verney** *about his son Ralph, aged almost seven. Mr Butterfield was looking after Ralph while his parents and elder brother John were in London.*   *England, 1721*

He is in perfect health and seems well content with his company, and the sweetness of his temper and vivacity of spirit, joined with the innocency of his age, renders him the delight of all about him. He lies in a little room hung with paper, which is a sort of alcove within ours, so that we are near at hand upon any occasion; and he has a bedfellow as my lady directed, but I hope his good angel, or rather that eye of providence, which neither slumbers nor sleeps, will be his continual guard. After prayers and dressing, betwixt the book and the top and other diversions, the hours pass smoothly and not unprofitably away; so that though he is every one's care and concern, he is a trouble to none. He pleases himself with imagination of his brother's being cooped up in a little house whilst he has the liberty of ranging the garden and the fields, and on church-days has the sole ringing of the bell, and the whole property of the newspapers. He was in great expectation of the drum and fiddle on Thursday night, and when the carrier delivered the one broken and the other lying at the bottom of the waggon, could not be come at, he bore the disappointment with the temper of a philosopher. [*(b) vol. 2, p. 173*]

Lord **Chesterfield** *writes to his eight-year-old son, Philip. (The original letter is in Latin.)*   *England, 1741*

This is the last letter I shall write to you as to a little boy, for tomorrow, if I am not mistaken you will attain your ninth year; so that, for the future, I shall treat you as a *youth*. You must now commence a different course of life, a different course of studies. No more levity: childish toys and playthings must be thrown aside, and your mind directed to serious objects. What was not unbecoming to a child, would be disgraceful to a youth. [*vol. 1, pp. 171–2*]

Frances **Boscawen** *writes to her husband of their two children, Edward, aged three, and Frances, aged twenty-two months.*   *England, 1748*

I don't carry the children into Hyde Park as usual, for I don't find time to go out in the morning, and I imagine 'tis not necessary in this airy Audley Street – at least, I'm sure they can't be better than

they are. I wish you could see us all supping together, for you must
know I always regale with your fine tea before I go abroad. And
with it enters two immense pieces of bread, which, being sopped
in very weak tea, are put into two different plates for Ned and
Fanny. The former feeds himself with great seriousness and
solemnity: the latter jumps and skips and sings, still minding the
main chance all the time. After they are satisfied, *c'est l'etiquette* to
have a great game of romps, in the height of which I escape and
gain my coach. [*p. 69*]

Scotland, 1774   John **Harrower** *advises his wife how to treat their daughter Elizabeth,
aged about eight.*

I suppose Betts is at home with yourself, pray keep her tight to her
seam and stocking and any other household affairs that her years
are capable of and do not bring her up to idleness or play or going
about from house to house which is the first inlet in any of the sex
to laziness and vice. [*p. 91*]

America, 1822   Susan **Huntington** *gives her opinion on what kind of play is suitable
for girls.*

I like a baby house for little girls, all that some sensible people
have said to the contrary notwithstanding. They may have a closet,
or part of one entirely to themselves, and the arrangements and
order of it be entrusted to their care. If they are required to keep it
neat and tidy, it will be employment and amusement for them. As
soon as children are old enough to understand what they read, the
difficulty of amusing them lessens. And I think it is desirable to
accustom them, as soon as may be to assist in doing what they can,
that they may learn the pleasure of being useful. To fold up the
baby's cradle clothes, or pick up threads on the carpet, or anything
else, however trivial, is something important for a child to do, if it
inspires the love of industry, and make her experience the
happiness of doing good. [*pp. 340–41*]

England, c.1830   Mary **Sewell** *outlines her views on children's play.*

All who have had to do with little children know how wearing it is
to the temper of mother or nurse to have to listen to children's
drawling exclamations and questions – 'What shall I do?' 'I don't
know what to play at'. 'Give me this or that,' etcetera. It is a great
point of wisdom so to arrange the periods of the day that this
weary time never comes: for this purpose, habitual regularity is
invaluable. At stated times the child should be set up at the table
to amuse itself quietly, without any assistance except being

furnished with its amusements for the time, and these should generally be the same. Children should not be accustomed to too much variety; they do not need it, and it is a waste of our resources. A child will amuse itself for a very long time in stringing beads, putting different kinds of seeds or beads into different divisions of a box, drawing, cutting, etcetera, etcetera. There should be a degree of perfectness, and even something approaching to business habits, encouraged and expected, even in these little amusements, to give a worth and interest to them. Perfect play is the anticipation of perfect work. Habitual restraint and self-dependence for an hour once or twice in the day will be invaluable as habits for the child, and a great relief for the parent. [pp. 103–4]

*Sara **Coleridge** considers how play may be given an educative function. (Herby is her five-year-old son.)* *England, 1835*

I would never turn all lessons into play; but without losing sight of this principle we may, perhaps, turn a child's play, to a certain degree, into lessons. For instance, when Herby looks over a book of coloured prints, I never attempt to make a task of the thing; but I draw his attention to such points as are of a general interest – the knowledge of which may come usefully into play afterwards. This flower is crimson, that is pink, that scarlet; I make him observe this difference, and his great amusement is to compare these different hues together. 'These birds have small wings and large bodies – that sort of birds the contrary.' In this way I think a child *may* be 'beguiled usefully' into the habit of observation – into the use of his mind; the particular facts are of little consequence, or less consequence; but they are not totally useless; they form a nucleus of knowledge – they give an interest to other facts; and this little knowledge is gathered at a time when, if that were not done, nothing else would be. [*vol. 1, p. 122*]

*Caroline **Richards**, aged ten, relates the disadvantages of one play-ground game. (Anna is her younger sister.)* *America, 1852*

We played snap the whip at recess to-day and I was on the end and was snapped off against the fence. It hurt me so, that Anna cried. It is not a very good game for girls, especially for the one on the end. [p. 28]

*David **Cairns** looks back on his childhood.* *Scotland, c.1870*

Snapshots of our games emerge as I look back into the past. John devised a railway system on our bare potato beds in winter with stations, signals and lines, and we all ran puffing along them. He had also an invention called 'the Happy Valley'. This was a dug-out space in the same ground, with model houses, a church, a plantation of twigs, roads, bridges and loch . . .

Some of our games were weird enough. One was the formation of a cemetery for dead birds discovered in the garden, with headstones of slates. We made mud pies, moulded in coconuts and set forth as a plum pudding with boxwood leaves for raisins. To imagine that our fine old elm was a ship was another. Yet another was to make a tent of chairs and rug and imagine ourselves nomad gypsies or Arabs . . .

Some of the keenest enjoyments of my youth were of skating, football and tennis.

But of all recreations the best beloved by me was trout fishing and guddling or gumping trout (i.e. hand poaching) . . . I shall never forget my unalloyed delight in capturing my first trout in the Linn Hole. [*pp. 53–4*]

England, 1879 Caroline **Head** *on her son Albert, aged two and a half.*

He constantly plays at being a gardener, or lamplighter, or engine driver, or coal-man, or man with organ and monkey. He is most imaginative, and such a chatterbox. [*p. 110*]

Scotland, c.1890 Catherine **Carswell** *recollects her childish pastimes.*

Even in town we were allowed the utmost freedom in almost every direction, and I cannot remember a time when we did not play in the streets as and with whom we pleased, so long as our comings and goings did not impinge on the simple home routine of meals, lessons, prayers and bedtime. We made our forays unburdened by warnings, moral instructions or questioning . . .

We did not only play at tops, marbles, 'peever', hoop-running (insisting upon iron hoops and hooks to match those of our street boy friends), ball, and road games, each in their season and correct circumstances; we fought in gangs with peashooters and catapults, rode madly on a tricycle horse, tore about on roller skates or trundling a cane 'mail-cart' crammed with passengers; we coasted the steep hills on wheels or sledges. We fished down gratings for queer objects; we scoured waste lands, dodged policeman, hung on to the back rails of horse trams, four wheelers and lorries in the traffic of Sauchiehall Street. There were, of course, no motor vehicles, but the traffic was brisk. We followed with mimicry and absurd gestures any passerby who appeared to us over-dressed or 'stuck-up'. [*p. 61*]

Recreation

England, 1614–17

*Hugh **Cholmley** on the pastimes of his youth; he had entered Cambridge University at the age of fourteen.*

Yet I did not spend my time so profitably as I might have done, for I was naturally given to all sports and recreations, and inclinable to play; wanting my old tutor to hold me to my studies, I did not follow it close here at Cambridge . . .

At seventeen years of age I left Cambridge and went into the country with my father, where I was so entered in hunting, hawking, and horse-races, that I could not easily put them out of my mind when, by riper years, I saw the vanity of them; and therefore I advise, not to let children have any taste of them, or be taught to game; but, as the wise man directs, 'train a child in his youth in such courses as are fit for him to practise when he comes to be a man'. [*pp. 37–8*]

England, c.1625

*Margaret **Cavendish** recalls the pastimes of her sisters and brothers.*

Their [my brother's] practice was, when they met together, to exercise themselves with fencing, wrestling, shooting, and such like exercises, for I observed they did seldom hawk or hunt, and very seldom or never dance, or play on music, saying it was too effeminate for masculine spirits; neither had they skill, or did use to play, for ought I could hear, at cards or dice, or the like games, nor given to any vice, as I did know, unless to love a mistress were a crime, not that I know any they had, but what report they did say, and usually reports are false, at least exceed the truth.

As for the pastimes of my sisters when they were in the country, it was to read, work, walk, and discourse with each other. [*pp. 7–8*]

Scotland, 1672

*John **Foulis**'s account book contains entries of money spent procuring amusements for his offspring. Jean was eighteen and Margaret nine.*

1672.	[£	s	d]
to the children to see the puppie [puppet?]			
play and for curds and whey at Leithwind craigs	1	5	0
for a coach to Ravelston and two babies to the bairns	0	3	8
to the children to get curds and whey	0	13	4

1680.			
left to my daughter Jean to give the fiddler			
and to play at cards	2	0	0
to Meg to to to the curds and whey	0	18	4
to Peter Birnie, fiddler, for playing to	0	13	4
the bairns	[*pp. 4, 5, 19, 45*]		

*Thomas **Isham**, aged sixteen, kept a diary outlining the day-to-day activities of his life. There follows a selection of entries for March to July 1673, illustrating how he and his brothers spent their free time. Justinian was aged fifteen and John fourteen.*

March.

Northampton Market.

I went coursing for hares with Lewis and Robert.

April.

The famous Harleston races were held, and Lord Lovelance was the winner.

A horse race at Rowell between Lord Cullen and Mr Washbourne for twenty pounds. Lord Cullen won.

Northampton Market.

Today my brother John caught a large carp in the fishpond with his rod.

May.

Brixworth Fair. My brothers Justinian and John went and there met Sir William Haslewood with Mr Saunders and Mr Ashfield, with whom they went to see a Punch and Judy show.

Mr Saunders, Mr Farmer and several others came to play at bowls.

We caught twenty-two perch in the fishpond with a hook, including two large ones.

June.

Boughton Fair: I went with Mother and my brothers and sisters.

My brother John killed a sparrow with a stone.

July.

Today Father and I set off for Oxford with my brother Justinian.

Being refreshed after our journey we went out to see the beauties of the city. Near Magdalen we saw a walk about five hundred yards long planted on each side with a row of beech trees. In the evening we saw many colleges.

Today in the theatre the doctors made their speeches full of wisdom clothed in ornate language. There the *Terrae filii* intersperse the proceedings with their quips and ribald jokes – one of them cracked his jokes with such ease and wit that I should have believed him to be speaking from memory if he had not kept his eye on his book the whole time.

Today we went to Paradise, a garden very pleasant and beautiful to look on and rich in everything to delight us.

We saw comedy and rope-walkers.
We saw a man eating fire.
We returned home today. [*Isham (b), pp. 201, 202, 207, 209, 215, 217, 221*]

Frances and Jane **Grimston**, *aged about ten and nine, on holiday at the   England, 1765
seaside, compose a poem for their father.*

Thanks to Papa for his kind card
A pleasing token of regard
The partridges and hare were good,
None better tasted since the flood.
So plentiful was your supply
As to enable us thereby,
Other friends to gratifye.

Our health is good, our spirits cheerfull,
Bathing we like . . . scorn to be fearfull.
We ride, we walk, we pick up shells
To day we guns have heard and bells
In honour of great George our King
You will suppose the bells did ring
That was indeed the very thing.

And now Papa, we pray excuse,
These infant babblings of our Muse,
The attempt is new, our time is short,
If it contributes to your sport,
Our end is answer'd; so shall We,
Ever remain most cordially
Your duteous daughters.

[*p. 101*]

Anna **Winslow**, *aged twelve, writes to her mother about a party she   America, 1772
attended.*

There was a large company assembled in a handsome, large, upper room in the new end of the house. We had two fiddles, and I had the honor to open the diversion of the evening in a minuet with Miss Soley . . . our treat was nuts, raisins, cakes, wine, punch, hot and cold, all in great plenty. We had a very agreeable evening from five to ten o'clock. For variety we wooed a widow, hunted the whistle, threaded the needle, and while the company was collecting, we diverted ourselves with playing pawns, no rudeness Mamma I assure you. [*pp. 16–17*]

England, 1772   *Thomas **Grimston**, aged eighteen, writes to his father from Harrow.*

I have been obliged to stay from school since Saturday evening last, as I had a quarrel with one of the boys, and we fought, and I had the ill luck to be conquered, receiving many blows on the face; it was swelled up very much, and I have got two black eyes . . . The boy I fought was bigger and stronger than I am. [*pp. 98-9*]

America, 1773   *Philip **Fithian** relates the pastimes of his pupils once they are freed from their lessons. Priscilla is aged fifteen; Nancy, thirteen; Robert, sixteen; Benjamin, eighteen; and Harry, sixteen.*

Miss Priscilla, and Miss Nancy rode this morning in the chariot over to Mr Turburvilles. Bob, every day at twelve o'clock is down by the riverside with his gun after ducks, gulls, etcetera. Ben is on his horse a riding, Harry is either in the kitchen, or at the blacksmith's or carpenter's shop. They all find places of rendez-vous so soon as the bell rings, and all seem to choose different sports. [*p. 49*]

England, 1796   *Eugenia **Wynne**, aged seventeen, confides to her diary her reaction on being informed of the possibility of a ball.*

General de Burgh is to give a ball for the new year day. These words make my heart beat as if it would jump out of my breast. Beat for anxiety, wish, fear. I wish to go, I fear to be asked, and if I am asked to stay at home, then I hope, then I fear again, and can think of nothing else. God forgive me if it be a sin.

The next day.

The ball, the ball always trots in my head. I cannot help it but I am always thinking of it. [*vol. 2, pp. 142–3*]

Eugenia's anxieties were not assuaged even after she had received an invitation.

On our return from church the Vicar made me as mad as possible in pretending that we should give up the ball, and make a sacrifice of it, take it as a mortification, etcetera and God knows what stuff. I made no answer, but thought, my friend, if instead of that black robe you had a petticoat on, if instead of the weight of fifty years you had only seventeen, you would not speak so. [*vol. 2, p. 144*]

In the event, Eugenia both attended and enjoyed the ball.

Elizabeth **Fry** *reflects on the problem of reconciling her adolescent children's desire for amusement with the restrictions imposed by her religious faith.*   *England, 1830*

My arrival at home was clouded by a party, to which my children were invited, and rather wished to go. We had some pains about it – my path is a very peculiar one; and, as to bringing my family up consistent Friends, a most difficult one. My husband not going hand in hand with me, in some of these things, and my children, in no common degree, disliking the cross of the minor testimonies of Friends, and, from deeply sorrowful circumstances, after having their faith in them tried, also their being exposed unavoidably, to much association with those, who do not see these things needful. My desire is, only to do what is for the real good of my children, and for the good of the cause which I love, and leave *myself* altogether out of the question whether it bring me into evil report, or good report. [*p. 403*]

Her children accepted the invitation.

Frederick **Post***, at the age of eleven, is taken to the zoo.*   *England, 1830*

I was much amused with the monkeys, who eat strawberries very dexterously. I saw the tigers – lions – bears etcetera, etcetera. I was afraid to touch the elephant's trunk, and, therefore, threw him some food to pick up – he directly threw back his trunk, and opened his mouth for me to throw the food in, which I did. [*p. 134*]

Mary **Haldane** *describes the recreational pursuits of herself and her sister as children.*   *England, 1835*

As a child I loved games of all kinds, and used to long to play cricket and go out spearing with the boys and to ride the hounds. But such was not them permitted, and we had practically no amusements. [*p. 47*]

I have very pleasant recollections of riding round the race-course with my sister on our ponies. The race-course was over a common covered with heath. At six o'clock in the morning we accompanied our father to drink the waters at the Spa, walking through the fields for upwards of a mile, which we greatly enjoyed ... Occasionally we spent a day with our cousins at Stonefall. [*p. 48*]

On the few occasions when we were free from nurse or preceptress we had a sunny, happy time walking on the moors and watching the lambs. We would go forth on our ponies under the old coachman's care, fording the streams and climbing the sides of those green hills. [*p. 65*]

We had something to eat, and at 7 a lady came and drove us to the Botanical Gardens. There are some lovely trees there and some very big bamboos. As were going back through the town we saw a man doing penance. He was dressed in black and had smeared himself with soot and ashes. He had a pot on his head with fire in it, and a great crowd of people were following him. He stopped at every house, and those who wanted to help him gave him some oil. The men here - at least the Bhuddists, - have long hair and tie it up in a knot behind. Some wear large tortoise shell combs. They look so very funny. Some of the people wear tall straw caps. The Bhuddists priests have their heads shaved and wear long yellow robes. - Then when we got back we had breakfast. When we got up Jack (who had been out first with Papa) - brought us some mangosteens and we ate these for breakfast. They are very nice. They are red outside and have a very thick skin. Inside they are white and have stones in the middle. At half past ten we went to see the temple of the tooth. When we got there we went up some steps and looked at the moat - it had some tortoises in it - and then went to the place where the tooth which is called Bhuddah's tooth is kept. It is kept in a tower in the middle of the building. This tower is painted outside with dragons and lions; its door has a brass lock and bolt beautifully carved. Inside there are some beautifully carved wooden pillars. We went upstairs and came to another room and from that we went into a smaller one. Its door, too, had a brass lock and bolt: then there was another very small room, the outside had ivory and brass carving. This room had a brass door; inside it was a grating, and behind that there was a large bell shaped gold case with a little chain hanging from it, and some big jewels set in it. There are seven gold cases one inside the other and inside that the tooth. In front of the bars there was a carved brass table covered with flowers which scented the room strongly, and in the anteroom there were two tables covered with flowers. The priests brought in the golden plates and bowls belonging to the temple. It was very hot indeed inside. Then we went to see

Extract from Rachael Hamilton-Gordon's diary, 1882

We had something to eat, and at 7 a lady came and drove us to
the Botanical Gardens. There are some lovely trees there and
some very big bamboos. As [we] were going back through the
town we saw a man doing penance. He was dressed in black
and had smeared himself with soot and ashes. He had a pot
on his head with fire in it, and a great crowd of people were
following him. He stopped at every house and those who
wanted to help him gave him some oil. The men here - at least
the Bhuddists, - have long hair and tie it up in a knot behind.
Some wear large tortoise shell combs. They look so very
funny. Some of the people wear tall straw caps. The Bhuddists
priests have their heads shaved and wear long yellow robes.
Then when we got back we had breakfast. When we got up
Jack - (who had been out first with Papa)
 brought us some mangosteens and we ate these for breakfast.
They are very nice. They are red outside and have a very thick
skin, inside they are white and have stones in the middle. At
half past ten we went to see the temple of the tooth. When we
got there we went up some steps and looked at the moat - it
had some tortoises in it - and then went to the place where the
tooth which is called Buddah's tooth is kept. It is kept in a
tower in the middle of the building. This tower is painted
outside with dragons and lions; its door has a brass lock and
bolt beautifully carved inside there are some beautifully
carved wooden pillars. We went up stairs and came to another
room and from that we went into a smaller one. Its door, too,
had a brass lock and bolt: then there was another very small
room, the outside had ivory and brass carving. This room had
a brass door; inside it was a grating, and behind that there
was a large bell shaped gold case with a little chain hanging
from it, and some big jewels set in it. There are seven gold
cases one inside the other and inside that the tooth. In front of
the brass there was a carved brass table covered with flowers
which scented the room strongly, and in the anteroom there
were two tables covered with flowers. The priests brought in
the golden plates and bowls belonging to the temple. It was
very hot indeed inside. Then we went to see

British Library, add mss 49271 f 218

My mother drove us to see the first balloon ascend, and we were greatly excited at the event. I was also much impressed by seeing the treadmill of the Newcastle prison; it seemed a barbarous form of punishment. [*pp. 69–70*]

England, 1841   *Frances **Wood** on her daughter Frances, aged four.*

We have found some nice fields where Baby can go; she revels in picking daisies and 'dandy elephants' (as she miscalls dande-lions). Primrose expeditions to the woods and paddling about the sands are great treats. I have had some difficulty in persuading her that the sea is not *alive*; and the first day that there was any surf, she begged to know 'who had been washing in the sea, for it was all over soap-suds'. [*pp. 322–3*]

England, 1843   *Sara **Coleridge**, on holiday with her thirteen-year-old son Herbert, relates his dissatisfaction with the situation.*

We were delayed in coming hither for some days by Herbert's prolonged stay at Rickmansworth, where he spent nearly three weeks in a sort of boy's paradise, bathing two or three times a day . . . Herbert thinks this place very *seedy*, and despises the bathing. The tide seems never in a state to please him; but the truth is, he wants companions, and does not like to be a solitary Triton among the minnows, or rather, as those are fresh-water fish, among the crabs and seaweed. However, he has got 'Japhet in Search of a Father' from the circulating library, reads a portion daily of Euripides, and has begun learning French; and it is quite right that a little *seediness* should come in its turn after 'jollity', and quietness and plain fare after 'splendid lark', with 'sock' of all sorts, that he may learn to cut out interests and amusements for himself out of home materials. [*vol. 1, pp. 284–5*]

America, 1847   *Henry **Longfellow** writes about his four-year-old son Charles.*

I took Charles into the circus. It did not amuse him. Coming out, a black kitten on a post, and a smith shoeing a horse, delighted him infinitely more. Children are most amused by the slightest things; they comprehend them most easily. [*Longfellow (a), vol. 2, p. 89*]

Four years later, Charles has a birthday party.

He is eight years old, and had a charming party with children wild with play among the haycocks; the seat in the old apple-tree turned into a fort; great scrambling for sugar-plums, and the like. All ending with supper and a dance in the drawing-room. [*Longfellow (a), vol. 2, p. 238*]

*Ellen **Parker**, aged twenty, describes a ball she attended.* *America, 1851*

The first thing was dancing, and then were passed around refreshments. I think the next operation was rolling the platter; then a game of euchre; then followed another dance, and some more kissing plays came next in order, in which there was *a great participation*. I can safely say I kissed the boys all I wished to. I don't remember what came next, but there is one thing I *do* remember, it was daylight when we *kissed* and parted; and another thing – it was nine when we got home. We all enjoyed ourselves very much. [*Parker (1), p. 155*]

*Caroline **Richards**, aged thirteen, relates the tale of an outing she and* *America, 1856*
her eleven-year-old sister Anna did not enjoy.

Anna and I were invited to go on a sleigh-ride, Tuesday night, and Grandfather said he did not want us to go. We asked him if we could spend the evening with Frankie Richardson and he said yes, so we went down there and when the load stopped for her, we went too, but we did not enjoy ourselves at all and did not join in the singing. I had no idea that sleigh-rides could make any one feel so bad. It was not very cold, but I just shivered all the time. When the nine o'clock bell rang we were up by the 'Northern Retreat', and I was so glad when we got near home so we could get out. Grandfather and Grandmother asked us if we had a nice time, but we got to bed as quick as we could . . . I know one thing, we will never run away to any more sleigh-rides. [*pp. 68–9*]

*Annie de **Rothschild**, aged fourteen, considers her attitude to parties.* *England, 1858*

I hope it is not wrong! No it cannot be wrong! to like a little amusement. There are very few girls who do not enjoy a little dance when it comes, so seldom, and I am not one of those hermit girls – though I shall never dote on my balls and parties like some people – God forbid that I should ever: women are put into the world to be useful and not to idle their time away. [*p. 83*]

*Mary **Hughes**, the only girl in a group of brothers, recollects her* *England, 1870s*
exclusion from their amusements.

The boys used to go to the theatre and music-halls. The latter sounded rather dull, but mother explained that they were not dull, only not very nice. However, it made no difference to me what they were like, since I was never allowed to go even to a theatre. [*p. 17*]

Strange as it seems I was never taken to anything more exciting than a picture gallery, not even to a pantomine at Christmas. Not even to the Tower or Crystal Palace or Madame Tussaud's – places to which the boys had to conduct country cousins, with profuse grumblings. [*p. 35*]

'How I wish I were a boy!' Mother caught me saying this aloud one day, and promptly told me that this was a wicked thought. She did not go on to give a reason, but merely insisted that it was splendid to be a girl, and with such exuberant enthusiasm that I was quite convinced. My father's slogan was that boys should go everywhere and know everything, and that a girl should stay at home and know nothing. [*pp. 37–8*]

America, 1872   Elizabeth **Drinker** *writes in her journal about her son William, aged fifteen.*

Billy came home about dinnertime, his face much bruised. He had been boxing with one of the Latin-school boys – an exercise that by no means suits him. [*Drinker (a), p. 144*]

England, 1890s   Eleanor **Farjeon** *recalls her childhood pastimes as the only girl in her family.*

Harry and Joe and Bertie go to Lord's; I too endure long days on a hard narrow seat with a packet of sandwiches. I learn to look at the game as the epic it is. I learn how to score for our home-made table-cricket games, played in all manner of ways. [*p. 292*]

TO KEEP CHILDREN IN THE PROPER STATE OF OBEDIENCE: PARENTAL ATTITUDES TO CHILDREN, CHILD-REARING AND DISCIPLINE

The Mansell Collection

Introduction

It is held by some historians of childhood that parents, especially those in the upper classes who could relinquish much of the responsibility to their servants, took very little interest in the upbringing of their children. The material presented in this chapter depicts a quite different state of affairs. Parents strove to understand their offspring, to protect them from the dangers of the outside world and to bring them up to the best of their ability.

Children were thought to be weak and in need of protection both from physical dangers and from mental corruption (Alice Thornton, p. 169, and Anne Bradstreet, p. 168). In some families the character and inclinations of each child had to be fully understood in order that the appropriate training regime be implemented (Ann Grant, p. 170, and Amelia Steuart, p. 171). In contrast, Bronson Alcott (p. 172) did not wish to control and regulate the lives of his children; instead, they were to be 'free'. He believed that internal regulation was more effective in ensuring conformity to social mores than external sanctions. Ideally, the company and presence of children should be enjoyed, although concern for their future could overshadow this sentiment (Frances Boscawen, p. 169, and Priscilla Johnston, p. 173).

Parenting, especially motherhood, was regarded as a vital duty, an indispensable obligation to be carried out by the mother (Dorothy Leigh, p. 174, and Susan Huntington, p. 179). Even in those homes where servants were employed to take on some of the chores of child-rearing, the role of the mother was still conceived to be one of paramount importance in a child's life (Grace Mildmay, p. 174). Despite the emphasis on the mother's position, fathers too were concerned with how their children should be brought up and some devised their own schemes for this purpose (Cotton Mather, p. 175, and John Taylor, p. 176). Parenting was not felt to be an easy task. Indeed, the carrying out of the parental duties caused mothers and fathers many moments of anxiety, to the extent that a few, for example Elizabeth Gaskell (p. 180) and William Lucas (p. 181), worried about their suitability for the role. It is also clear that parents did not approach the task of child-rearing in a haphazard fashion. They had a goal, an end in view to the process, which they desired to reach. While endeavouring to make their children happy in the present, they aimed to produce useful members of society for the future. Sometimes the two aims were not compatible, as the extracts on discipline illustrate.

Discipline is the yardstick against which the parenting practices of the past have been measured and found wanting. Whenever physical chastisement was imposed, it has been argued, children were subject to a severe regime under cruel parents. The matter of punishment, particularly physical, has been given undue prominence in historical works and the treatment of the topic has been bereft of subtlety. Little attempt has been made to place punishment within the entire spectrum of parental attitudes to children or within the function of the parental role. Thus, we have been presented with a distorted, misleading history of repressed children brought up under the threat of the rod.

Discipline was undoubtedly a problem. It was, and is, no easy matter either to devise the correct course or to keep it, especially when parents were dealing with their own children, with whom they had a deep emotional involvement (Margaret Woods, p. 187, and Hannah Allen, p. 190). Punishing a child was not something a parent enjoyed doing but, as Thomas Cobden-Sanderson points out (p. 192), concern for the future conduct of a child led them to try and eradicate what they saw as bad habits. Whippings (this, or 'correction', referred to physical punishment of any sort before the nineteenth century, when the term 'spanking' was introduced) were certainly inflicted. It is true, too, that in a few families attempts were made to break a child's spirit, although even in such cases the situation was rarely as bleak as has been depicted (Roger North, p. 182). In the main, whippings were reserved for a cumulation of faults (Samuel Sewall, p. 183), or for a specific offence which the parents deplored, such as lying (James Boswell, p. 186), and above all for outright defiance of a parental command (Bronson Alcott, p. 189, and Lucy Lovell, p. 189). Parents definitely wished for obedient children and chose a path which they hoped would procure this end, but controlling children through fear was not condoned (Cotton Mather, p. 183, and Sara Coleridge, p. 188).

Parents inflicted punishment because they were trying to rear a responsible being who would conform to acceptable standards of behaviour, and in certain situations corporal punishment seemed the best way to achieve this. However, the acceptance of the necessity of physical chastisment for specific transgressions is not the same as the approval of severe correction in general. As the extracts from Adam Martindale (p. 193) and James Erskine (p. 194) illustrate, parents condemned others, such as schoolmasters, who administered a harsh beating to their child. At the same time they did not wish their child to go unpunished for offences he or she had committed, since all the training and discipline they had so far imparted would then have been in vain (Mary Woodforde, p. 193, and Claver Morris, p. 195). The harshness of some of the English public schools in the nineteenth century has been well documented. It was not, however, the continuation of an established tradition of cruelty in schools. The regulations for the schools of Dunbar and Penn Charter (p. 193 and p. 195) make it clear that mild disciplinary regimes operated in some educational establishments. School punishments do seem to increase in severity during the nineteenth century (John Epps, p. 197), and this is accompanied by a growing reluctance on the part of some parents to intervene in these matters, even though they might deplore the regime, as did Charlotte Guest (p. 198).

Views on Children

America, 1658 Anne **Bradstreet** *laments the departure of her children from home.*

I had eight birds hatcht in one nest,
Four cocks there were, and hens the rest,
I nurst them up with pain and care,
Nor cost, nor labour did I spare,
Till at the last they felt their wing,
Mounted the trees, and learn'd to sing;

. . .

If birds could weep, then would my tears
Let others know what are my fears
Lest this my brood some harm should catch
And be surpriz'd for want of watch,

. . .

O would my young, ye saw my breast,
And knew what thoughts there sadly rest,
Great was my pain when I you bred,
Great was my care, when I you fed,
Long did I keep you soft and warm,
And with my wings kept off all harm,
My cares are more, and fears then ever,
My throbs such now, as 'fore were never:
Alas my birds, you wisdom want,
Of perils you are ignorant,
Oft times in grass, on trees, in flight,
Sore accidents on you may light.
O to your safety have an eye,
So happy may you live and die:

[*pp. 401–3*]

England, 1658 *Gervase* **Holles** *dedicates his family history to his sixteen-year-old son Frescheville.*

From you (I bless God) I have other hopes; whose childhood (which you are scarce yet past) hath given me no other arguments but of a good nature and disposition and of principles not insusceptible of good impressions, which that God may be pleased more and more to enlarge and adorn with fair and honest characters is and shall be the daily prayer of your most loving and most carefull father. [*p. 6*]

Henry **Newcome** *muses on the disadvantages of being a parent.*   *England, 1659*

I consider the sad things that befall parents about children. May not one beg of God, that if it be His will, He will save us from such afflictions, and if He sees it good:

1. That my children may be kept in health, or from sad and grievous distempers.

2. However not to die immaturely, if God see it good, especially not untimely deaths.

3. That they may not die while they live; nor be a cross and exercise to us, by rebellious untowardliness. [*p. 105*]

Alice **Thornton** *considers the hazards incident to childhood.*   *England, 1660*

If His divine providence did not send His angels to keep and guard little children, they could not continue nor be preserved from all evil accidents and casualties incident to that feeble and weak estate of infants and childhoods. For although their innocency be not capable of offending others, yet that innocency and harmlessness is not able to defend them from injurious dealings from evil persons, neglects and brutishness of nurses, and carelessness of others, not to mention those infinite hazards of overlaying, and badness of their food and evil milk. [*pp. 3–4*]

Frances **Boscawen** *relates her hopes for the future to her husband.*   *England, 1756*

Thus, I presume sometimes to look forward to future years, when you will be wrinkled and I shall be grey. Place each by the other's side in our warm, well-built mansion, surrounded with these your old friends; each will have his neat cabin to the rising sun; a large room and a good fire for all to assemble. We shall talk of old stories, admire the young plants, our sons and daughters. Set them to dance, or laugh round about a commerce table, with good cheer, good hours, good humour and good wine. Perhaps we may yet add *a little tiny* one, which though last, won't be least beloved – the plaything of the house. [*p. 207*]

Margaret **Woods** *writes to a friend.*   *England, 1777*

I am now sitting with my dear little cares, watching them in their evening's repose. They (as thou justly observest) attach us strongly to life; and without a guard over ourselves, we are in danger of centring too much of our happiness in them. They may, indeed, in various way, be deemed uncertain blessings, their lives are very precarious, and their future conduct proving as one could wish, not less doubtful. I already often look forward with anxiety, and the most ardent wishes for their welfare, in a state of permanent felicity. They are now pretty playthings, and pleasing calls of attention, and should be received with grateful hearts, as additions to our present comfort; but we should consider, that they may be blessings only lent for a time. [*p. 85*]

Scotland, 1782

Ann **Grant**, *moving to another area, left her baby daughter behind with her grandparents. She writes to a friend.*

You inquire if I left Mary at Fort Augustus; I durst not do otherwise, she is so firmly established in the affections of the good old people, that it would be a breach of the peace to deprive them of her. This does not please her father, who is afraid of his dear daughter being spoiled, but, in fact, very unwilling to part with her, though he affects to be too manly to be fond of an infant; but he wants a pretence to lament her absence without descending from his dignity. For my own part, I honestly confess, that my heart ached at parting with her. I would not wish these human flowers to breathe their first fragrance on any breast but my own. [*Grant (1) (a), vol. 2, p. 83*]

Eight years later she describes her offspring.

They are all artless and disinterested: no traces of mean cunning or selfish grasping. This is an indication of an enlarged mind; and, besides the future promise, has a present good effect. Whatever they have they share with each other with readiness and pleasure; so there is one source of wrangling and debate stopped. They all give pretty strong proofs of feeling as well as understanding; and it is by the management of these feelings that I propose, in a great measure, to sway them, till their minds open and strengthen: so that one may reason with them without teaching them parrotism. This, perhaps, might not be a safe way in the world; but, if ever children can be brought up with uncorrupted hearts, they have a chance of being so. Their number, and being altogether strangers to those indulgences which wealth and ease admit of, will entirely prevent their being softened into a sickly sensibility, by those feelings being exercised. For the art lies in directing them to those ends for which it is presumed they were bestowed. In the first place, I am at the utmost pains to fix their affections; we should be unhappy if we thought they loved any one near so well as their parents. [*Grant (1) (a), vol. 2, pp. 213–14*]

England, 1794

William **Jones**, *in great financial difficulties, writes.*

My poor dear children little know what passes in my mind, and I am truly glad of it. May they ever rejoice, but never weep when I weep! May their cheerful spirits remain as long as possible unbroken! . . . At any rate while my dear, dear, children are under my protection and roof, let me not envy them all the little happiness which they can possibly enjoy! May no impatience or fretfulness arising from my painful feelings ever check their sweet smiles or interfere with their innocent cheerfulness! Never let me grudge them all the happiness they can enjoy!! [*Jones (2), p. 102*]

Samuel Taylor **Coleridge** *describes his two children, Hartley aged seven and Sara under a year, to a friend.* *England, 1803*

Hartley is what he always was, a strange, strange boy, 'exquisitely wild', an utter visionary, Like the moon among thin clouds he moves in a circle of light of his own making. He alone is a light of his own. Of all human beings I never saw one so utterly naked of self. He has no vanity, no pride, no resentments; and, though very passionate, I never yet saw him angry with anybody. He is, though seven years old, the merest child you can conceive; and yet Southey says he keeps him in perpetual wonderment; his thoughts are so truly his own. His dispositions are very sweet, a great lover of truth, and of the finest moral nicety of feelings; and yet always dreaming. . . . If God preserves his life for me, it will be interesting to know what he will become; for it is not only my opinion, or the opinion of two or three, but all who have been with him talk of him as a thing that cannot be forgotten.

My meek little Sara is a remarkably interesting baby, with the finest possible skin, and large blue eyes; and she smiles as if she were basking in a sunshine, as mild as moonlight, of her own quiet happiness. [*vol. 1, pp. 4–5*]

Amelia **Steuart** *writes in her diary about her children, Margaret aged nine, John aged seven, and Charles aged three.* *Scotland, 1806*

Margaret Harriet is a very amiable child – but too ready to shed tears. She is very affectionate and quite distressed if I am displeased with her. She is very sensible and thoughtful (that is to say not so thoughtless as most children) only she is not yet *orderly* which I wish her to be. She is not talkative and has no pleasure in carrying tales from one to another. She has a great deal of carefulness about fire or anything dangerous which is occasioned by her being rather of a timid fearful disposition. She finds it very unpleasant to command her attention to any study for any length of time, but she is rather better as to this than she was. She very easily conquers bad habits and tricks such as biting her nails, lolling when reading or repeating. . .

John *has much* resemblance to his sister in many of these things

– but he is more ready to carry tales and he is not so ready in his obedience and sometimes delays a long while doing what he is desired. He is exceedingly affectionate too and though hasty and soon angry he is pleased in a moment. It is very difficult to find a punishment for him when he does wrong as he receives it with a sort of indifference and good humour that makes it quite thrown away upon him. Margaret seems cleverer than John but he can appear as much so when he exerts himself . . .

Charles promises to be the cleverest of the three though I am sure neither of the others are deficient. He is very good tempered but if once he takes it into his head to refuse doing what he is desired it is incredible how long he will hold out even though whipped soundly and frequently. This however happens very seldom and at very long intervals, for he remembers it well. [*MS983, ff. 93–4*]

America, 1831   *Amos Bronson* **Alcott** *on his first child Anna, aged three months. Anna had been subject to crying fits.*

To some these might seem like indications of passion, to which criminality is attached. They might regard them as the beginning of anger, and think it is their duty to check and overcome them in their early weakness. The will, they might believe, should be only subjected to their own; and thus obedience, that virtue so often imposed in infancy, be made habitual from the beginning. But this view of infant nature, seems to me essentially erroneous and the consequences which flow from it, in education, most injurious to the mind and character. Liberty is a primary right of all created natures, and the love of it inherent in all . . . The *child* must be *treated* as a *free*, self-*guiding*, self-*controlling being*. He must be allowed to feel that he is under his own guidance, and that all external guidance is an injustice which is done to his nature unless his own will is intelligently submissive to it . . . He must be free that he may be truly virtuous, for without freedom there is no such thing as virtue. [*Alcott (b), pp. 14–15*]

England, c.1835   *Mary* **Haldane** *recollects a moment of intense disappointment in her childhood when the family home had to be rebuilt.*

The Manor house of Jesmond was pronounced to be in a dangerous condition owing to the undermining of the colliery, and it was entirely to be rebuilt and a new foundation stone laid. This was done to the great disappointment of my sister and myself, because our names were not placed on the stone, but only my brother's. From that time forward the fact of being merely a daughter rankled in my mind, and during my childhood, and for years afterwards, I used to feel as if I was nothing to anybody. [*pp. 46–7*]

*Priscilla **Johnston** reflects on her children.*　　　　　　　　*England, 1844*

How little does this book convey any idea of the almost ceaseless engrossment of my heart, mind, and time about them! Every day seems marked by care about the body, conduct, or circumstances of one or other of these precious, anxious treasures! I sometimes think if I were taken away, it would be almost a pity they should have no more record of my travail of spirit for and about them. [*p. 166*]

Of her eldest son she writes.

O what a new world is unlocked, as it were, by having a child ten years old! It seems gradually to engross and occupy so large a portion of one's mind: I cannot say how many more thoughts they take as they grow older. I often think that as children in the charms and fascinations of their first years are like the blossoms, so they go through the state of unripe fruit, their infantine charms, are gone, and the full fruit is far from being come: yet this is not true fully; for though unripeness and hope for the future may predominate, yet how large a measure of enjoyment is there from them in all stages! I am much impressed with the duty of enjoying them, as well as labouring for them; and I believe this spirit (of dwelling with thankful hope on them, and cultivating them in love and encouragement) would often produce greater fruit than the more careful one which is my nature. [*pp. 168–9*]

*Mary **Hughes** recalls the difference in her parents' attitude to their*　　*England, 1870s*
sons and daughter. She was the youngest child and the only girl.

I suppose there was a fear on my mother's part that I should be spoilt, for I was two years younger than the youngest boy. To prevent this danger she proclaimed the rule 'Boys first'. I came last in all distribution of food at table, treats of sweets, and so on. I was expected to wait on the boys, run messages, fetch things left upstairs, and never grumble, let alone refuse. All this I thoroughly enjoyed, because I loved running about, and would often dash up and down stairs just to let off my spirits. Of course mother came in for some severe criticism from relations in this matter, but I have never ceased to thank her for this bit of early training. [*pp. 6–7*]

The Parental Role

England, 1618 *Dorothy **Leigh** composed a work of instructions for her sons George, John and William. In her preface she explains why she did so.*

I being troubled, and wearied with fear, lest my children should not find the right way to Heaven, thought with my self that I could do no less for them than . . . to write them the right way that I had truly observed out of the written word of God, lest for want of warning they might fall where I stumbled, and then I should think my self in the fault, who knew there were such downfalls in the world, that they could hardly climb the hill to Heaven without help, and yet had not told them thereof. [*pp. A2–A5*]

England, 1618 *Grace **Mildmay** considers the necessity for parental care.*

Parents have much to answer for before God, who neglect their duty in bringing up their children, or prefer any care, labour or delight in the world before that natural and most necessary employment. [*Mildmay (2), p. 128*]

England, 1622 *Elizabeth **Joceline**, pregnant and fearing she might die in childbirth, wrote* The Mother's Legacie to her Unborne Childe.

Having long, often and earnestly desired of God, that I might be a mother to one of his children, and the time now drawing on, which I hope he hath appointed to give thee unto me: it drew me into a consideration both wherefore I so earnestly desired thee, and (having found that the true cause was to make thee happy) how I might compass this happiness for thee.

I knew it consisted not in honour, wealth, strength of body or friends (though all these are great blessings) therefore it had been a weak request to desire thee only for an heir to my fortune. No, I never aimed at so poor an inheritance for thee, as the whole world. Neither would I have begged of God so much pain, as I know I must endure, to have only possesed thee with earthly riches, of which today thou mayest be a great man, tomorrow a poor beggar. Nor did an hope to dandle thy infancy move me to desire thee. For I know all the delight a parent can take in a child is honey mingled with gall.

But the true reason that I have so often kneeled to God for thee, is, that thou mightest be an inheritor of the kingdom of heaven. To which end I humbly beseech Almighty God thou mayest bend all thy actions, and (if it be his blessed will) give thee so plentiful a measure of his grace, that thou mayest serve him as his minister, if he make thee a man. [*pp. 1–4*]

*Mary **Rich** became the guardian of her three nieces after their parents'*   *England, 1659*
death.

I promised to have while I lived as great a care of them as if they
had been my own, and that promise I can truly say I have
performed, for I have from the time of their father's death, that I
took them home to me, with the same care bred those three ladies,
who were all left to my care young, as I could have done if they had
been my own children, studying and endeavouring to bring them
up religiously, that they might be good, and do good afterwards in
their generation. [*p. 27*]

*Cotton **Mather** records in his diary his intentions with regard to the*   *America, 1711*
rearing of his family.

I would carefully observe the tempers of each of my children. And,
first, I would warn them against the peculiar indiscretions and
temptations whereto they may be exposed in their tempers. Then I
would see, whether I can't suit their tempers with motives that
may encourage and animate their peity. [*Mather (b), vol. 8, p. .1*]

If any little occasion for my anger, do occur by any neglect, or by
something amiss, in my family, I would with all possible decency
govern my passion. My anger shall not break out, into any
froward, peevish, indecent expressions. I will only let them see,
that I don't like what I take notice of. [*Mather (b), vol. 8, p. 127*]

I must with the help of grace resolve upon it, that it shall be my
custom, to be at home with my family, about nine o'clock in the
evenings; and employ an hour, in instructing of the children, and
conversing with them, on the several points, wherein I should be
desirous of their becoming excellent. The time so spent with them,
will turn to much better account, than what I have sometimes
allowed in sitting with my neighbours. [*Mather (b), vol. 8, p. 227*]

*Eliza **Pinckney** after the birth of her first child considers how she will*   *America, 1745*
bring him up.

I am resolved to be a good mother to my children, to pray for them,
to set them good examples, to give them good advice, to be careful
both of their souls and bodies, to watch over their tender minds, to
carefully root out the first appearing and buddings of vice, and to
instil piety, virtue and true religion into them; to spare no pains or
trouble to do them good, to correct their errors what ever uneasiness it may give myself and never omit to encourage every virtue I
may see dawning in them. [*p. 117*]

England, late
18th century

*John **Taylor** outlines the principles he employed in the upbringing of his children.*

My Behaviour to My Children

1. I own my imperfections in best attempts, both in this and other duties. I am sincerely troubled that I had done no better. But I can truly say, that I have laboured in this great business, as a father, to understand the Divine Directory on it. I have thought a deal on 'Train up a child in the way he should go'. I have considered the New Testament precepts on the same subject; and I have endeavoured to practise them.

2. When I was bringing up my children, I recollected my being a child myself; how I behaved to my father and how he behaved to me. Much of my father's method, in this respect, was laudable; but it was, in a degree, like his son's, imperfect. I endeavoured to avoid his imperfections and to imitate his excellencies. I took notice also of other families in the neighbourhood, and attempted to derive some improvement from them.

3. I laboured to preserve the love, esteem, and affection of my children. I considered this rational and, from our directory, I saw it my incumbent duty. 'Fathers, provoke not thy children to anger, lest they be discouraged.'

4. I endeavoured not to overburden them with work; though sometime it could hardly be prevented. But when this was the case, and I observed it, I was overburdened too, for if I could not ease them I pitied them sincerely. Thus also when they were afflicted with sickness, exercised by cross providences, or abused by unreasonable and wicked men, I deeply sympathized with them. This is the case with me still, with respect to those who are spared alive for my comfort, how far soever they are separated from me. If I know of their misery, I cannot but be miserable too.

5. I was especially determined to keep them from following any course of sin, and from sinful companions. I always understood it to be necessary to keep them from the latter, if I wished to preserve them from the former. I was, in this great design peculiarly assisted, by their good mother. I bless the gracious God for it; and I can never bless him enough. I was anxious to preserve my children from bad company; partly because I myself had suffered so much from it, partly because I clearly saw the same circumstances constantly recurring to others, and partly because of the heedlessness of persons professing religion on this important subject; but chiefly on account of the admonition of the Holy Book on this head.

6. I was particularly desirous of assisting my children in learning to read. It has often cost me study and anxiety to procure them

opportunity for this. Sometimes I laboured when I otherwise would not, that they might have leisure for this. I knew the honour and benefit of learning to read when young; and it would have been almost infinite trouble to me, if they had not enjoyed the same advantages . . .

7. I made a practice of talking with my children, to instruct them and to impress their minds. I have, I acknowledge, been very imperfect in this also; but I then understood how unreasonable and cruel it was in parents to scold and beat their children for acting in such and such a manner; when they had taken no pains to instruct them that such actions were wrong. When a child is born, he knows nothing. Knowledge is attained gradually; and often very slowly, even when proper methods are employed. If parents will not be persuaded to endeavour to make their children wise, then mankind must remain as they are. I bless God for disposing me to aim at something of this, unqualified as I always have been for such a work.

8. I made a constant and daily practice of praying with my children. As soon as the first child was able to kneel at prayer, she did kneel; and she and all the rest, as they became able, constantly attended to it, as long as they abode with me. I never had such a notion as some have of teaching my children to *say their prayers*; either the Lord's prayer, or any other form. I am well persuaded that the Lord Jesus did not intend to teach his disciples to use those precise words. But suppose it were true, that his disciples and so all Christians were taught to use that form, it is really a wonder if any sober man can believe, that those words are really fit for children or ignorant wicked men. Besides praying with my children, I prayed very frequently for them, when they were not present. I have considered this a great duty, and I have found my affections so united to my children, that both nature and conscience urged the necessity and propriety of earnest constant prayer with them and for them. [*pp. 118–20*]

Nancy **Shippen** *devises her own scheme for the upbringing of her seventeen-month-old daughter Margaret.*   America, 1783

I thought seriously this morning about my sweet child's education. I formed many schemes which I believe it would be very difficult to put in execution. I wish in some particulars that it may differ from mine. In some respects I wish it may be as good. I have her welfare at heart more than any earthly object. God grant she may be in every respect what I wish her. I have met with sentiments on that head that please me. I will insert them here that I may not forget them:

Some Directions Concerning a Daughter's Education

1st. Study well her constitution and genius.

2nd. Follow nature and proceed patiently.

3rd. Suffer not servants to terrify her with stories of ghosts and goblins.

4th. Give her a fine pleasing idea of good, and an ugly frightful one of evil.

5th. Keep her to a good and natural regimen of diet.

6th Observe strictly the little seeds of reason in her, and cultivate the first appearance of it diligently.

7th. Watch over her childish passions and prejudices, and labour sweetly to cure her of them.

8th. Never use any little *dissembling* arts, either to pacify her or to persuade her to anything.

9th. Win her to be in love with openness, in all her acts, and words.

10th. Fail not to instil into her an abhorrence of all 'serpentine' wit.

11th. If she be a brisk witty child do not applaud her too much.

12th. If she be a dull heavy child, do not discourage her at all.

13th. Seem not to admire her wit, but rather study to rectify her judgement.

14th. Use her to put little questions, and give her ready and short answers.

15th. Insinuate into her the principles of politeness and true modesty, and Christian humility.

16th. Inculcate upon her that most honourable duty and virtue, *sincerity*.

17th. Be sure to possess her with the baseness of telling a lie on any account.

18th. Show her the deformity of rage and anger.

19th. Never let her converse with servants.

20th. Acquaint her in the most pleasant and insinuating manner, with the sacred history, nor let it seem her lesson, but her recreation.

21st. Set before her the gospel in its simplicity and purity, and the great examples of antiquity unsophisticated.

22nd. Explain to her the nature of the baptismal sanction.

23rd. Prepare her in the best manner for confirmation.

24th. Animate, and instruct her for the holy communion.

25th. Particularly inform her in the duties of a single and married state.

26th. Let her be prepared for the duties and employment of a city life, if her lot should be among citizens.

27th. See she be informed in all that belongs to a country life.

28th. Discreetly check her desires after things pleasant, and use* her to frequent disappointments. *Rousseau

29th. Let her be instructed to do every thing seasonably and in order, and whatever she is set to do let her study to do it well, and peaceably.

30th. Teach her to improve everything that nothing may be lost or wasted, nor let her hurry herself about any thing.

31st. Let her always be employed about what is profitable or necessary.

32nd. Let nothing of what is committed to her care be spoiled by her neglect.

33rd. Let her eat deliberately, chew well, and drink in moderate proportions.

34th. Let her use exercise in the morning.

35th. Use her to rise betimes in the morning, and set before her in the most winning manner an order for the whole day.

When wisdom enters into her heart, and knowledge is made pleasant to her soul, 'discretion shall preserve her, and understanding shall keep her'. [pp. 147–9]

Susan **Huntington** *the mother of two young children confides to her*   America, 1813
diary.

There is scarcely any subject concerning which I feel more anxiety, than the proper education of my children. It is a difficult and delicate subject; and the more I reflect on my duty to them, the more I feel is to be learnt by myself. The person who undertakes to form the infant mind, to cut off the distorted shoots, and direct and fashion those which may, in due time, become fruitful and lovely branches, ought to possess a deep and accurate knowledge of human nature. It is no easy task to ascertain, not only the principles and habits of thinking, but also the causes which produce them. It is no easy task, not only to watch over our actions, but also to become acquainted with the motives which prompted them. It is no easy task not only to produce correct associations, but to remove improper ones, which may, through the medium of those nameless occurrences to which children are continually exposed, have found a place in the mind, but such is the task of every mother who superintends the education of her children. Add to this the difficulty of maintaining that uniform and consistent course of conduct which children ought always to observe in their parents, and which alone can give force to the most judicious discipline, and verily, every considerate person must allow, that it is no small matter to be faithful in the employment of instructors of infancy and youth. [pp. 88–9]

Six months later she reflects on the importance of motherhood.

What a delicate office is that of a mother! How wary should be her footsteps, how spotless her example, how uniform her patience, how extensive her knowledge of the human heart, how great her skill in using that knowledge, by the most vigilant and strenuous application of it in every variety of occurring circumstances, to enlighten the understanding and reform the heart! Legislators and governors have to enact laws, and compel men to observe them; mothers have to implant the principles, and cultivate the disposi- tions, which alone can make good citizens and subjects. The former have to exert authority over characters already formed; the latter have to mould the character of the future man, giving it a shape which will make him either an instrument of good to the world, or a pest in the lap of society. Oh that a constant sense of the importance and responsibility of this station may rest upon me! that grace may be given faithfully to discharge its difficult duties. [*p. 100*]

England, 1835   *Elizabeth* **Gaskell** *began a diary after the birth of her first child, Marianne, to record her development.*

To my dear little Marianne I shall 'dedicate' this book, which, if I should not live to give it her myself, will I trust be reserved for her as a token of her mother's love, and extreme anxiety in the formation of her little daughter's character. If that little daughter should in time become a mother herself, she may take an interest in the experience of another; and at any rate she will perhaps like to become acquainted with her character in its earliest form. I wish that (if ever she sees this) I could give her the slightest idea of the love and the hope that is bound up in her. [*p. 5*]

The day after tomorrow Marianne will be six months old. I wish I had begun my little journal sooner, for (though I should have laughed at the idea twelve months ago) there have been many little indications of disposition, etcetera already; which I can not now remember clearly. I will try and describe her *mentally*. I should call her remarkable good-tempered; though at times she gives way to little bursts of passion or perhaps impatience would be the right name. She is really very firm in her own little way occasionally; what I suppose is obstinacy really, only that is so hard a word to apply to one so dear. But in general she is so good that I feel as it I could hardly be sufficiently thankful, that the materials put into my hands are so excellent, and beautiful, and yet it seems to increase the responsibility. If I should misguide from carelessness or negligence! *wilfully* is not in a mother's heart.

From ignorance and errors in judgement I know I may, and probably shall, very often. But, Oh, Lord! I pray thee to lead me right (if it by thy will) and to preserve in me the same strong feeling of my responsibility which I now feel. And you too, my dearest little girl, if when you read this, you trace back any evil or unhappy feeling to my mismanagement in your childhood, forgive me, love! [*pp. 5–6*]

William **Lucas** *deprecates his abilities as a parent. His eldest child was*   *England, 1847*
aged fifteen.

I feel at times much depressed from not being able to make myself so companionable as I ought to be with my children. I never had the art of winning children or getting free with them and I do not think I now can expect to do it. It is so difficult to put up with their extreme vivacity, and so difficult to remember what we once were at their age, and to make due allowance for it. Christian humility and command of temper are great requisites and difficult attainments. When I look upon my seven boys I feel an inexpressible anxiety that they may turn out well, and feel how much depends upon my own example and character. The remembrance of the high and lovely nature of my dear Father and the Christian integrity and conscientious moderation of his Father makes me hope that my children may never act so as to bring disgrace upon their name. I shall never be able to do more than assist them to exert their industry and abilites in providing things honest as regards their worldly concerns, and I have no desire to see them raised above the middle rank of life, which allows the fullest cultivation of the mind, and every innocent pleasure of life, society of the most desirable sort, whilst the necessity for exertion is the surest foundation for usefulness and respectability. I think there is a desire to please us, and evidence of right feeling in some respects in our children. They are not much inclined to Quakerism, and I often doubt whether I ought to be more strict in regard to their language, dress etcetera, but on the whole I am satisfied to leave these things to their own decision, wishing them to be Friends but more anxious that they should be Christians, and men of integrity. [*Vol. 2, p. 395*]

Parental Modes of Punishment

Margaret **Cavendish** *recalls the method by which she and her sisters were brought up.*

We were bred tenderly, for my mother naturally did strive to please and delight her children, not to cross and torment them, terrifying them with threats, or lashing them with slavish whips; but instead of threats, reason was used to persuade us, and instead of lashes, the deformities of vice was discovered, and the graces and virtues were presented unto us. [*p. 4*]

Thomas Meautys writes to his sister Jane **Cornwallis** *about his young daughter.*

Now I pray, give me leave to ask you a question, and that is, How you like my little girl that is with my wife? I must tell you that she hath been lapt in the skirts of her father's shirt, for she is beloved where she comes, and I love her very well, and so doth she me; and yet sometimes I can whip her and love her too. You must excuse me for using this language, for, when I cannot see my children it does me good to talk of them. [*p. 253*]

Roger **North** *recalls his upbringing.*

The government of us was in general severe, but tender; our mother maintained her authority, and yet condescended to entertain us. She was learned (for a lady) and eloquent. Had much knowledge of history, and readiness of wit to express herself, especially in the part of reproof, wherein she was fluent and pungent, and not only her children but servants dreaded her reproof, knowing how sensibly she would attag them, and in the most nice and tender articles that concerned them. But without occasion given to the contrary, she was debonair, familiar, and very liberal of her discourse to entertain all, and ever tending to goodness, and morality. This saved us that were children, and of stubborn spirits, as such usually are, the trouble, and inconvenience of contesting points with her, for we knew beforehand, from the steady conduct of her authority, that submission was the best course, and comported accordingly. . . . We had, as I said, stubborn spirits, and would often set up for ourselves, and try the experiment, but she would reduce us to terms by the smart of correction; and which was more grievous would force us to leave crying, and condescend to the abject pitch of thanking the Good Rail, which she said was to break our spirits, which it did

effectually. I need not hint the perpetual care she took we should
contract no ill habits by conversing with servants, especially lying,
which she always preached against, as well as hardly forgave,
when discovered. [*vol. 3, p. 4*]

Samuel **Sewall** *whipped his sons Samuel aged ten and Joseph aged*   America, 1688
four.

Corrected Samuel for breach of the ninth commandment, saying
he had been at the writing school, when he had not.

1692.

Joseph threw a knop of brass and hit his sister Betty on the
forehead so as to make it bleed and swell upon which; and for his
playing at prayer-time, and eating when return thanks, I whipped
him pretty smartly. When I first went in, (called by his Grandmother) he sought to shadow and hide himself from me behind
the head of the cradle, which gave me the sorrowful remembrance
of Adam's carriage. [*vol. 5, pp. 225, 369*]

Cotton **Mather** *relates how he attempts to regulate his offspring.*   America, 1705

I mightily endeavour it, that the children may betimes, be acted by
principles of *reason* and *honour*.
    I first beget in them at high opinion of their Father's love to
them, and of his being best able to judge, what shall be good for
them.
    Then I make them sensible, 'tis a folly for them to pretend unto
any wit and will of their own; they must resign all to me, who will
be sure to do what is best; my word must be their law. I cause
them to understand, that it is an *hurtful* and a *shameful* thing to do
amiss. I aggravate this, on all occasions; and let them see how
amiable they will render themselves by well doing. The *first
chastisement*, which I inflict for an ordinary fault, is, to let the child
see and hear me in an astonishment, and hardly able to believe
that the child could do so *base* a thing, but believing that they will
never do it again.
    I would never come, to give a child a *blow*; except in case of
obstinacy: or some gross enormity.
    To be chased for a while out of *my presence*, I would make to be
looked upon, as the sorest punishment in the family . . .
    The *slavish* way of *education*, carried on with raving and kicking
and scourging (in *schools* as well as *families*), 'tis abominable; and a
dreadful judgement of God upon the world. [*Mather (b), vol. 7, pp.
535–6*]

Honoured Sr.

           I had this day the favour of yours and
Mr. Bush had one from mama with such a severe
sentence on me just as we was going to dinner that I
could not taste one bit neither shall I have one moments
peace of mind I own my fault and ask mamas Pard[o]n
for doing any thing against her orders but as I think
I have and ever shall be obedient to her in every thing els
hope she will take that most unkind word off of not
forgiving me and pardon my crime I could not have
believed she would have bin so angry where my health
and ease depended I thought mama loved me better
then to order me to be put to so much pain to have four
teeth drawn if I must be so hurt I beg it may be by a safe
hand and with her self for nobody here can do it I shall

Letter from Nicholas Carew, 1736

Honoured Sr:
I had this day the favour of yours and Mrs Bush had one from
mama with such a severe sentence on me just as we was going
to dinner that I could not taste one bit neither shall I have one
moments peace of mind. I own my fault and ask mamas
pardon for doing any thing against her orders but as I think I
have and ever shall be obedient to her in every thing else [I]
hope she will take that most unkind word off of not forgiving
me and pardon my crime. I could not have believed she would
have bin so angry where my health and ease depended. I
thought mama loved me better then to order me to be put to
so much pain to have four teeth draw[n] if I must be so hurt I
beg it may [be] by a safe hand and with herself for nobody
here can do it. I shall

British Library add mss 29599 f 312

England, 1755   *Frances* **Boscawen** *writes to her husband about their son William, aged three. William had been inoculated against smallpox six weeks previously.*

Billy is now perfectly recovered, I thank God. Purging discipline all over, but *my* discipline to begin, for it has been slackened so long it is unknown. How perverse and saucy we are, and how much we deal in the words won't, can't, shan't, etcetera. Today he would not eat milk for breakfast, but the rod and I went to breakfast with him, and though we did not come into action, nor anything like it, yet the bottom of the porringer was very fairly revealed and a declaration made by him; indeed he could not but say it was very good milk. [*p. 179*]

America, 1766   *Landon* **Carter** *describes a domestic squall involving his young grandson, Landon, his son and his daughter-in-law.*

We had this day a domestic gust. My daughters, Lucy and Judy, mentioned a piece of impudent behavior of little Landon to his mother; telling her when she said she would whip him; that he did not care if she did. His father heard this unmoved. The child denied it. I bid him come and tell me what he did say for I could not bear a child should be saucy to his Mother. He would not come and I got up and took him by the arm. He would not speak. I then shook him but his outrageous father says I struck him. At breakfast the young gentleman would not come in though twice called by his father and once sent for by him and twice by me. I then got up, and gave him one cut over the left arm with the lash of my whip and the other over the banister by him. Madam then rose like a bedlamite that her child should be struck with a whip and up came her knight errant to his father with some heavy God damning's, but he prudently did not touch me. Otherwise my whip handle should have settled him if I could. Madam pretended to rave like a madwoman. I showed the child's arm was but commonly red with the stroke; but all would not do. Go she would and go she may. [*Carter (a), vol. 1, p. 310*]

Scotland, 1780   *James* **Boswell** *on his son Alexander (Sandie), aged three.*

I this morning beat Sandie for telling a lie. I must beat him very severely if I catch him again in falsehood. I do not recollect having had any other valuable principle impressed upon me by my father except a strict regard to truth, which he impressed upon my mind by a hearty beating at an early age, when I lied, and then talking of the *dishonour* of lying. I recollect distinctly having truth and honour thus indelibly inculcated upon me by him one evening in our house. [*vol. 14, p. 20*]

*Martha **Bayard**, while visiting a friend, writes in her journal.*   *America, 1795*

She has two sweet children and manages them after my system, which I was so much blamed for at home; but these are a proof that gentleness is by far the best, with reasonable tempers. [*p. 96*]

*Margaret **Woods** on the difficulty of choosing the right disciplinary path.*   *England, 1799*

The love of liberty and independence is strongly implanted in the human mind. How far it should be indulged in the education and conduct of youth, will, by many people, be differently determined. Some parents throw the reins on the necks of their children at a very early period, and hold them with a very slack hand; while others seem scarcely willing to loosen them a little, so long as they are able to keep hold of them. Either extreme, I believe, is prejudicial. Too tight a curb sometimes makes young people fret under it, and produces an impatience to be entirely free, when more gentle discipline might have produced submission. Little benefit can arise from mere compulsion, either in doing or forbearing, futher than as it may gain time for the understanding and judgement to ripen; and if they can be kept in the practice of good, and preserved from evil, till that time, it will be a great point gained. The body acquires strength and the power of its movements but by slow degrees; and the mind still more slowly; both want the assistance of superior strength and intellect, to bring them forward, and instruct them in the means necessary to attain the end they aim at. [*pp. 205–6*]

Sixteen years later she writes to a friend.

To keep children in the proper state of obedience, without having them stand in too much awe, is sometimes difficult. I have always wished that they should be afraid of doing wrong, but not afraid of me. I would encourage them to lay open their little hearts, and speak their thoughts freely; considering that by doing so, I have the best means of correcting their ideas, and rectifying whatever may be amiss. I am, from judgement, no great disciplinarian; if I err, I had rather it should be on the lenient side. Fear and force will, no doubt, govern children while little, but having a strong hold on their affections will have most influence over them in their progress through life. Obedience I do consider as an indispensable thing in education; but perhaps it would be imprudent to call it forth too frequently on trivial occasions. [*p. 427*]

Scotland, 1806   *Amelia* **Steuart** *describes how she punishes her children, John, aged seven, Charles, aged three, and Margaret, aged nine.*

John was getting up from table before his time (which is when ever the cloth is removed); I desired him to sit down again, but he would not do it for a moment till he had got to his Papa to put him in mind of a pear he brought from — . He was not allowed to have any of the gooseberries Mag brought from — nor any plums or pears. Seemed more sorry to miss the fruit than that he had done wrong.

Charles cried very much last night upon being disturbed by Peggy leaving the nursery and I told him this morning that he was to have no fruit today – which he kept in mind – and told Peggy he was not to have any. His other punishment was not being allowed to come into my bed this morning as he used to do.

Her daughter had been told twice to fetch her shoes from the nursery.

'They're not in the nursery' [she said] and added low 'I tell you' which I did not hear but John told it and she did not deny it. She cried very much when she found I was angry and was to expose her by not allowing her to have a plum after dinner . . . I think by what she said, nothing of the kind will happen again. It is very unusual with her to be impudent. [MS983, ff. 92, 93]

America, 1814   *Susan* **Huntington** *explains her attitude to discipline to a friend.*

You ask my advice about the correction of children. I feel that I am not qualified to direct in a thing of so much importance. I will however remark, that I do not like the punishment of whipping, unless when the child exhibits strong passion, or great obstinacy. It ought to be the last resort. Neither do I like those punishments which are chiefly directed to the selfish principles of our nature, as depriving a child of cake, sweetmeats etcetera. I should rather aim to cherish feelings of conscious rectitude, and the pleasure of being loved. I would have a child consider his parent's declaration that he is not good, his worst punishment. For instance, if your little boy has done very wrong, I would tell him he must not stay with mamma, or must not take a walk, or see the company, or that he must eat his dinner alone; and all, because he is not good enough to be indulged in these usual privileges. But there are some cases in which the use of the rod is indispensable. [p. 109]

England, 1835   *Sara* **Coleridge** *writes to Miss Trevenen.*

My aim is something far beyond extorting obedience in particular instances. Unless the wayward *will* is corrected, what care I for the *act*; unless the fount is purified, what care I for an artificial cleansing of the draught which falls to my portion this day or the next? If I thought that to force compliance by terror would induce a salutary habit by which the heart might be bettered, it might be my duty to take this painful course. But I do not think so. I believe the experiment to be worse than dangerous; for the improvement of our children's moral nature I put my trust in no methods of discipline; these may answer well for a warring prince or general who has a particular external object to gain, and cares not for his instruments, except *as* instruments . . . I do not strictly *put my faith* in anything but the power of grace in the heart. What I mean is, that I hope more from favourable influences of this kind I have mentioned than from any mechanical routine; and I really think that 'you shall be beaten unless you do it, or you shall be mortified and annoyed till you look and speak humbly,' *is* a sort of external force which does not touch the heart. [*vol. 1, pp. 140–41*]

Amos Bronson **Alcott** *on his daughter Louisa, aged two. Louisa wished*　　America, 1834
to sit on her mother's lap to eat rather than in her chair.

I told her that I should place her in the chair if she did not get in herself. She refused saying, 'No! No!' with her usual force of expression, raising her tones and giving me to understand that the decision was made in her mind, I placed her in it, notwithstanding her struggles. The cry was heightened and prolonged; the persistance more decided and obstinate. I told her she must stop crying and sit in the chair, or I should punish her – hurt her – for she 'must mind *father*.' 'No! No!' she exclaimed with more decided vehemence than before. I said, 'Father must *spank* Louisa if she does not do as he says. Will she?' 'No! No! Sit with mother,' she reiterated. I *spanked her*. She cried the louder, I then told her that she must sit on her little chair by the side of her mother, and be still, or I should punish her more. She was unwilling to give up her purpose, and set up crying again. I repeated the punishment, and did not attain peace and quiet for her, till I had repeated it again. She then became quiet and continued talking with me and her mother till her supper was brought in, when, as I had promised her, she . . . sat at the table to eat it. [*Alcott (b), p. 33*]

Lucy **Lovell** *recalls how she chastized her one-year-old daughter*　　America, 1840
Caroline.

When Caroline was about a year old it became necessary for me to teach her her first lesson in obedience. The shovel and tongs seemed to fascinate her and she would take them and carry them around the house. I forbade her to touch them. She seemed perfectly to understand me, but continued to get them. I tried various ways to dissuade her from her purpose and finally concluded the best method was to divert her attention to some other object . . . But she had yet to learn obedience. When she was nearly two years old she one day took a cushion out of a chair and was bringing it across the room. I told her to carry it back and put it in the chair. She did not obey, and after repeating the requisition several times, to no purpose, I felt obliged to use corporal punishment. She had never before heard of such a thing, and of course knew nothing about it. So that it was some time before I could make her understand that there was any connection between the correction and the fault. But she finally yielded. During all this time she did not seem angry in the least, and indeed I do not know that I have ever seen her so. [*p. 52*]

We wished to train her to a habit of implicit compliance with our directions, and so on this account we frequently had occasion to correct her in such a way as we thought would best promote this object. [*p. 84*]

England, 1849 *Hannah **Allen** on the difficulty of disciplining one's own children.*

It is one thing to look upon their errors and failings as a disinterested party but quite another to do for the best as each occasion arises for the varying dispositions of children and their different temperaments . . .

As little as possible correct them before others; speak to them privately on any matter. Loud reproof may sometimes provoke to wrath instead of leading to repentance, though of course there are occasions when instant rebuke *is* needful. [*pp. 110–11*]

England, 1872 *John **Russell** writes to his wife Kate about the difficulties he is experiencing in controlling their son Frank, aged seven, whom he has taken to stay with some friends.*

Even if I speak to him in the gentlest way to ask him not to do something troublesome (as throwing about his big ball with a great noise in the dining room when he has a large front hall to do it in) he at once does it all the more; while he addresses his orders to me in the most peremptory tone and is furious if they are not at once obliged. This morning he began very well; was very affectionate and nice when he first woke and I wished him joy, and after breakfast sat down quietly to write to you. I sat in the chair reading and told him the words he did not know how to spell, till Mrs Story came in and then he commanded me to come close to him each time he wanted to know something. Twice I went up to him, and the second time retreated to my chair while telling him the word 'birthday'. No, he said I must not move away, but stand close to him. As he was asking something every instant, I said I could not keep going to him, but either I would tell him there, or he might come to me and ask (this was because he did not like Mrs Story to hear). However neither would suit him, and as I could not be called up every minute as I was talking to Mrs Story he said he would write no more. So I told him I did not care at all whether he did, and I took up the unfinished letter to send you, but he seized it and tore it. As he would not write to you I have told him to write his copybook before dinner. Of course he said he would not, and he *would* have his dinner in spite of me. So I left him and said I did not the least care whether he did it or not, but if not done in time for our dinner the things could not be kept and he would have dry bread. At dinner-time he came down rather crestfallen and when I asked him agreed to write if I could get out the copybook from behind the drawers where he had thrown it. This I did, and he got down after writing in time for dinner. I find the best way is to leave him alone to think over things, till he gets it right . . .

Frank has just smashed a window in the drawing-room by his violence, not intentionally. It is very tiresome. You have no idea how dispirited I feel about it. [*vol. 2, pp. 507–8*]

Mary **Hughes** *remembers the family rules in operation during her childhood.*   England, 1870s

I cannot remember that we were ever punished severely. An occasional putting in the corner for me, and a threatened 'slippering' of the boys by my father if they were too noisy – these were the usual penalties. When one of the boys had really annoyed mother, she would address him as 'Sir', and send him to have his hair cut. This does not sound so bad as it in fact was. Our only available hairdresser had a strange habit of keeping a customer waiting for a half to three-quarters of an hour. There was nothing to do but stare at a fern and a picture of Cromwell sitting at his daughter's death-bed.

A kind of family 'common law', an unwritten code, seemed to have existed from the beginning of time and was accepted as inevitable by us all. One rule was that we went to bed the moment the word was said, without argument or plea. Another was that one ate up everything on one's plate. Tom once had to finish the mustard which he had too liberally taken, and I can still recall the swelling in my throat as I bolted my last piece of blancmange. Another law was that we must never be rude to servants. Beyond these there was nothing criminal, except perhaps taking mother's scissors for our private ends.

So infrequent were my own punishments that I recall vividly the two occasions when I deserved them and obtained them. One morning I was bored with my lesson, looked round for some little drama, and proclaimed myself thirsty. Already I suppose I had discovered that a mother can require resistance to hunger, but not to thirst. 'Run downstairs then, dear, and ask cook to give you a glass of water.' Down I went, and after a decent delay returned with the report that cook had refused to give it to me. Now, thought I, for some fireworks. Alas! mother didn't even send for the cook or institute inquiries, or even appear disturbed at all. She said, 'Write in your diary, "I told a lie today".' There was no escaping it, my beautiful diary had to be thus disfigured, staring at me. And to this day I think the punishment was excessive. The other disgrace was still more memorable because it was a strain, and the only one, between me and my father. Charles was reading Hans Anderson: I wanted the book, asked for it, fussed for it, and finally broke into tears. This brought my father into the room, and I hoped for the best. But he became dreadfully serious, led me upstairs, and administered a whipping. Then he explained that it is as bad for a girl to cry for what she wants as for a boy to plant a blow. I might cry a little if I was badly hurt, but never, never, must I cry just to get something. [pp. 35–6]

England, 1886   *Thomas* **Cobden-Sanderson** *relates how he deals with the tantrums of his son Richard, aged eighteen months.*

Our anxiety for his future makes us careful in ridding him of bad habits and making his will 'supple' as Locke – whom we are now reading – would say. The other night he cried after being put to bed, not of course from pain, but mere contrariness. I tried to induce him to be quiet and failed. I then took him out of bed and whipped him, and as he cried out even more, pressed him close to me, and held his head and bade him to be quiet. In a moment, after a convulsive sob or two, he became quite quiet. I put him back into his cot, told him to be quiet and to go to sleep, and left him. Not a sound more did he make, and he went to sleep. The next day at noon he cried again when put to bed. I went to him, told him he must not cry, that he must lie down – he stands up in bed on such occasions and usually is found arranging his blanket over the rails of his cot – be quiet and go to sleep. I placed him properly in bed, spread the clothes over him and left him. He became and remained perfectly quiet, and went to sleep. He now goes to bed noon and night and to sleep without a cry. If this can be done, how much more may not be done? What a responsibility! What a superb instrument, gymnast of virtue and of beautiful conduct, may not a man be made early in life. [vol. 1, pp. 246–7]

Non-parental Modes of Discipline

*Adam **Martindale** recalls a schoolmaster he had as a child.*   *England, c.1631*

His worst fault while he stayed there was, that he was humorous and passionate, and sometimes in these moods he would whip boys most unmercifully for small or no faults at all. He once bestowed a severe correction on me for nothing in the world but defending myself from a great sloven (much older, taller, and stronger than myself), who abused me intolerably and incessantly with a besome as had been fit to have been given to one that had picked a pocket. This I concealed; yet at last it came out, and mightily offended my father, but the schoolmaster crying *peccavi* and promising to do so no more, all was well again. [*p. 14*]

*Mary **Woodforde** is anxious that her son Jack should accept the punishment due to him for his part in a school rebellion.*   *England, 1687*

This evening I had the cutting news that my second boy was in rebellion at the college of Winton, where he and all his companions resolved not to make any verses, and being called to be whipped for it several of them refused to be punished, mine amongst the rest. Some of them did submit, amongst which was cousin John Woodforde, and if the others do not, they must be expelled. God I beseech thee subdue their stubborn hearts, and give them grace to repent and accept of their punishment due to their fault, and let them not run on to ruin, for Christ's sake. [*p. 15*]

*School regulations for a school in the burgh of **Dunbar**. The first part of the document has not survived.*   *Scotland, 1679*

25. What ever public damage the scholars do either to glass windows (especially about the church or school) or by breaking the desks, locks or any thing in the school, they are to make up the same: and if the particular person can not be found out, then are they all to contribute for the damage done, and if he be afterwards known, then to receive double punishment.

26. Whosoever shall through [blot] turn fugitives, it shall be lawful for the masters to cause hail them to school, and punish them as he shall judge convenient.

27. All those that refuse to submit to discipline; but maliciously rebel against their masters, the masters with the greatest severity are to make them an example to the rest, and if the stubborn party be too strong then to call for help from the magistrate.

28. If children may be won by words or threatenings, 'tis

expected that the masters will make use of prudence in their actions, and to spare the rod as long as it may consist with the good of the children; but if neither fair words, nor threats will gain them, then shall the masters show both by their words and countenance an aversion to passion and a dislike to the action, with suitable expression to that purpose, in which humour they may correct. But not to be passionate when they correct, mere necessity (being for the welfare of the children) compelling them to it; but not for every trifle to stupefy them with strokes.

29. That the masters assume nothing to themselves, that may render them obnoxious to the clamour of the vulgar, as they are to instruct and correct according to our order and command; so by the same authority they are to give the accustomed liberty to their scholars. That the children be not used as slaves; but as freeborn and that their labour may be sweetened unto them, upon every Tuesday and Thursday the days being fair, they shall be suffered to play at the place appointed for that end, from half three till four afternoon, after which time they are to return to school, where they are to remain till six. These days being unfit for recreations, it may be delayed until the first fair season, with every Saturday's afternoon, together with the accustomed festival days observing the ancient rites of their oblations (to testify their thankfulness) to their masters. At and after which times, the scholars may with a kindly homeliness mediate for the play by the mouth of their victor; as also at the entry of a new scholar (if earnestly entreated) they may have it for all night. The like may be granted to any of the masters' superiors, or for a compliment to strangers, or when any necessary occasion require it, that thereby the masters show their clemency to their scholars and gain them by such demonstrations of their affection towards them; but the masters shall no ways give them whole day's play without they be permitted, or commanded by their superiors. [B18/box 1/5]

England, 1712   *James **Erskine** is angered by a complaint from his son's tutor that Charles, aged seven, displayed a 'perverseness'.*

As to the perverseness of the poor young child, it rarely is unconquerable in a boy so very young, if proper methods be taken. I know the boy had a wantonness, as such of his age use to have, and is more pliable by persuasion than by rough treatment. But Cumming's crabbed peevish temper made him use the last method, and often to beat him severely for trifles, and sometimes when the boy was more in the right than he, till I put a stop to it, and now he says himself that the boy does well. Lord be thanked he learns well and would learn better if he had a more painful and better tempered master. [*Erskine (2), pp. 73–4*]

*Cover **Morris** is concerned about reports of harsh whippings inflicted on his son William, aged fourteen, by his schoolteacher.*   *England, 1724*

I went about ten o'clock to Sherborn to be fully informed, whether the report of Mr Wilding's excessive severity to my son under his instructions, was true. I found he had been often whipped since Christmas, but not above three lashes; not fourteen at a time as he was before I had desired him to be more moderate in his discipline. Mr Wilding showed me his exercises in one of which there were thirty literal faults; but none of false concord or very improper words. He read about ten lines of English, and made him piece by piece turn them into Latin off hand; which he did very well. He then examined him, in Latin and Greek, being late put into the Greek testament. He made him decline a Greek verb, conjugate it through all the moods, and give account [of] the characteristics, and variations which he did exactly, to the greatest satisfaction to me imaginable. At last Mr Wilding said, he would compare him with any boy of England of his standing, and did not doubt but he should make him an incomparable scholar, and the best that ever went from his school. He loved him heartily, for he had no fault but one, and that was he would not take pains, which he endeavoured by his often whipping to break him of, and he had almost compassed his desire. If he would but search his dictionary, they should never fall out. Mr Wilding then bid him to go out a little while and divert himself . . . He professed to me, he had not given him above three lashes at a time since I talked with him about it. He said also I should tell his Mother he would whip him no more. I answered him, then all would be spoiled that way. No I did not desire that; but only moderate correction, which to him a good-natured and flexible, though lazy, boy I hoped would be effectual. I desired also he would keep him in the school at playtime when the other boys were at liberty. He said that would [be] no manner of punishment to him; for he would sit in his chamber by himself many hours together. However, I answered it might be grievous to him when he was forced to do so. [*pp. 103–4*]

*Rules for conduct at the **Penn Charter** School*   *America, 1748*

That no boy shall presume to absent himself from the school without producing a note from one of his parents.

That strict obedience shall be paid to the monitor[s] in discharge of their office, and that none shall take the liberty of entering into any dispute with them, but if any boy conceives himself aggrieved, he shall make his complaint to the master.

That in coming to school and returning home every one shall behave with decency and sobriety.

That in all their conversation they shall use the plain language
... and shall be careful never to utter any rude or uncivil
expression, nor to call their schoolmates or others by any nick-
name or term of reproach.

That in their hours of leisure, they shall avoid ranting games
and diversions, and every occasion of quarrelling with each other.
That none shall at any time play or keep company with the rude
boys of the town, but shall converse, as much as they can, with
their own schoolfellows. That no boy of this school shall be
allowed to go into the backyard, during schooltime, unless he be
sent on an errand by the master. [p. 122]

America, 1774   *Philip* **Fithian** *describes how he was called upon to whip one of his
pupils, Robert, aged sixteen. (Nancy is Robert's thirteen-year-old sister
and Harry his sixteen-year-old cousin.)*

Bob and Nancy before breakfast had a quarrel. Bob called Nancy a
liar; Nancy upbraided Bob, on the other hand, with being often
flogged by their Papa; often by the masters in college; that he had
stolen rum, and had got drunk; and that he used to run away,
etcetera. These reproaches when they were set off with Miss
Nancy's truly feminine address, so violently exasperated Bob that
he struck her in his rage. I was at the time in my chamber; when I
entered the room each began with loud and heavy complaints, I
put them off however with sharp admonitions for better behaviour ... Immediately after breakfast Ben came over with a
message from Mr Carter, that he desired me to correct Bob severely
immediately. Bob, when I went into school sat quiet in the corner,
and looked sullen, and penitent; I gave some orders to the
children, and went to my room. I sent for Bob. He came crying. I
told him his father's message; he confessed himself guilty. I sent
him to call up Harry. He came. I talked with them both a long time,
recommended diligence, and good behaviour, but concluded by
observing that I was obliged to comply with Mr Carter's request. I
sent Harry therefore for some whips. Bob and poor I remained
trembling in the chamber (for Bob was not more uneasy than I it
being the first attempt of the kind I have ever made.) The whips
came! I ordered Bob to strip! He desired me to whip him in his
hand in tears. I told him no. He then patiently, and with great
deliberation took off his coat and laid it by. I took him by the hand
and gave him four or five smart twigs; he cringed, and bawled and
promised. I repeated them about eight more, and demanded and
got immediately his solemn promise for peace among the children,
and good behaviour in general. I then sent him down. He
conducts himself through this day with great humility, and
unusual diligence, it will be fine if it continues. [pp. 66–7]

*Marjory **Fleming**, aged seven, relates the problems her temper posed her cousin and tutor Isabella.*   *Scotland, 1811*

I confess that I have been more like a little young devil than a creature for when Isabella went up the stairs to teach me religion and my multiplication and to be good and all my other lessons, I stamped with my feet and threw my new hat which she made on the ground and was sulky and was dreadfully passionate but she never whipped me but gently said, Marjory go into another room and think what a great crime you are committing letting your temper get the better of you but I went so sulkily that the devil got the better of me; but she never never whips me so that I think I would be the better of it and the next time that I behave ill I think she should do it, for she never does it but she is very indulgent to me but I am very ungrateful to her. [*Fleming (b), pp. 40-2*]

The next day.

Today I have been very ungrateful and bad and disobedient. Isabella gave me my writing. I wrote so ill that she took it away and locked it up in her desk where I stood trying to open it till she made me come and read my Bible, but I was in a bad humour and read it so carelessly and ill that she took it from me and her blood ran cold but she never punished me. She is as gentle as a lamb to me an ungrateful girl. [*Fleming (b), pp. 43–4*]

*John **Epps** remembers the punishments he received at school.*   *England, c.1818*

At this school there were several masters. I more generally received my punishment from a revered gentleman. This was the principal, but he was a man, I never could like. I fear he was a selfish man; and certainly he evinced a spiteful disposition. But he is gone, and I hope to heaven. When he saw me hold out my hand with firmness, he would raise his arm the higher, and would bring down his cane with the additional force imparted by anger. When he had exhausted his venom without being able to move me, he was obliged to say, 'Go to your seat, sir.' This master used to have cobbler's cord wound round the end of his cane, so that the poor schoolboy might suffer more. [*p. 46*]

*Mary **Haldane** recollects the harsh discipline imposed by her governess.*   *England, c.1835*

She was a very strict disciplinarian, and we were vigorously punished when we infringed the laws of the schoolroom. She had rooms in a house adjoining that which we occupied while my father was building West Jesmond, his new house, and we went

Boys Praise. When I work to write I have no ink. I have no place to keep my pens &c &c. I hope you will either bring me one if you come or send me one soon. Mr Langley lets a pieman to come every Saturday & we may all spend sixpence — if we like but no more and for fear of making ourselves sick we must have 3 worth to spend on Monday. Today most of us bought a muffin which we had for Tea. Please tell me when Mr King & Mr Mclean come home and where Mr King is when he comes home for I want to write to him. If you could tell me his address in London I would be very glad. Mr Langley gives 3 prizes the Conduct prize the

(the Examination Prize. Mr Langley gives 1 prize for good Conduct at Table (in the house. If we do any thing wrong she gives us a mark & whoever has fewest marks gets the prize. Mr Langley gives a good 1 but the bad marks are one has 0 the good marks are marked with figures if we behave well we get 12 marks every day. I am in great want of a pen can for I have lost the pen of the one my Isabella Erskine gave me. I had a letter from Hannah this morning (she was quite well. To think you shall come to see me in spring (for I wrote the first part of my letter on Saturday evening) it will be very nice. Will you send me a Bun &c. give with Bun at Christmas

Letter from William Stirling, 1859

[I am sadly in want of a deske which most of the] boys have. When I wish to write I have no ink & I have no place to keep my pens & c & c. I hope you will either bring me one if you come or send me one soon. Mr Langley lets a piewoman to come every Saturday & we may all spend sixpence if we like but no more and for fear of making ourselves sick we must have 3d worth to shew on Monday. Today most of us bought a muffin which we had for tea. Please tell me when Mr King & Mr Mclean come home and where Mr King is when he comes home for I want to write to him. If you could tell me his address in London I would be very glad. Mr Langley gives 3 prizes the conduct prize the lesson prize & the examination prize. Mrs Langley gives a prize for good conduct at table & in the house. If we do any thing wrong she gives us a mark & whoever has fewest marks gets the prize. Mr Langley gives us good & bad [marks] the bad marks are thus O the good marks are marked wih figures; if we behave well we get 12 marks every day. I am in great want of a penc[il] case for I have lost the pen of the one miss Isabella Erskine gave me, I had a letter from Hannah this morning & she was quite well. Do [you] think you shall come to see me in spring (for I wrote the first part of my letter on Saturday evening) it will be very nice. Will you send me a bun a good rich bun at Christmas

Strathclyde Regional Archives T-SK 13/11/5.11

and came to and from her apartment, spending twelve hours of every day there under her supervision. The system of the day was to administer corporal punishment. We, or rather I, as my sister escaped from having had scarlet fever and being pronounced delicate, were shut up for a day at a time and fed only on bread and water. Sometimes it was in an empty room, and once in a room never opened in a so-called haunted house which my father had taken for the shooting season. I remember to this hour the sound of the closing heavy door. It was done for good, but I question whether it was good. It did me no harm, however, as far as I am aware, though I was naturally afraid of rats. [*pp. 43–4*]

Scotland, 1835   *John Wilder writes to William **Gordon-Cummings**, defending the punishment administered to the latter's son Roualeyn at Eton. (Dr Hawthey was the Provost at Eton.)*

In justification of the measures adopted by Dr Hawthey in the punishment of your son, I need not again enter into the minute details of his offence. I stated them most fairly and fully in my last letter; and notwithstanding Lady Gordon-Cummings' conviction that there are many extenuating circumstances to my report if I knew all the truth, I can assure you that the facts were precisely as I stated them, and that I did not act hastily or without due consideration, but I took very great pains to investigate the truth from beginning to end by examining witnesses etcetera as well as by hearing your son's own defence, as to the 'punishment being too severe for the offence' ... Dr Hawthey and all those in authority in the place, and especially *the boys themselves* ... [were] unanimous in their view of the nature of the offence, and of the justice of the punishment inflicted. [*dep. 175/2/160/4*]

Roualeyn left Eton the following year because of continued disciplinary problems.

England, 1845   *Charlotte **Guest** is unhappy about sending her ten-year-old son Ivor to public school.*

When I thought of all the sorrow and temptation my poor boys would have to go through in that place I quite shuddered and prayed that assistance might be granted them from above. It seems a sad prospect, but everybody says it is the only way to bring up boys; and what is to be done? How can I, a poor weak woman, judge against all the world? [*p. 164*]

Introduction

Childhood was considered to be a period of profound importance for the formation of a sound character, the development of intellectual skills, and the acquisition of a staunch religious faith. As a stage of life it offered rich opportunities for improvement (Zadoc Long, p. 214). The prevailing belief through the centuries was that children could be moulded in the right way while young and malleable; they could be trained to follow the paths of virtue (Henry Newcome, p. 207, and Mary Sewell, p. 212). Young people were to be dutiful, respectful, and not to waste valuable time (Elizabeth Saltonstall, p. 207, and Reginald Heber, p. 211). Parents took a primary role in this socialization process, regarding it as a main parental duty (Cotton Mather, p. 209, and Bronson Alcott, p. 213). Children, though, were not schooled in compliance only through the method of external regulation; their consciences too were shaped so that they participated in the training process. The development of a system of internal discipline was encouraged since this was seen as a more effective means of socialization than the mere obeying of parental commands (Mary Sumner, p. 207).

The religious education given to children in previous centuries could be intense, especially if their parents were of the Puritan, Methodist or Evangelical faith. Haunted by the fear that their child would go to hell, parents who adhered to these forms of piety urged on their children an early awareness of sin and death. As children were considered to be innately sinful, the only way to escape perdition was to induce them to strive for salvation from an early age. Death could strike at any time and the young must be made ready (Samuel Sewall, p. 215). The intensity of the preparation for salvation and the dwelling on the sinful nature of mankind produced a religious crisis in some children (Samuel Sewall, p. 215, and Mary Haldane, p. 220). Though religious indoctrination could be harsh, it is important to realize that most parents sympathized with a child's distress, and were prepared to soften their approach if the child became too upset (Mrs Housman, p. 217).

Not all children were brought up in an atmosphere of intense religious struggle, although most would be given some form of scriptural knowledge. In some households children were entertained as well as instructed by religious teachings (Roger North, p. 215, and James Boswell, p. 218). By the nineteenth century some parents disapproved of children being made aware of sin too early (Mary Sewell, p. 220). The religious education of daughters posed something of a problem in the nineteenth century, since the Bible was not felt to be an entirely suitable textbook for girls (Fanny Burney, p. 219).

This difference in the education of sons and daughters becomes more marked in academic education. A few girls, like Lucy Hutchinson (p. 222), could be taught Latin, but in general a classical education was regarded as inappropriate for girls. Whereas the sons of the well-to-do were thoroughly grounded in Latin and other elements of a good education, in order to secure advancement in life, daughters made do with singing, writing, music, dancing, needlework and French (Ralph Verney, p. 226). It was not that parents were uninterested in their daughter's education or progress (Unton Dering, p. 223, and Aaron Burr, p. 233), nor even that a girl's education was similar to a boy's with the classics omitted, but rather that daughters were provided with different goals to strive for. They were to be fully accomplished in all the social graces, and to be competent in housekeeping skills; in short, they were trained to be suitable wives and good mothers (Charlotte Papendiek, p. 236). Thus, teaching a girl Latin was felt to be a waste of time not only because it was unnecessary for her role in life, but also because it hindered her from attaining perfection in those attributes which were considered to be essential for women (Lucy Hutchinson, p. 222). It may be that the intellectual content of the education given to girls worsened during the nineteenth century as the costs of boys' education rose (Elizabeth Pratt, p. 239, and Blanche Dundas, p. 241)

In the Stuart period children were taught to read first and then to write. Learning to write was a separate skill with its own place in the syllabus and many of the poor ended their education without acquiring it. Children generally began by learning their letters from a horn-book, progressing to a primer and then on to the Bible. Some of the teaching methods proposed – for example, the flash-card system of teaching children the alphabet suggested by Thomas Tryon (p. 227), and the learning-by-doing system put forward by Thomas Cobden-Sanderson (p. 244) 11 seem surprisingly modern. By the nineteenth century the value of practical play as a component part of the learning process was realized (Mary Sewell, p. 238).

The school day in educational establishments as well as for those tutored at home could be long and the timetable monotonous (Frank Dryden, p. 237). From the grammar schools of the seventeenth century to the public schools of the nineteenth, the classics, especially Latin, formed the core of the curriculum (Sydney Smith, p. 238). Great faith was placed in the superior mental and intellectual training offered by the classics: to such an extent that more than three-quarters of a public schoolboy's time in the early nineteenth century would be spent in studying Latin, Greek, ancient history and geography. The grammar schools of the nineteenth century, although still offering Latin, concentrated on

English, mathematics and French, an education thought to be more appropriate for a commercial or professional career. Regular scientific instruction in either type of school did not begin until 1849, and even then it was on a modest scale.

The Moral Training of Children

England, 1620s *Margaret **Cavendish** recalls her mother's insistence that her daughters be virtuously bred.*

We were bred with respectful attendance, every one being several-ly waited upon; and all her servants in general used the same respect to her children, (even those that were very young) as they did to herself; for she suffered not her servants either to be rude before us, or to domineer over us, which all vulgar servants are apt, and oftimes which some have leave to do; likewise she never suffered the vulgar serving-men to be in the nursery among the nurse-maids, lest their rude love-making might do unseemly actions, or speak unhandsome words in the presence of her children, knowing that youth is apt to take infection by ill examples, having not the reason of distinguishing good from bad; neither were we suffered to have any familiarity with the vulgar servants, or conversation: yet caused us to demean ourselves with an humble civility towards them, as they with a dutiful respect to us . . .

As for tutors, although we had for all sorts of virtues, as singing, dancing, playing on music, reading, writing, working and the like, yet we were not kept strictly thereto; they were rather for formality than benefit; for my mother cared not so much for our dancing and fiddling, singing and prating of several languages, as that we should be bred virtuously, modestly, civilly, honourably, and on honest principles. [*pp. 4–6*]

England, 1640s *Roger **North** considers how the inclination to idleness in mankind can be avoided.*

Those general inclinations which tend to deprave mankind, are well enough obviated in youth, by the common methods used in education of children. For that case which always happens in a concern so universal as breeding children, must needs be pro-vided for by a traditional method of proceeding in it. And this with careful parents is constantly done, by impressing in their tender minds duty to parents, enforced by the universal custom of asking blessing, learning to read, being put to school, and kept to it all their youth, and then handed into manly employments, as they become capable, without allowing any vacancy or idle time. [*vol. 3, p. 5*]

*Henry **Newcome** comments in his diary.*   *England, 1661*

Mr Heyrick's children with us this night. From the example I see in their mannerliness, and from what I read in Bentivolio, p. 92, 93 etcetera, I see I have cause to look after my children, that they may be well bent when young. [*p. 300*]

*Elizabeth **Saltonstall** writes to her young daughter Elizabeth while the*   *America, 1680*
latter is away from home attending school.

Betty, – Having an opportunity to send to you, I could do no less than write a few lines to mind you that you carry yourself very respectively and dutifully to Mrs Graves as though she were your Mother: and likewise respectively and lovingly to the children, and soberly in words and actions to the servants: and be sure you keep yourself diligently employed either at home or at school, as Mrs Graves shall order you. Do nothing without her leave, and assure yourself it will be a great preservative from falling into evil to keep yourself well employed. But with all and in the first place make it your daily work to pray earnestly to God that he would keep you from all manner of evil. Take heed of your discourse at all times that it be not vain and foolish but know that for every idle word you must certainly give account another day. Be sure to follow your reading, omit it not one day: your father doth propose to send you some copies so that you may follow your writing likewise. I shall say no more at present but only lay a strict charge upon you that you remember and practise what I have minded you of: and as you desire the blessing of God upon you either in soul or body be careful to observe the counsel of your parents and consider that they are the words of your loving and affectionate mother. [*Earle (c), pp. 100–1*]

*Mary **Sumner**, as a child, keeps a record of all her misdeeds, as well as*   *America, early*
her good behaviour.   *18th century*

Black leaf
July

    8. I left my staise [stays] on the bed.
    9. Misplaced sister's sash.
    10. Spoke in haste to my little sister, spilt the cream on the floor in the closet.
    12. I left sister Cynthia's frock on the bed.
    16. I left the brush on the chair; was not diligent in learning at school.
    17. I left my fan on the bed.

19. I got vexed because sister was a-going to cut my frock.
22. Part of this day I did not improve my time well.
30. I was careless and lost my needle.

August

5. I spilt some coffee on the table.

White leaf
July

8. I went and said my catechism today. Came home and wrote down the questions and answers, then dressed and went to the dance, endeavoured to behave myself decent.
11. I improved my time before breakfast; after breakfast made some biscuits and did all my work before the sun was down.
12. I went to meeting and paid good attention to the sermon, came home and wrote down as much of it as I could remember.
17. I did everything before breakfast; endeavoured to improve in school; went to the funeral in the afternoon, attended to what was said, came home and wrote down as much as I could remember.
25. A part of this day I parsed and endeavoured to do well and a part of it I made some tarts and did some work and wrote a letter.
27. I did everything this morning same as usual, went to school and endeavoured to be diligent; came home and washed the butter and assisted in getting coffee.
28. I endeavoured to be diligent today in my learning, went from school to sit up with the sick, nursed her as well as I could.
30. I was pretty diligent at my work today and made a pudding for dinner.

August

1. I got some peaches for to stew after I was done washing up the things and got my work and was middling diligent.
4. I did everything before breakfast and after breakfast got some peaches for Aunt Mell and then got my work and stuck pretty close to it and at night sat up with sister and nursed her as good as I could.
8. I stuck pretty close to my work today and did all that sister gave me and after I was done I swept out the house and put the things to rights.
9. I endeavoured to improve my time today in reading and attending to what brother read and most of the evening I was singing. [*pp. 167–9*]

*Cotton **Mather** notes in his diary:*

Some special points, relating to the education of my children.

i. I pour out continual prayers and cries to the God of all grace for them, that He will be a Father to my children, and bestow His Christ and His grace upon them, and guide them with His counsels, and bring them to His glory.

And in this action, I mention them distinctly, every one by name unto the Lord.

ii. I begin betimes to entertain them with delightful stories, especially *scriptural* ones. And still conclude with some *lesson* from the *story*. And thus, every day at the *table*, I have used myself to tell a *story* before I rise; and make the *story* useful to the *olive plants about the table*.

iii. When the children at any time accidentally come in my way, it is my custom to let fall some *sentence* or other, that may be monitory and profitable to them.

This matter proves to me, a matter of some study, and labour, and contrivance. But who can tell, what may be the effect of a *continual dropping*?

iv. I essay betimes, to engage the children, in exercises of piety; especially *secret prayer*, for which I give them very plain and brief *directions*, and suggest unto them the *petitions*, which I would have them to make before the Lord, and which I therefore explain to their apprehension and capacity. And I often call upon them; *Child, Don't forget every day, to go alone, and pray as I have directed you!*

v. Betimes I try to form in the children a temper of *benignity*. I put them upon doing of services and kindness for one another, and for other children. I applaud them, when I see them delight in it. I upbraid all aversion to it. I caution them exquisitely against all revenges of injuries. I instruct them, to return good offices for evil ones. I show them, how they will by this *goodness* become like to the good God and the glorious Christ. I let them discern, that I am not satisfied, except when they have a sweetness of temper shining in them.

vi. As soon as 'tis possible, I make the children learn to *write*. And when they can *write*, I employ them in writing out the most agreeable and profitable things, that I can invent for them. In this way, I propose to fraight their minds with *excellent things*, and have a deep impression made upon their minds by such things . . .

vii. I would have them come to propound and expect, at this rate, *I have done well, and now I will go to my father; he will teach me some curious thing for it.* I must have them count it a *privilege*, to be taught; and I sometimes manage the matters so, that by refusing to teach them sometime, is their *punishment*. [*Mather (b), vol. 7, pp. 534-6*]

America, 1718   Mr **Colman** *writes to his ten-year-old daughter Jane.*

My dear Child, – I have this morning your letter which pleases me very well and gives me hopes of many a pleasant line from you in time to come if God spare you to me and me to you. I very much long to see your Mother but doubt whether the weather will permit today. I pray God to bless you and make you one of his children. I charge you to pray daily and read your Bible, and fear to sin. Be very dutiful to your Mother, and respectful to everybody. Be very humble and modest, womanly and discreet. Take care of your health and as you love me do not eat green apples. Drink sparingly of water, except the day be warm. When I last saw you, you were too shamefaced; look people in the face, speak freely and behave decently. I hope to bring Nabby in her grandfather's chariot to see you. The meanwhile I kiss your dear Mother, and commend her health to the gracious care of God, and you with her to His Grace. Give my service to Mr A. and family and be sure you never forget the respect they have honoured you with. Your loving father. [*p. 92*]

England, 1742   Lord **Chesterfield** *counsels his son Philip, aged ten.*

Your promises give me great pleasure; and your performance of them, which I rely upon, will give me still greater. I am sure you know that breaking of your word is a folly, a dishonour, and a crime. It is a folly, because nobody will trust you afterwards; and it is both a dishonour and a crime, truth being the first duty of religion and morality: and whoever has not truth, cannot be supposed to have any good quality, and must become the detestation of God and man. Therefore I expect, from your truth and your honour, that you will do that, which, independently of your promise, your own interest and ambition ought to incline you to do; that is, to excel in everything you undertake. When I was of your age, I should have been ashamed if any boy of that age had learned his book better, or played at any play better than I did; and I would not have rested a moment till I had got before him. Julius Caesar, who had a noble thirst for glory, used to say, that he would rather be the first in a village than the second in Rome; and he even cried when he saw the statue of Alexander the Great, with the reflection of how much more glory Alexander had acquired, at thirty years old, than he at a much more advanced age. These are the sentiments to make people considerable; and those who have them not, will pass their lives in obscurity and contempt; whereas those who endeavour to excel all, are at least sure of excelling a great many. The sure way to excel in anything, is only to have a close and undissipated attention while you are about it; and then you need not be half the time that otherwise you must be; for long plodding, puzzling application, is the business of dullness: but good parts attend regularly, and take a thing immediately. Consider, then, which you would choose; to attend diligently while you are learning, and thereby excel all other boys, get a great reputation, and have a great deal more time to play; or else not mind your book, let boys even younger than yourself get before you, be laughed at by them for a dunce, and have no time to play at all; for, I assure you, if you will not learn, you shall not play. What is the way, then, to arrive at that perfection, which you promise me to aim at? It is, first, to do your duty towards God and man; without which, everything else signifies nothing: secondly, to acquire a great knowledge; without which, you will be a very contemptible man, though you may be a very honest one; and lastly, to be very well bred; without which, you will be a very disagreeable, unpleasing man, though you may be an honest and a learned one.

Remember then these three things, and resolve to excel in them all; for they comprehend whatever is necessary and useful for this world or the next; and in proportion as you improve in them, you will enjoy the affection and tenderness of, Yours. [*vol. 1, pp. 211–13*]

Reginald **Heber** *instructs his son Richard.*   *England, 1783*

You will, I trust, my dear, endeavour to deserve the continuance of your worthy tutor's favour and good opinion and I am sure you will be very happy and improve greatly under his care. A ready obedience to his commands, diligent attention to his instructions, and assiduous application to your business will infallibly ensure you the applause, love, and affection of your master. Than which nothing in this life can afford greater satisfaction to me, and the rest of your friends. It has pleased God, the giver of every good gift, to bless you with a capacity which makes learning much easier to you than to many: you can never be too thankful my dear for this blessing, and it would be very ungrateful and culpable in you not to cultivate and improve the talents, the bounty of heaven has bestowed upon you. I make no doubt you have many clever boys in your class and I doubt not you will feel and be incited by an honest emulation to keep pace with the best of them in running the race of honour and improvement in learning that is set before you . . .

Let me repeat my earnest request to you my dearest child never to omit your own prayers morning and evening to Almighty God for his blessing and protection without which all human endeavours will be vain and fruitless. I know, my love, you have now an honest and a good heart, and I trust and hope by God's grace it will be preserved. [*Eng. letter C.203, ff. 7–8*]

Nathaniel **Saltonstall** *writes to his daughter Mary, aged thirteen, who is attending school in Boston.*

Dear Mary, – I was glad to hear that the alteration of the plan for the improvement of your time, whilst in Boston, was agreeable to you – hope therefore that you will be attentive to your schooling and gain all possible instruction; and consider that at your time of life, such a foundation ought to be laid, as will raise such a superstructure as will be useful in the future period of your life.

I hope that you are contented in your present situation; if not, I wish to be informed, for I desire not to keep you in Boston unless it is agreeable to you; but when you reflect on the advantages you may reap from a proper improvement of your time there, I think it must calm every uneasy reflection which naturally arises in young minds in their first absence from their parents.

I expected that you would have wrote us, but we have not yet been favoured with a line. I would recommend your writing and depend on it that any grammatical error or deficiency in any respect, shall be viewed with parental candour. Letter writing, (Polly) is one of the most useful branches of education and which I most earnestly desire you to attempt and doubt not you'll do yourself honour in your first endeavour. If you are not fully acquainted with spelling, I would advise you to a small pocket dictionary and in every doubtful word, apply thereto for information . . .

I wish you to be very observant to Mr Turner's instruction and endeavour, if time will allow it, to get some knowledge of a minuet, although I do not suppose that he can put you forward faster than the class you are in. Let your manners be free and easy – your conversation agreeable and sensible and in every deport-ment through life so conduct [yourself] as to be distinguished for your amiable qualities; this will be advantageous to your self and pleasing to your parents. [*vol. 2, pp. 28–9*]

Mary **Sewell** *on her two children, Anna and Philip.*

As very little children I accustomed them to playing in the dark. Many a game of hide-and-seek have I had with them in room bordered by dressing-room and two closets, and admitting of all kinds of surprises. They were never afraid of any kind of insect, would handle beetles, spiders, earwigs, etcetera, with pleasure, and were much amused if any one was afraid of them. [*p. 59*]

She also composed sets of instructions which were presented to her children on their birthdays.

To Anna.

Anna Sewell has this day completed her ninth year, and is in many respects a delight and comfort to her mother, who, that she may be able to test her progress from year to year, wishes now to write a short account of her attainments in her learning, and of the qualities of her mind, etcetera . . . Much disposed to idle over lessons and work. She needs to get the habit of a cheerful surrender of her own will – to give up entirely telling tales of her brother. She begins to be useful to her mother, but is not tidy. In *everything* her mother hopes she will be improved by another year. [*pp. 85–6*]

To Philip.

More persevering in play than in work: he has an awkward habit of repeating what other people say; can neither sit nor stand still; takes no pains to speak distinctly. Altogether he is a nice little boy and his mother hopes by this day twelve months he will have lost all his bad habits, and increased his good ones. [*p. 86*]

Mary had firm views on the necessity of training a child's character.

The metal of a child's character must be formed early. The soul must be trained to govern the body, and not to be its slave. A noble life of truth, humanity, and reverence should be lived before him, and its influence will fall upon the ductile nature that is gathering in its character, and moulding itself after the pattern of its surroundings. [*p. 101*]

*Bronson **Alcott** gives counsel to his daughter Louisa on her tenth birthday.* *America, 1842*

My Daughter, – This is your birthday: you are ten years of age today. I sought amidst my papers for some pretty picture to place at the top of this note, but I did not find anything that seemed at all expressive of my interest in your well-being, or well-doing, and so this note comes to you without any such emblem. Let me say, my honest little girl, that I had had you often in my mind during my separation from you and your devoted mother, and well meaning sisters, while on the sea, or the land, and now that I have returned to be with you and them again, meeting you daily at fireside, at table, at study, and in your walks and amusements, in conversation and in silence being daily with you, I would have you feel my presence and be the happier, and better that I am here. I want, most of all things, to be a kindly influence on you, helping you to guide and govern your heart, keeping it in a state of sweet and loving peacefulness, so that you may feel how good and kind is that love which lives always in our breasts, and which we may always feel, if we will keep the passions all in stillness and give up ourselves entirely to its soft desires. I live, my dear daughter, to be good and do good to all, and especially to you and your mother and sister[s]. Will you not let me do you all the good that I would? And do you know that I can do little good or none, unless you are disposed to let me; unless you give me your affections, incline your ears, and earnestly desire to become daily better and wiser, more kind, gentle, loving, diligent, heedful, serene. The good spirit comes into the breasts of the meek and loveful to abide long; anger, discontent, impatience, evil appetites, greedy wants, complainings, ill-speakings, idleness, heedlessness, rude behaviour, and all such, these drive it away, or grieve it so that it leaves the poor misguided soul to live in its own obstinate, perverse, proud, discomfort; which is the very *pain of sin*, and is in the *Bible* called the worm that never dies, the growing worm, the sting of *conscience* while the pleasures of love and goodness, are beyond all description – a peacefulness that passes all understanding. I pray that my daughter may know much of the last, and little of the first of these feelings. I shall try every day to help her to the knowledge and love of this good *spirit*. I shall be with her, and as she and her sisters come more and more into the presence of this spirit, shall we become a family more closely united in loves that can never sunder us from each other. [*Alcott (c), pp. 92–3*]

America, 1849   *Zadoc* **Long** *wrote this note in his eleven-year-old son's diary.*

John Davis, wake up! Perform your duties better. Let not your time be wasted and lost. *Consider.* Can these bright days and these rich opportunities of your boyhood return to you? If you do not improve them in acquiring knowledge and in fitting yourself for a useful and happy life, will it not cause you bitter remorse as long as you live? *Wake up*, I say. It is not yet too late. [*p. 41*]

Religious Education

*Samuel **Mather**, aged twelve, writes to his father* America, 1638

Though I am thus well in body yet I question whether my soul
doth prosper as my body doth, for I perceive yet to this very day,
little *growth* in grace; and this makes me question whether grace
be in my heart or no. I feel also daily great unwillingness to good
duties, and the great ruling of sin in my heart; and that God is
angry with me and gives me no answer to my prayers; but many
times he even throws them down as dust in my face; and he does
not grant my continued request for the *spiritual blessing of the
softening of my hard heart*. And in all this I could yet take some
comfort but that it makes me wonder what God's *secret decree*
concerning me may be: for I doubt whether even God is wont to
deny grace and mercy to his chosen (though uncalled) when they
seek unto him by prayer for it; and therefore, seeing he doth thus
deny it to me, I think that the reason of it is most like to be because
I belong not unto *the election of grace*. I desire that you would let
me have your prayers as I doubt not but I have them. [*Mather (c),
pp. 239–40*]

*Roger **North** remembers the religious training given by his mother.* England, 1640s

And for the part of learning to read, and bringing us to it at set
hours, leaving the intervals to remission, which is absolutely
necessary to younglings and making all possible impressions in
the way of religion; by discoursing and answering wisely, when
we were talkative and to show how virtue may be mixed with
delight, she used to tell us tales, always concluding in morality, to
which as children use, we were most attentive. On Sundays also
she would comply when we solicited for a story, but it must be a
Sunday one, as she called it, and then would tell some scriptural
history which was more pleasing to us because more admirable
and extraordinary than others. Nothing could be more apropos,
than this method, for forming the minds of children to a prejudice
in favour of what was good. [*vol. 3, pp. 4–5*]

*Samuel **Sewall** attempts to prepare his son Samuel, aged eleven, for
death.* America, 1689

Richard Dumer, a flourishing youth of nine years old, dies of the
smallpox. I tell Samuel of it and what need he had to prepare for
death, and therefore to endeavour really to pray when he said over
the Lord's Prayer: He seemed not much to mind, eating an apple;

but when he came to say, Our Father, he burst out into a bitter cry, and when I asked what was the matter and he could speak, he burst out into a bitter cry and said he was afraid he should die. I prayed with him, and read scriptures comforting against death, as, O death, where is thy sting, etcetera. [*vol. 5, pp. 308–9*]

Later, he records the religious crisis of his fifteen-year-old daughter Elizabeth in his diary.

When I came in, past seven at night, my wife met me in the entry and told me Betty had surprised them. I was surprised with the abruptness of the relation. It seems Betty Sewall had given some signs of defection and sorrow; but a little while after dinner she burst into an amazing cry which caused all the family to cry too. Her Mother asked the reason, she gave none; at last said she was afraid she should go to Hell, her sins were not pardoned. She was first wounded by my reading a sermon of Mr Norton's; about the 5th of January. Text John 7.34, Ye shall seek me and shall die in your sins, ran in her mind and terrified her greatly. And staying at home January 12, she read out of Mr Cotton Mather – Why hath Satan filled my heart, which increased her fear. Her mother asked her whether she prayed. She answered Yes, but feared her prayers were not heard, because her sins were not pardoned. Mr Willard was sent for to comfort Elizabeth. [*vol. 5, pp. 419–20*]

Six weeks after this, Elizabeth experiences a new crisis.

Betty comes into me almost as soon as I was up and tells me the disquiet she had when waked; told me was afraid [she] should go to Hell, was like Spira, not elected. Asked her what I should pray for, she said, that God would pardon her sin and give her a new heart. I answered her tears as well as I could, and prayed with many tears on either part; hope God heard us. I gave her solemnly to God. [*vol. 5, pp. 422–3*]

America, 1706   *Cotton* **Mather** *sets out the way he performs the religious training of his children.*

viii. Though I find it a marvellous advantage to have the children strongly biased by principles of *reason* and *honour*, (which, I find, children will feel sooner than is commonly thought for:) yet I would neglect no endeavours, to have *higher principles* infused into them.

I therefore betimes awe them with the *eye* of God upon them. I show them, how they must love Jesus Christ; and show it, by doing what their parents require of them.

I often tell them for the *good angels*, who love them, and help them, and guard them; and who take Notice of them: and therefore must not be disobliged.

Heaven and *hell*, I set before them, as the consequences of their behaviour here.

ix. When the children are capable of it, I take them *alone*, one by one; and after my charges unto them, to fear God, and serve Christ, and shun sin, *I pray with them* in my study and make them the witnesses of the agonies, with which I address the throne of grace on their behalf.

x. I find much benefit, by a particular method, as of *catechising* the children, so of carrying the *repetition* of public sermons unto them.

The answers of the *catechism* I still explain with abundance of brief *questions*, which make them to take in the meaning of it, and I see, that they do so.

And when the sermons are to be *repeated*, I choose to put every *truth*, into a *question*, to be aswered still, with, *yes*, or, *no*. In this way I awaken their *attention*, as well as enlighten their *understanding*. And in this way I have an opportunity, to ask, *Do you desire such, or such a grace of God*? and the like. Yea, I have an opportunity to demand, and perhaps obtain their *consent* unto the glorious articles of the *new covenant*. The spirit of grace may fall upon them in this action; and they may be seized by Him, and held as His *temples*, through eternal ages. [*Mather (b), vol. 7, pp. 536–7*]

Mrs **Housman** *notes her method of teaching religious precepts to her eight-year-old daughter.* England, 1732

I have had this evening, my dear child with me in my closet, conversing with her, endeavouring to awaken her, and convince her of her sin and misery, by nature and practice. The child was seemingly affected and melted into tears, and in distress; so much that I was fain to turn my discourse, and tell her that God was good, and willing to pardon and receive sinners, especially those children that were willing to be good betimes, and in their younger days set themselves to love and serve God. I told her she must pray to God to pardon her, and give her Grace to serve him. The child seemed willing to pray, but wanted words to express herself; I asked her if I should help her, and teach her to pray. [*p. 81*]

Elizabeth **Mascall** *urges an early awareness of sin on her offspring.* England, 1738

I have been sometimes endeavouring to my utmost to convince my children of their natural sinful state, and the necessity of a saviour, and to teach them what to believe and practice that they may be saved ... while others are mourning over the sins and follies of their children, I have the pleasure to hear mine mourn in secret over their own sins, and this they acknowledge to me has been occasioned by my talking seriously and affectionately to them; oh blessed be God for setting home instructions upon young minds. [*p. 13*]

Scotland, 1777   James **Boswell** *had many conversations about religion with his young daughter Veronica, aged four.*

I had a most pleasing conversation with my dear Veronica, sitting with her on the floor of my dining-room while the sun shone bright. I talked to her of the beauties and charms of Heaven, of gilded houses, trees with richest fruits, finest flowers and most delightful music. I filled her imagination with gay ideas of futurity instead of gloomy ones, and she seemed to lift her eyes upwards with complacency. Yet when I put it to her if she would not like to die and go to Heaven, the *natural* instinctive aversion to death, or perhaps the *acquired*, by hearing it mentioned dismally made her say, 'I hope I'll be spared to you.' I for the first time mentioned *Christ* to her; told her that he came down to this world for our good; that ill men put him to death; that then he flew up with silver wings and opened the great iron gates of heaven, which had long been shut, and now we could get in. He would take us in. She was delighted with the idea, and cried 'O I'll kiss him'. One cannot give rational or doctrinal notions of Christianity to a child. But it is a great blessing to a child to have its affections early engaged by divine thoughts. [*vol. 12, pp. 180–81*]

In 1779

At night, after we were in bed, Veronica spoke out from her little bed and said, 'I do not believe there is a God'. 'Preserve me', said I, 'my dear what do you mean?' She answered, 'I have *thinket* it many a time, but did not like to speak of it'. I was confounded and uneasy, and tried her with the simple arguments that without God there would not be all the things we see. It is He who makes the sun shine. Said she, 'It shines only on good days'. Said I: 'God made you'. Said she: 'My Mother bore me'. It was a strange and alarming thing to her Mother and me to hear our little angel talk thus. But I thought it better just to let the subject drop insensibly tonight. I asked her if she had said her prayers tonight. She said yes, and asked me to put her in mind to say them in the morning. I prayed to God to prevent such thoughts from entering into her mind.

The next morning.

By talking calmly with Veronica, I discovered what had made her think there was not a God. She told me, 'she did not like to die.' I suppose as she has been told that God takes us to himself when we die, she had fancied that if there were no God, there would be no death; so 'Her wish was Father to the thought' – 'I wot through ignorance.' I impressed upon her that we must die at any rate; and how terrible would it be if we had not a Father in Heaven to take care of us. I looked into Cambray's *Education of a Daughter*, hoping to have found some simple argument for the being of God in that piece of instruction. But it is taken for granted. [*vol. 14, pp. 5–6*]

*Fanny **Burney** writes to Mrs Burney. (Alexander is Fanny's son, aged   England, 1801
seven.)*

With respect to the grand subject of your letter, religious instruction for dear little E—, I would I could help you better than I can! Had my Alex been a girl, I could have had a far greater chance of hitting upon something that might serve for a hint; for then I should have turned my thoughts that way, and have been prepared with their result; but I have only weighed what might be the most serviceable to a boy. And this is by no means the same thing, though religion for a *man* and a *woman* must be so precisely. Many would be my doubts as to the Old Testament for a girl, on account of the fault of the translators in not guarding it from terms and expressions impossible – at least utterly improper, to explain. With respect to Alex, as I know he must read it at school, I think it best to parry off the danger of his own conjectures, questions, or suggestions, by letting him read it completely with me, and giving such a turn to all I am sorry to let him read as may satisfy his innocent and unsuspicious mind for the present; and, perhaps – 'tis my hope – deter him from future dangerous inquiries by giving him an internal idea. He is already well informed upon the subject. So much, however, I think with you that religion should spring from the heart, that my first aim is to instil into him that general veneration for the creator of all things, that cannot but operate, though perhaps slowly and silently, in opening his mind to pious feelings and ideas. His nightly prayers I frequently vary; whatever is constantly repeated becomes repeated mechanically: the Lord's Prayers, therefore, is by no means our daily prayer; for as it is the first and most perfect composition in the universe, I would not have it lose its effect by familiarity. When we repeat it, it is always with a commentary. In general the prayer is a recapitulation of the error and naughtiness, or forbearance and happiness, of the day. [*vol. 6, pp. 223–4*]

England, 1830s   Mary **Sewell** *details her views on the religious training of children.*

> The first thing to teach a little child is that he has a Father in heaven who loves him and wishes him to be as happy as he can be – as happy as the little birds that sing and fly about; as merry as the lambs that frolic with one another, and eat the grass that has grown for them, and lie down in safety by their mother's side. Do not too early impress upon the mind of a little child that he is a sinner; let him discover this by his own experience. When he has done wrong, let the natural consequences of wrongdoing fall upon him. Do not shield him from the consequences of ignorance or disobedience; let them fall with their full weight, but let them be the only penalties. Let him distinctly feel in himself the difference between obedience and disobedience. Cultivate a quick and tender conscience. Require prompt obedience. Refer constantly to the happiness and obedience of the insect and animal world.
>
> Do not let the atonement for sin through the sacrifice of our adorable Saviour be presented early to a child – he is not at first able to conceive of the malignity of sin, which made the extremity of sacrifice needful. Presenting it to him when it is impossible for him to feel it properly, can hardly act otherwise than to make both sin and sacrifice appear light matters. God begins in His first teaching to the human race with the law. By the law is the knowledge of sin. We must begin as He begins. Never think to lower the standard of the law by way of bringing it nearer the capacity of the child. The law is God's appointed schoolmaster to bring us to Christ. It is through 'The broken vow, the frequent fall' we learn our need of the righteousness of Another.
>
> Self-denial, the milder form of sacrifice, may be touchingly and effectively taught, by various examples from the animal world, by facts and anecdotes, and whenever possible, from living human example. Let the Bible be always at hand, also books of natural history with good pictures. Both from God's Word and His works let the truth be ever impressing itself on the mind of the child, that every living thing around him belongs to the great family of God, and that He watches over all. Gradually let him understand his responsibility for the power he possesses, in God's creation, for making happiness or misery, and that all cruelty or injury inflicted is displeasing to Him who made His creatures to be happy, and who has provided for their being so. [*pp. 105–6*]

England, 1830s   Mary **Haldane** *recollects the religious training of her youth.*

> I used to have passages of the Bible to learn, or poetry, if I misbehaved. For a Sunday transgression I had to learn the 139th Psalm, and the words of that Psalm sank deeply into my mind. I

was often kept awake by thought of the sinfulness of my nature and with the sense that at any moment judgement might be passed upon me. I knew and felt that I was a great sinner and that God was my judge and must condemn me. I used to try to keep the Commandments of God, which I learned by heart, but constantly failed, and I was miserable. We were always at home on Sundays, as we did not go to church, and our father wrote two catechisms for us, which we learned; one was on the Lord's Prayer, the other on the general doctrines of the Bible. I think now that both were rather beyond us. [*pp. 4–5*]

Frances **Wood** *writes about her four-year-old daughter Frances.*   *England, 1841*

She asked me yesterday whether when chimney-sweeps die they become 'black angels'! She also asked 'If God has not got a great many pieces of people ready to make up into whole people'! How difficult it is to make so young a child understand anything clearly of the attributes of the Almighty; the omnipresence of the Deity puzzles her much; on hearing a story of two men who were drowned she said, – 'Well, Mama, God cannot catch their souls, for they are at the bottom of the sea'! [*p. 322*]

Catherine **Carswell** *describes the amount of religious instruction she*   *Scotland, 1879*
had imbibed by the age of thirteen.

By that age, for at least eight years, I had heard two sermons every Sunday, had often accompanied my parents to the Wednesday night prayer meetings. I had been taken to revival and other religious gatherings. At least once I had been moved to hold up my hand as a signal to Messrs Torrey and Alexander – or was it Gipsy Smith? – that here was a soul convicted of sin and anxious to repent. I calculate that I had heard with attention near one thousand carefully prepared exhortations, many of them appealing to the mind, others effectively addressed to the emotions. In addition I had hearkened, more or less since I could remember, to the converse of missionaries, and had twice daily participated – about six thousand times – in family prayers, which with us involved reading the Bible, verse and verse about, from beginning to end, over and over again, as the years proceeded. I knew most of the psalms and many hymns by heart. I could recite my shorter catechism, and chapters from the Old and New Testaments. I won a Bible at my Sunday school for the most word perfect and intelligent rendering of the twelfth chapter of Romans. I had read and enjoyed a number of godly books, including the *Pilgrim's Progress* and *Foxe's Booke of Martyrs* (this last my favourite Sabbath reading when still of a tender age). [*pp. 35–6*]

Academic Education

England, 1624   *Lucy* **Hutchinson** *recalls her intellectual achievements as a child.*

My father and mother fancying me then beautiful, and more than ordinarily apprehensive, applied all their cares, and spared no cost to improve me in my education, which procured me the admiration of those that flattered my parents. By the time I was four years old I read English perfectly, and having a great memory, was carried to sermons, and while I was very young could remember and repeat them exactly, and being caressed, the love of praise tickled me, and made me attend more heedfully. When I was about seven years of age, I remember I had at one time eight tutors in several qualities, languages, music, dancing, writing, and needlework, but my genius was quite averse from all but my book, and that I was so eager of, that my mother thinking it prejudiced my health, would moderate me in it; yet this rather animated me than kept me back, and every moment I could steal from my play I would employ in any book I could find, when my own were locked up from me. After dinner and supper I still had an hour allowed me to play, and them I would steal into some hole or other to read. My father would have me learn Latin, and I was so apt that I outstripped my brothers who were at school, although my father's chaplain that was my tutor was a pitiful dull fellow. My brothers who had a great deal of wit, had some emulation at the progress I made in my learning, which very well pleased my father, though my mother would have been contented, I had no so wholly addicted myself to that as to neglect my other qualities; as for music and dancing I profited very little in them and would never practise my lute or harpischords but when my masters were with me; and for my needle I absolutely hated it. [*vol. 1, pp. 25–6*]

England, 1636   *Thomas Meautys writes to his sister Jane* **Cornwallis***, who is taking care of his children while he is abroad. His eldest daughter is aged about ten.*

I am sorry to read in your letter to my wife, that my son is so hard to learn, but I hear it proceeds not from dullness of spirit, but rather from wildness, which time may alter in him; for, if I be not deceived, he is like unto his second sister, whom I praise God for, is a fine quick spirited child, but something hard to learn; but then my eldest girl is much the contrary, and of a good memory, and learns more than I can find means to have taught her, and I may say hath already sowed all her wild oats, so much a woman is she grown, God bless her. [*p. 277*]

Henry **Slingsby** *on the education of his son Thomas, aged four.*   *England, 1640*

I also committed my son Thomas into the charge and tuition of Mr Cheny whom I intend shall be his schoolmaster, and now he doth begin to teach him his primer; I intend he shall begin to spell, and read Latin together with his English, and to learn to speak it, more by practice of speaking than by rule; he could the last year, before he was four years old, tell the Latin words for the parts of his body and of his clothes . . . I will make trial of this way teaching my son Latin, that is without rule or grammar; and herein I do follow the pattern of Michael Montaigne a Frenchman who as he himself saith was so taught Latin, that he could at six years old speak more Latin than French. But I want that means which he had, having those about him that could speak nothing but Latin; him I do take to be my pattern herein of educating my son. [*pp. 53–4*]

His daughter Barbara, aged five, was taught by her mother.

She is able already to say all her prayers, answer to her catechism, read and write a little. [*p. 3*]

Unton Dering to Henry **Oxinden** *on the suitability of a school for his*   *England, 1647*
two daughters, Elizabeth, aged eleven, and Margaret, aged twelve.

According to your desire, I have spoken with Mr Beven of Ashford concerning your daughters being with him; he is very willing to do you and them any service in his power, and I am confident you will receive very good satisfaction in your charge, for he is a conscienable, discreet man, and one that stands upon his credit; and so industrious for the benefiting of his scholars as if they be willing to receive, he will spare no pains to bring them to perfection; as I can witness by experience, when he taught my daughter. And besides the qualities of music both for the virginals and singing (if they have voices) and writing (and to cast account which will be useful to them hereafter) he will be careful also that their behaviour be modest and such as becomes their quality; and that they grow in knowledge and understanding for God and their duty to Him, which is above all. For truly he is able to perform all this exceeding well: and 'tis his delight as well as his duty. They shall want no attendance or ought else necessary for them, for his wife is an excellent good woman, and his daughter a civil well qualified maid, and both work very well. I presume you will think £30 a year for both reasonable, when you consider the hardness of the times and that there is more trouble with girls than boys; and receive assurance from me that these qualities shall not be taught superficially but really, if your daughters will be industrious. [*Oxinden (b), p. 128*]

Sweete Sister.

Vpon the sight of your letter to my Lady I could not
rest vntill I had obtayned her favour to learne to wright
And such is her Motherly care of vs, as she will incourage
and further vr desires for attayning any good quallitie.
And although I have practised but three weekes, yet I
have presumed these powr lynes to your view, hoping that
as I mend, wee shall often converse by letters being the
chiefast meanes of absent freinds And me you shall indeere
mee as I am.

Your most affectionate Sister
Elizabeth Isham

Lamport
May: 2th 1645

Letter from Elizabeth Isham, 1645

Sweete sister
Uppon the sight of your letter to my Lady I could not rest
untill I had obtayned her favour to learne to wright. And such
is her Motherly care of us, as she will incourage and further
our desiers for attaynning any good quallitie; And although I
have practised but three weekes, yet I have presented these
poore lynes to your view, hoping that as I mend, wee shall
often converse by letters being the cheifest means of absent
freinds. And soe you shall indeere mee (as I am)
your most affectionate sister
Elizabeth Isham

Letter from Justinian Isham, 1622

Most deare father though I am u[n[sckilful in writing of
epistles never the lesse I thought it good to write somthing to
you allthough it will abounde with many faults where in I will
certifie you what I have profited you in the studie of good
letters for now I am newly entred in the exercise of making
s[c]hoole epistles but I pray you accept of it beeing the first
epistle that ever I made. My grandmother and my mother and
all the rest of the household are veri well hoping that you are
well too but I praye you remember my dutie to my aunt
denton and to my unkle Washucton and my aunt and all the
rest of my kindred. I have obeayed your comanndiment
which you tooke order with my mother and maister that I
shoulde keepe mee within the compose of the yards. I shoulde
bee very glad to see you at home and there I lave you with god
your obeydient son
Justinian Isham
I woulde have written this epistle in latin but time would not
serve mee

Northamptonshire Record Office, IC 251, 154

England, 1651   *Ralph **Verney** writes to Dr Denton about the education of the latter's*
daughter Nancy, Ralph's goddaughter.

Let not your girl learn Latin, nor shorthand; the difficulty of the
first may keep her from that vice, for so I must esteem it in a
woman; but the easiness of the other may be a prejudice to her; for
the pride of taking sermon notes, hath made multitudes of women
most unfortunate. Doctor, teach her to live under obedience, and
whilst she is unmarried, if she would learn anything, let her ask
you, and afterwards her husband, *at home.* Had St Paul lived in our
times I am most confident he would have fixed a shame upon our
women for writing (as well as for their speaking) in the Church.
[*(b) pp. 500–1*]

Nancy, however, is not to be dissuaded, and repeats her determination
to learn Latin and Greek in a letter to her godfather. He replies.

My dear child, – nothing but yourself, could have been so welcome
as your letter, nor have surprised me more, for I must confess I did
not think you had been guilty of so much learning as I see you are;
and yet it seems you rest unsatisfied or else you would not
threaten Latin, Greek, and Hebrew too. Good sweetheart be not so
covetous; believe me a Bible (with the Common prayer) and a
good plain catechism in your mother tongue being well read and
practised, is well worth all the rest and much more suitable to your
sex; I know your father thinks this false doctrine, but be confident
your husband will be of my opinion. In French you cannot be too
cunning for that language affords many admirable books fit for
you as romances, plays, poetry, stories of illustrious (not learned)
women, receipts for preserving, making creams and all sorts of
cookery, ordering your gardens and in brief all manner of good
housewifery. If you please to have a little patience with yourself
(without Hebrew, Greek, or Latin) when I go to Paris again I will
send you half a dozen of the French books to begin your library.
[*(a) pp. 501–2*]

America, 1698   *William **Fitzhugh** writes to George Mason, a merchant, about his son*
Henry, aged eleven.

Sir, – By this comes a large and dear consignment from me, the
consignment of a son to your care and conduct. I am well pleased
and assure my self of a careful and ingenious manage, if you will
please to undertake it; the general good character of your most
virtuous lady, who I must esteem the cape merchant in the
adventure, puts me under the assurance, that he will be as well, if
not better, under your conduct there, than he can be possibly with
us here. He is furnished with clothes only for his sea voyage, for I

thought it was needless to make him up clothes here for his wear there, because it might be there better and more suitably done, therefore I shall refer to you for furnishing of him with what is fit and decent, as befits an honest planter or farmer's son, not with what's rich or gaudy, I shall refer that to your own discretion. Now Sir to tell you that he is eleven years and a half old, and can hardly read or write a word of English might make you believe that either he was a dull boy, or that I was a very careless and neglectful parent. Indeed it's neither carelessness in me nor dullness in him, for although he cannot read or write English, yet he can both read, write and speak French, and has run over the rudiments of the Latin grammar, according to the French method, for he has been a considerable time with a most ingenious French gentleman, a minister who had the government and tutorage of him, and indeed did it singularly well, but the unhealthfulness of his seat and the sickliness of the child, occasioned his remove from thence. Therefore if it could be as Captain Jones tells me it may, I would have him put to a French schoolmaster, to continue his French and learn Latin. Now Captain Jones tells me there is such a school or two, about three or four miles from Bristol, and if it could conveniently be done, I would have him boarded at the school-master's house. Now Sir, I have told you my mind and how I would have him managed if I could, I must at last say in general terms, that I refer the whole to your discreet and prudent manage, assuring my self that if you are pleased to undertake the trouble, you will do by him as if he were a child or relation of your own, and shall without more saying, refer him wholly to your conduct, and hope within a week after his arrival you will contrive him to his business; what's necessary for him, either for books, clothes or now and then a little money to buy apples, plums, etcetera is left solely to your self and all charges shall be punctually answered you and thankfully acknowledged. [*pp. 361–2*]

Thomas **Tryon** *advises how to teach children to read and write.*   *England, late 17th century*

At a year and a half, or two years old show them their letters, not troubling them in the vulgar way, with asking them what is this letter, or that word; but instead thereof, make frequent repetitions in their hearing, putting the letters in their sight. And thus in a little time, they will easily and familiarly learn to distinguish the twenty-four letters, all one as they do the utensils, goods, and furniture of the house, by hearing the family name them. At the same time, teach your children to hold the pen, and guide their hand; and by this method, your children, unaccountably to themselves, will attain to read and write at three, four or five years old . . .

In learning, languages, sciences, arts or trades, observe this method viz: so many sciences or arts your child learns, divide the day into so many parts; if he learns two, divide the day in two parts; if three divide the day in three parts, and so on. Set each child his task, and let it be rather too little, than too much, that the child may be easy, and no ways discouraged.

When your children are of dull capacities, and hard to learn, reproach them not, nor expose them, but taking them alone, talk to them familiarly; and give them sweet and soft words, show them the advantages of learning, and how much it will tend to their advancements; intermixing in your discourse the praise of all ingenious men, which your children will know. [pp. 117–18, 121–3]

America, 1706   *Coitton **Mather** writes in his diary about his son Samuel, aged six.*

About this time, sending my little son to school, where the child was learning to read, I did use every morning for diverse months, to write in a plain hand for the child, and send thither by him, a *lesson* in *verse*, to be not only *read*, but also got my heart. My proposal was, to have the child improve in *goodness* at the same time, that he improved in reading. [*Mather (b), vol. 7, p. 555*]

In 1710 he notes of his daughters.

To accomplish my little daughters for housekeeping, I would have them, at least once a week, to prepare some new thing, either for diet, or medicine; which I may show them described in some such treatise as the *Family Dictionary*. [*Mather (b), vol. 8, p. 51*]

When Samuel reached eleven, Cotton decided . . .

[To] entertain *Sammy* betimes, with the first rudiments of geography and astonomy, as well as history; and so raise his mind above the sillier diversions of childhood. [*Mather (b), vol. 8, p. 473*]

America, 1711   *Timothy **Edwards** writes to his wife about the education of his son Jonathan, aged eight, and his five younger daughters.*

I desire thee to take care that Jonathan don't lose what he hath learnt, but that as he hath got the accidence and about two sides of Propia quae maribus by heart, so that he keep what he hath got, I would therefore have him say pretty often to the girls. I would also have the girls keep what they have learnt of the Grammar, and get by heart as far as Jonathan hath learnt; he can keep them as far as he had learnt. And would have both him and them keep their writing, and therefore write much oftener than they did when I was a home. I have left paper enough for them which they may use to that end. [*p. 93*]

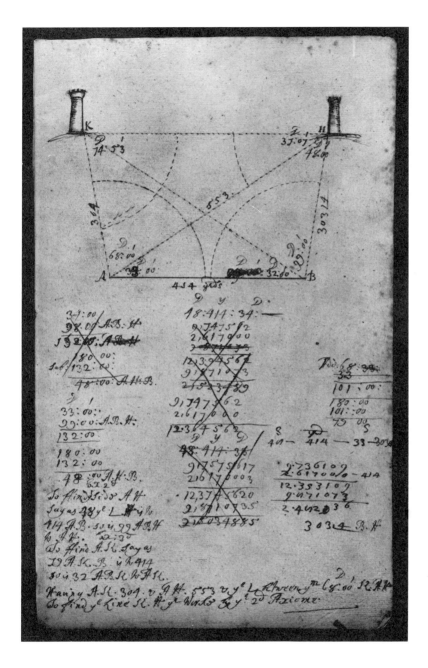

Extract from the mathematics exercise book of a child of the
Barrell family, c1700.

England, 1719   *Extract from the accounts for the education and maintenance of John* **Dryden** *while a student at Christ Church, Oxford.*

1 February.	[£	s	d]
A week's allowance	0	10	6
Putting up pegs for cloths and moving things	0	1	6
For coals	0	12	0
A basin, plates and pitcher	0	1	10
To the university beadle	0	2	6
Bought *The gentleman's calling*	0	2	6

15 February.			
A fortnight's allowance	1	1	0
For 3 pair of gloves	0	3	9
Bringing the bureau from London	0	4	0
An hat and hat box	0	12	6
Bought *Gordon's Geograph Grammar*	0	5	0
Oats and beans 13s 6d, six poor men 1s	0	14	6

22 February.			
A week's allowance	0	10	6
Coals 4s, new key 1s 6d	0	5	6

29 February.			
A week's allowance	0	10	6
Gilt paper 5s, a basin 3d	0	5	3

7 March.			
A week's allowance	0	10	6
A pair of buckles	0	1	0
For Sir John's first letter	0	5	0
Oats and beans	0	13	6

14 March.			
A week's allowance	0	10	6
A tea kettle	0	5	0
For coals	0	8	0
A velvet cap for riding	0	15	0

21 March.			
A week's allowance	0	10	6
Making the best gown	1	1	0
Paid the mercer's bill for that gown	27	16	0
For 3 pair of thread stockings	0	10	6
Poor debtor's box 1s, a letter 3d	0	1	3

30 March.

Week's allowance	0	10	6
A chamber pot 6d, faggots 18d, shoe brush 2d	0	2	2
To the laundress this quarter	1	0	0
To the bedmaker ditto	1	0	0
To the servitor ditto	0	1	0
To the barber ditto	1	0	0
For a natural wig	2	10	0
Cleaning a sword etcetera, 2s, dyeing silk stockings 1s	0	3	0
For chamber rent this quarter	2	2	0
Dancing master ditto	1	10	0
Battles in the buttery ditto	3	8	0
For commons ditto	2	16	8
For tuition	5	5	0
For standing of the mare	2	10	0
For boots and shoes	0	16	0
[Total	108	3	8]

[D(CA) 311]

*Mary **Grafton**, sent to school in Philadelphia, writes to her father in Delaware.* America, 1739

Honoured Sir, – Since my coming up I have entered with Mr Hackett to improve my dancing, and hope to make such progress therein as may answer to the expense, and enable me to appear well in any public company. The great desire I have of pleasing you will make me the more assiduous in my undertaking, and if I arrive at any degree of perfection it must be attributed to the liberal education you bestow on me. I am with greatest respect, dear Papa, Your dutiful daughter. [*p. 111*]

*Ephraim **Williams** instructs his son Elijah at Princeton College.* America, 1750s

I would entreat you to endeavour daily to improve yourself in writing and spelling; they are very ornamental to a scholar and the want of them is an exceeding great blemish.

I desire you would observe in your writing to make proper distances between words; don't blend your words together, use your utmost endeavours to spell well; consult all rules likely to help you; such words as require it always being with a capital letter, it will much grace your writing. Try to mend your hand in writing every day all opportunities you can possibly get. Observe strictly Gentleman's method of writing and superscribing, it may be of service to you: you can scarce conceive what a vast disadvantage it will be to leave the college and not be able to write and spell well. Learn to write a pretty fine hand as you may have occasion. [*pp. 158–9*]

England, 1769   *William Whately writes to John **Grimston** about the merits of Harrow for Thomas Grimston's education.*

Your favourite accomplishment of drawing is not taught at Harrow and indeed besides the usual school learning and writing etcetera, I believe nothing is taught but dancing and Tassonic the dancer being lately engaged as dancing master to the school, your son is to receive his instructions ... The entrance fees to the master tutors etcetera vary according to the parent's circumstances and desires and I chose in this respect to put your son upon a footing with the best in the school, a little money on these occasions is I always think well bestowed. [*pp. 85–6*]

America, 1771   *Henry **Laurens** writes to his daughter Martha, aged twelve.*

I have recollected your request for a pair of globes, therefore I have wrote to Mr Grubb to ship a pair of the best eighteen inch, with caps and a book of directions, and to add a case of neat instruments, and one dozen Middleton's best pencils marked M.L. When you are measuring the surface of the globe remember you are to cut a part in it, and think of a plum pudding and other domestic duties. [*p. 78*]

America, 1772   *Richard **Lee** writes to his brother about his two sons, Ludwell, aged eleven, and Thomas, aged thirteen. He has decided to send them to England for their education.*

'Tis the care of my dear boys that I recommend to you with true parental warmth. Their welfare you may be sure is deeply at my heart. Great reflection, aided by observation, and my own experience, sufficiently convince me, that education is much cheaper obtained in England, than in any part of America, our college excepted. But there, so little attention is paid either to the learning, or the morals of boys that I never could bring myself to think of William and Mary.

In either of the Northern Colonies, the avowed charge with their various items will be more than an hundred sterling per annum. The sum beyond which I cannot afford now to go, is £30 sterling apiece for board, clothing and education. This sum either at St Bees, Warrington in Lancashire, or with the gentleman near Bristol will certainly do, as well from the accounts you have given me as from the information [I have?]. Whichever of these will best answer the purpose of education, there I would have them sent without delay, because, at their time of life, they forget very quickly, and now, they are good scholars so far as they have gone. I propose Thomas for the Church, and Ludwell for the Bar. A tolerable share of learning is requisite for either of these professions. About fifteen years old Ludwell may be entered of one of the Inns of Court, and actually come there to study law at eighteen. So that he may return with the Gown at twenty-one. We shall hereafter consider the cheapest, and fittest place for the eldest, until the time comes that he can be ordained. He is fourteen years old next October, and Ludwell twelve the same month. I am sorry the schools mentioned are so far removed from you, because I well know how apt they are to neglect boys at a distance. You will infinitely oblige me, by falling on the best possible plan to remedy this too common and pernicious evil. If some gentleman living near the place, could be persuaded to observe how they proceed, or when any of your acquaintance may be passing by the place, to call and enquire. But above all, frequently to remind the master of his duty, and know often from the boys themselves (for they can write well) how they go on, and what books they are reading. They have never yet learned arithmetic, it may be proper soon to have them entered in this branch. [*Lee (1), vol. 1, pp. 70–72*]

Theodosia **Burr** *informs her husband Aaron of the progress of their eight-year-old daughter.*   America, 1791

Theodosia is quite recovered, and makes great progress at ciphering. I cannot say so much in favour of her writing. I really think she lost the last month she went to Shepherd. She has not improved since last spring. She is sensible of it, is the reason she is not very desirous to give you a specimen. We now keep her chiefly at figures, which she finds very difficult, particularly to proportion them, and place them straight under each other. [*vol. 1, pp. 301–2*]

Aaron Burr was exceedingly interested in his daughter's education, writing to his wife three months later.

Theodosia must not attempt music in the way she was taught last spring. For the present, let it be wholly omitted. Neither would I have her renew her dancing till the family are arranged. She can proceed in her French, and get some teacher to attend her in the house for writing and arithmetic. She has made no progress in the latter, and is even ignorant of the rudiments. She was hurried through different rules without having been able to do a single sum with accuracy. I would wish her to be also taught geography, if a proper master can be found. [*vol. 1, pp. 304–5*]

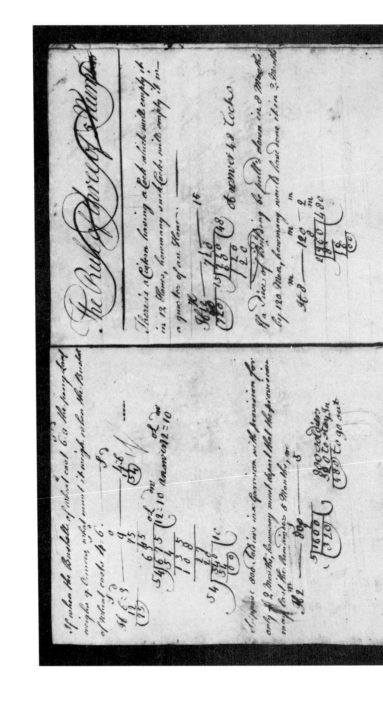

The Rule of Three of Numbers

There is a Cistern having a Cock which will empty it
in 12 Hours, how many such Cocks will empty it in
a quarter of an hour? —

$$\frac{70}{12}$$ 16

answer 48 Cocks

If a Sieve of Wheat... be fill'd down in 8 Months
by 120 Men, how many men would have done it in 3 Months?

When the Bushells of wheat cost 6:3 the firry [firkin?]
weight, 7 ounces, what must it weigh when the Bushel
of wheat costs 4:6 —

answer 12:10

Extract from John Bach's mathematics exercise book, 1774

If when the bushell of wheat cost 6s:3d the peny loaf weighs
9 ounces, what must it weigh when the bushell of wheat costs
4s:6d

. . .

answer 12 oz = 10dr

Suppose 800 soldiers in a garrison with provision for only
2 months, how many must depart that the provision may last
the remainder 5 months,

. . .

800 soldiers
320 to stay in
– – –
480 to go out

There is a cistern having a cock which will empty it in 12
hours, how many such cocks will empty it in a quarter of an
hour

. . .

answer 48 cocks

If a piece of building be pull'd down in 8 months by 120 men,
how many would have done it in 2 months

Northamptonshire Record Office, T(KEL) 106

As Theodosia grew older she studied Latin and Greek and was required by her father to keep a daily journal for his inspection. He used her letters to him as teaching material. For instance, in 1794 he writes.

When your letters are written with tolerable spirit and correctness, I read them two or three times before I perceive any fault in them, being wholly engaged with the pleasure they afford me; but, for your sake, it is necessary that I should also peruse them with an eye of criticism. The following are the only misspelled words. You write *acurate* for *accurate*; *laudnam* for *laudanum*; *intirely* for *entirely*; this last word, indeed, is spelled both ways, but entirely is the most usual and the most proper.

Continue to use all these words in your next letter, that I may see that you know the true spelling. And tell me what is laudanum? Where and how made? And what are its effects? [*vol. 1, p. 370*]

England, 1791   *Charlotte **Papendiek** recollects how she tried to provide her children with a good education.*

Our children were growing up, and their education becoming a matter of importance; and then followed the consideration of how this was best to be accomplished . . .

Schools at that time, for girls, as well as boys, were resorted to for every rank, from the nobility to the lowest classes . . . My desire was that my girls should remain as day scholars with Mrs Roach, where they would continue under my guidance, and I could watch their daily progress, knowing at the same time that they were with a woman of strict principle if not altogether of the ornamental manner of good breeding. In addition to this very great advantage, we were surrounded by superior masters in all branches of education, of whose talents and instruction we could avail ourselves without difficulty.

Frederick for the present was going on remarkably well at Mr Ward's, and we hoped to be able to keep him there. Female and household duties that had been early inculcated at Streatham, and not neglected at home, I hope I followed up, not only from the bent of my mind, but from the desire of acting rightly; and these duties I looked forward to imparting to my girls as soon as they were old enough to profit by my instructions.

All these desires, I am thankful to say, I have been enabled to fulfil, and I am sure that my daughters will give me credit for having done my best to bring them up as useful and right-minded members of society. In starting young people in the world it was necessary then, as now, that they should have a good education or some fortune. As we could not amass the latter, we determined that our children should have as good an education as we could possibly manage to give them, and in this matter I assisted as far as in me lay. I was constantly looking after the progress they made, urging them to perseverance, and exhorting them against any inclination to indolence; idleness, or self-will. This earnestness in me may be termed severity, and perhaps it savours of it, but to do my duty was ever my favourite theme. I loved my children more than life – I wished them to excel, and if I made them sometimes unhappy or uncomfortable they know now, indeed they knew then, that all was done in affectionate zeal for their welfare and that I sincerely regret any undue impetuosity. [*vol. 2, pp. 279–82*]

Nathaniel **Saltonstall** *writes to his son Leverett, aged thirteen.*   *America, 1796*

Dear son, – I hope you are contented in your present situation and that every thing is agreeable to your expectation. It would give me great pleasure to hear of your good behaviour and that you love and prosecute your studies, that in the youthful period of your life, such a foundation for knowledge may be fixed, as will, in fortune, distinguish you as a valuable and eminent member of society. Although I desired that you might apply to the languages, yet I hope it will not be to the neglect of writing, English grammar and whatever else that can with propriety be taught to a Latin scholar – but in these, it's probable your preceptor will dictate, yet there is knowledge to be gained by your applications in some of your leisure hours, and I think you will not be called an idle lad, but make such improvements, as will do you honour. [*vol. 2, p. 30*]

He writes to Leverett again in 1797.

I am pleased with your progress in the Latin and hope that equal advances are made in the Greek and every other branch of literature. I should be more gratified in perceiving a greater improvement in writing; but your late letters appear to be wrote with inattention and in great speed, which ought never to be done more especially by a youth; but the greatest care and exactness ought to be attended to, yea, with as much endeavour as if you were exerting yourself for a high position, for the approbation of your parents ought ever to be esteemed equal to any reward you can receive. Therefore [I] repeat my request you pay [as] great attention to writing as well as arithmetic, both of which are absolutely necessary to complete the scholar. [*vol. 2, p. 41*]

The curriculum for Frank **Dryden** *tutored at home by Mr Denison.*   *England, early 19th century*

Before breakfast 7 to 9
After [breakfast] from 10 to 1
After dinner from 4 to 6

	Before Breakfast		After Dinner		
Monday	Greek Homer	Mathematics	French history	Cicero	Latin verse
Tuesday	Greek prose	Logic	French history	Virgil	Rhetoric
Wednesday	Greek Homer	Mathematics	French history	Cicero	Latin verse
Thursday	Greek prose	Logic	French history	Virgil	Rhetoric
Friday	Greek Homer	Mathematics	French history	Cicero	Latin verse
Saturday	Greek prose	Logic	French history	Virgil	Rhetoric

Mr Denison to give Frank a theme alternately in Latin and English from history to compose of an evening, beginning first with narration and thus progressively to the higher species of composition to finish it for Mr Denison's examination in the morning. [D(CA) 283]

England, 1817   *Sydney **Smith** to J.A. Murray enquiring about a possible school for his son Douglas, aged twelve.*

Mr Pillar's method appears to be very good, but the great consideration is the ultimate result; to what age do boys who go through the school stay? Can they during the two last years of their stay construe (I allude to a boy of fair abilities) any of the plays of Sophocles and Euripides? Can they construe Homer, Herodotus – and the narrative part of Thucydides, what ever part of these authors their examiner may choose to turn to? Can they write decent Latin verse and prose? Are these things done publicly in the annual examination of the first class? [*vol. 1, pp. 281–2*]

England, c.1830   *Mary **Sewell**, as a mother, sets out her views on the education of children.*

I should be very glad to see the art of drawing from nature more systematically and thoroughly carried out in the education of young girls. I have often thought if half the time were given to that which is now all but exclusively devoted to music, it would prove, if not a more valuable acquisition, at any rate to the full as valuable – I think far more valuable to those who are likely to have the care of children, which all may expect in some way. A lady who has a free use of her pencil, and able to make a ready sketch of any living thing she sees, is sure to attract a group of delighted children around her. [*pp. 106–7*]

Children, she suggests, should be taught the art of observation.

The value of the habit of accurate observation is not to be told, nor the unceasing occupation and interest it has given to children. In the way a child obtains the power of using his own mind, and he

learns the value of current language and description. There would
be no end to lessons of this kind, including all natural and artificial
objects, and each one bringing fresh knowledge and, if the teacher
be skilful and cheerful, both moral and spiritual instruction . . .

Children led on after this manner will daily become less
troublesome and more interesting: they will find their own
amusements, and the more they learn, the more independent will
they become of toys and nursemaids . . .

Again, give them a piece of quicklime and a little water, a
handful of sand and the same, a lump of clay, and so on. Draw
their attention to effervescence, absorption, moulding, etcetera.
Show them then the effect of an acid on an alkali; give different
simple experiments in dyeing, extraction of colour, going on step
by step (for you can scarcely set one intelligent step in natural
history but another must follow it), and before you are aware, your
little ones are on the borders of science – yes, they have got their
little feet within the charmed line before they can even read.

Weighing and measuring are quite within the compass of a
child under eight years old, and with scales and weights and a
marked measuring line, and a little, a very little, calm distinct help,
they will learn the rudiments of long measure and avoirdupois
weight much more delightfully and intelligently than in the
visionary tables of weights and measures submitted to the jaded
memory. The relative weights connected with the bulk of different
materials would amuse children for many an hour. [*pp. 109–11*]

Elizabeth **Pratt**, *aged eleven, writes to her brother who has been sent to school in England.*   America, 1832

I find you have got the start of me in learning very much, for you
write better already than I can expect to do as long as I live; and
you are got as far as the rule of three in arithmetic, but I can't cast
up a sum in addition cleverly, but I am striving to do better every
day. I can perform a great many dances and am now learning the
sibell [?] , but I cannot speak a work of French. [*p. 195*]

Sara **Coleridge** *to her husband on their son Herbert, aged three.*   England, 1833

Herby begins his lesson now with 'Oo shan't dodge me!' but I tell
him (or tell myself rather) that without dodging no scholar was
ever made. Short instructions at a time, and thorough cross-
examination of those given, is the system I would go upon
teaching. Be sure that the first step is *really* taken before you
attempt to proceed, and don't fancy that children will listen to
lectures, either in learning or morality. [*vol. 1, p. 66*]

She describes to Mrs Plummer in 1835 the intellectual attainments of her son.

Herby is reported to be a forward child, and we have many admonitions against pushing, cramming, and over refining, which are all very just and sensible, and will, I hope, keep us from straying into the wrong path. But I cannot think we have been betrayed into it yet; neither would our admonishers think so, if they understood the whole state of the case. The child in question has a show of Coleridgian quickness, and bookishness, and liveliness of mind. He retains what he learns pretty well, and is mighty fond of sporting it afterwards, which he does with great vehemence and animation. For instance, he informs every one he meets that Chimborasco, whatever Coley may say on the subject, is not so high as Dhawalagiri, the highest of the Himalayas; and that he is not certain that the wedding of Mr and Mrs Day (domestics at his Uncles Patteson's, in Bedford Square), was not nearly so grand as that of Peleus and Thetia, on Mount Pelion. He is at this moment bent upon making bilberry preserve at Keswick, and rosefruit-jam from hips that must be gathered on Mount Caucasus. Hearing him talk in this way gives some people a notion that he is *crammed*. I can only say that I put no food into his mind which is not prepared as carefully for his childish digestion as the pap and panada which are recommended for infants; and he certainly never has any more of it at a time than he has the fullest appetite for. He hears certain stories about Troy and other antiquities over and over again, and looks at coloured plates of flowers which are lent me, and gradually learns some of their names; and he is actually fond of poring over maps, and tracing the course of rivers. But what is there in all this (*done in the way he does it!*) which can strain the intellect, or over load the mind of a young child? I assure you nobody can be more careful than I am not to err on these points, for I am fully aware of the mischief both to body and mind which may be caused thereby; but at the same time we all know that there is much in habit, in the gradual training both of hand and muscles. My boy will have to go through the mental labour required in a public school, and in after-life he will have to gain his bread by head-work. I cannot therefore follow the advice of those who say, Let him run about all day, and leave books entirely alone. I feel sure that such a plan would not be for his welfare, either for the present or in the long run. [*pp. 125–6*]

England, 1838 *Priscilla* **Johnston** *considers how children should be taught.*

I think it is right to take pains to cultivate the eyes and ears of children for nature – the flowers, clouds, sea, birds, all help. I do not so much point out to my children as express my own pleasure and admiration, and it is caught in a moment; also I think if young children are afraid of the dark, the weakness ought to be most tenderly dealt with, by perhaps walking about the house together without a candle, talking and telling stories, and enjoying the quiet dark. Our lessons are very pleasant; we have today finished the second page of three-letter words, and I think shall begin them again. We spell, look at pictures in infantine knowledge, read over the alphabet, and, for a treat, find and mark all the o's or any other letter in a page. Then Scripture illustrations; we look at a picture and talk about it – one picture lasts us several days. Sunday is made very much of a treat: the cake, clean clothes, a large picture Bible, walks with papa and mamma in the garden – we quite count the days till it will be Sunday. [*p. 142*]

*Lucy **Lovell** on her daughter Caroline, aged four.*   *America, 1841*

She has learned almost wholly of her own accord, the alphabet, and the figures, and reads and spells in words of two letters, counts and recites the multiplication table through the first line, for amusement. [*p. 73*]

It was very interesting to teach her, because she received ideas so readily, and although we did not attempt to give her regular school learning, and never sent her to school except during one summer to sabbath school, yet she was always learning. [*p. 80*]

She loved to count, and one day said she was going to count a thousand. I did not think she would have patience to go through with it, and should have been glad to have her desist from such a protracted effort of the mind. But she persevered until she had accomplished it, which she did, I think in the course of an hour, with a very little help from me. [*p. 80*]

*Blanche **Dundas** writes to her friend Sara Wilson, who has been sent to*   *England, 1871*
a finishing school.

I am curious to know how you like your new way of life . . . I shall hope to hear from you when you are settled that you like it and are working hard – I wish I had had your chance of improving myself but brothers howsoever charming they may be are expensive creatures and take *all* the money, and the sisters have to grow up ignorant and make their own dresses, neither of which processes is pleasant nor am I enamoured of either; so take the sage advice of one of twenty-four years and *make the most of your time*, when next we meet I shall expect a prodigy of accomplishments, having no brother to swallow up all the money you can stay as long as you like. [*DDPH242*]

Geography continued

21 State particulars respecting Chelsea, Windsor
Lincoln, Wolverhampton Leeds Liverpool
Chelsea Hospital for old and disabled sailors arsenal ships built
Windsor Usual residence of The Sovereing
Lincoln fine roman gateway Cathedral acient town
Wolverhampton Steam Engines locks and keys
Leeds Broad cloth
Liverpool ship building word pork
22 What kind of country is Scotland?
Poor compared to England and in some parts good
23 State the capes of Scotland?
St Abbs ness, Fife Ness, Buchan Ness, Kinnardo Hd,
Dunnet Hd, Tarbet Ness. Burrow Hd., Wrath Mull of
Galoway, Hebberidees.
24 Name the Principal Islands?
Orkenys Shetlands and the Hebiridies Arran Bute
25 What kind of State is Ireland?
In a backward state
26 State some particulars respecting the Irish people?
They are very rebellious out of every 100 more than
one third are roman catholic.
27 Wheat of the Globe is Ammerica?
North West
28 Why is Ammerica called the new world?
Beacaud it as lakly be discovered
29 Why is Europe Asia and Africa called the old world
Because it is been long Discovered
30 State what direction is Europe lies from Australia
and Asia from Africa?
South West. North East. South West.

H. Bonham

Extract from the geography test given to H Bonham, C19th

[The teacher's corrections are placed in brackets]

Geography continued

21 State particulars respecting Chelsea, Windsor, Lincoln,
    Wolverhampton, Leeds, Liverpool
    Chelsea (hospital) for old and disabled sailors arsnal ship
    builders
    Windsor Usual residance of the Sovereing
    Lincoln fine roman gateway cathedral ancient town
    Wolverhampton Steam engines locks and keys
    Leeds Broad cloth
    Liverpool ship building second port

22 What kind of country is Scotland?
    Poor compared to England and in some parts good

23 State the capes of Scotland?
    St Abbs ness, Fife Ness, Buchan Ness, Rinndards Hd
    Dunmett Hd, Tarbet Ness, Burrow Hd, Wrath Mull of
    Galloway, Hebberidees.

24 Name the principal islands?
    Orkennys Shetlands and the Heberidies Arran Bute

25 What kind of (state) is Ireland?
    In a backward state

26 State some particulars respecting the Irish people?
    They are very rebellious out of every 100 more than
    one third is (are) roman catholic

27 What of the globe is Ammerica?
    North West

28 Why is Ammerica called the new world?
    Because it as lately be discovered

29 Why is Europe Asia and Africa called the old world?
    Because it is been long discovered

30 State what direction is Europe lies from Australia and
    Asia from Africa?
    South West. North East. South West

Northamptonshire Record Office ZB 556/21/2

England, 1889 *Thomas* **Cobden-Sanderson** *records in his diary his plan for the education of his son Richard, aged five.*

It occurs to me that I must bestir myself and do something for Dickie in the way at once of amusement and education. And the following media suggest themselves.

Folding paper along ruled lines and cutting with scissors and paper knife. Hammering nails into board to make a pattern – dotting the nails beforehand: also pushing in drawing pins. Also driving in screws for ditto: also sticking pieces of wood together. Making windmills and teaching him to make them for himself. Making boxes. Brick building. Balancing. Standing on heights. Lifting small weights. Gymnastics (book of gym). Tracing letters and outlines. Cutting out big letters (posters) and pasting on letters. Before sewing teaching to prick holes with big needle. Sewing with coloured threads through dotted holes in cardboard to make patterns to hang on nursery walls. Knot making. Needle-threading. Buckling. Fastening up parcels (coats, etcetera, with straps). Arranging pressing boards carefully one above the other. Sorting pressing boards, etcetera into sizes. Sawing wood. Carrying (horizontally with small weights on) longish pressing boards from one end of the room to the other. Drawing straight lines with pencil, straight edge and square. Measuring distances with dividers or rather adjusting dividers to given lengths of distances.

Acting little stories and parables and fables. Reading stories with pictures, parables and fables, etcetera. Teaching him to tell them to me again. Reading to him little poems. Teaching him to learn accurately by heart:

Politeness	Unselfishness	Application
Kindness	Fortitude	Attention
Obedience	Courage	Modesty
Patience	Truthfulness	Reverence
	Self-control	

[*vol, 1, pp. 277–8*]

I WOULD THERE WERE NO AGE BETWEEN 10 AND 23: INTERGENERATIONAL CONFLICT AND OTHER PROBLEMS

Introduction

Parents in the propertied classes saw it as their duty to provide a framework of instruction to guide their offspring through life. They wished to warn inexperienced youths of the pitfalls and hazards which would be encountered in the world, as well as supplying them with the rules of behaviour essential for social success. Advice to sons and, occasionally daughters, became a recognized genre, popular from the sixteenth to the eighteenth centuries. These works illustrated the ideal of manners and behaviour of an age, the standards of conduct which parents hoped their son or daughter would attain, and the ruling principles upon which they hoped their children would base their future life pattern. The texts were typically a mixture of religious instruction, admonitions and exhortations, combined with practical, more worldly counsel. The selections given in this chapter are from parental instructions contained in family paper collections. These – as is the case with Sarah Cowper (p. 250) who copied Lord Burghley's popular instruction manual – could be plagiarized from printed books.

Throughout the centuries, certain themes reverberate. There was an insistance on honesty and integrity, and an emphasis on honour and the necessity of comporting oneself with dignity and breeding. They considered youth to be a valuable learning period in which a sound foundation for a young person's later progress through life could be constructed. Thus, there was a stress on avoiding idleness, of instead devoting the time to self-improvement, and endeavouring to bring the golden promise of these years to fruition. For women the emphasis was on modesty, reticence, delicacy and virtue. Justinian Isham's daughters were to be chaste, obedient, meek, modest, silent, affable and frugal (p. 249). Guidelines were set out for the handling of all aspects of adult life: choosing a wife, running an estate or business, organizing the home, bringing up children, making oneself socially acceptable and borrowing or lending money. Parents were not only presenting their sons or daughters with a code of conduct to ease the transition from childhood to adulthood, but also attempting to maintain some control over their adult offspring, or at least to exert some influence over their behaviour. How much authority parents wished to retain, and how much autonomy young people sought, is the topic of 'Intergenerational Conflict'.

Conflict between parents and children arose over many issues: among them marriage, money, employment choice, and a lack of consideration for parental wishes. Marriage among the propertied classes not only involved the transference of property but was also a means of expanding the circle of kin who could be asked for help. It was therefore a matter of too great importance to leave only to the desires of the young couple involved. These marriages have been labelled 'arranged', and this does suggest that parents had the first and final say in the matter. A recognition that parents in the upper classes would wish to exercise some power over their offspring's choice of spouse, and an acknowledgement that children agreed that their parents were entitled to wield some influence, does not, however, imply that the children's rights in this matter were negligible. The choice of marriage partner was undoubtedly a major bone of contention through the centuries, but young people were rarely forced into a match against their will. They may, as in the case of Mary Rich (p. 259), have had to withstand severe parental pressure, but ultimately parents faced with a determined child would concede defeat. In most families matters would not get this far, since most parents appreciated that there was no point in forcing two people to marry, and create unhappiness for all concerned. Parents were more likely to be angered by a child marrying someone they disapproved of than by a child refusing someone the parents approved of (Landon Carter, p. 274, and Caroline Capel, p. 275). The same sentiment influenced their reaction to a child's dislike of a career favoured by the parents: if the son disliked the employment, compelling him to stay could only bring more problems (Henry Oxinden, p. 261).

Parents were reluctant to cast off an erring child, and were distressed by long periods of conflict. They were certainly prepared to threaten disinheritance (Ludovic Gordon-Cummings, p. 267, and Nicholas Blundell, p. 271), or even to exact a financial penalty if a child disobeyed them (Mary Rich, p. 259), but the complete exclusion of a child from the family's society and wealth was rarely put into practice. It was the last weapon for ensuring conformity possessed by parents, and they were exceedingly reluctant to use it (Ralph Josselin, p. 265). In stalemate situations, when neither child nor parent was prepared to compromise, outsiders would step into the breach on the side of the child (Anne Halkett, p. 262). Parents could also ask a wayward child to leave home, but even here they kept in contact, ensured the child had somewhere to live and a sufficient income for maintenance (John Skinner, p. 276). Though parents may have wished for obedience from older offspring, it is clear from the quotations that this was a privilege and not a right. Adult offspring were to be dutiful only to reasonable parents, and were prepared to remind parents of their obligations if it was felt they had failed in their duty (Charles Hatton, p. 263). The relationship between adult offspring and their parents was much more reciprocal, and much less parent-dominated, than has been envisaged by many historians.

Advice to Older Offspring

*Justinian **Isham**'s code of conduct for his daughters, the eldest of whom* England, 1642
is aged nine, composed after the death of their mother.

To my children, Jane, Elizabeth, Judith, Susan.

The uncertainty of man's life, of his course and condition whilst he is living, as also of the state of things where he lives; are motives sufficient to neglect no time, yes (so far as may be) to forerun time itself in the discharge of such duties especially which God and nature require of us. To you therefore (though now tender infants yet already half orphaned) I write this, which whether you live to read and observe, or my self to instruct you in, yet it will not repent me to have done my utmost both for the discharge of myself, and the manifestation of that dearest affection I bear towards you. But here let not be expected any general or exact treatise of a complete woman, but only a brief mention of what is most necessary relating chiefly to yourselves as my children whom I am first of all to instruct in the knowledge of another Father, the Father and Creator of all things. Him you may learn both in His word and works, as of the latter you are daily eye witnesses, so of the first you cannot be too diligent either readers or hearers, but then lean not wholly to your own sense of it, or make too much reasoning about it, but after your earnest prayers to be enlightened from above, go that way which the blessed spirit and your mother church shall guide you in . . . At all times therefore to have recourse unto God by prayer but especially in trouble, and he will hear you, by granting what you ask, or what he knows better for you. Prayers, meditations, and such like holy treatises, I rather commend unto you than knotty disputes; and although your sex is not so capable of those stronger abilities of the intellect, to make you so learned and knowing as men ought to be; yet be sure to keep your hearts upright and your affections towards God unfeigned and there is no doubt but that will be more acceptable unto him than all the wisdom of the whole world besides. St Augustine's Meditations, Kempe on The Imitation of Christ and Gerard's Meditations I commend unto you, as also Doctor Fealtie's Handmaid to Devotion and divers treatises of Doctor Sibbs often read over by your mother who was a religious and discreet woman. And this I believe, that no women in England have fairer examples to follow of their own sex and kindred on both sides (God be praised for them) than you have whose good names I doubt not will be still fresh unto you, that you as 'twere receiving light from them, will I hope shine as clear as they did upon those who may succeed you. Your imitation of divers of them (of one of which, Lady to the Lord Edward Mountague, you may chance meet with some observations of mine in a letter to her) will save me a labour of giving many precepts to you, there having been of our house both maids, wives and widows, all of a very virtuous and exemplary life. And this let me tell you, though a fair fortune and a fair face will never want suitors to them; yet I cannot say whether they have oftener availed, or betrayed their owners. However I am sure the internal graces of the mind will be your best and surest portion, both unto your selves, and unto men of such discretions as I believe you would willingly give yourselves unto. A virtuous woman is a good portion (saith Siracides) which shall be given as a gift to such as fear the Lord, so hear you see the best way to get a good husband, unto whom being virtuous you will be a very possession, nay more his crown and glory.

And now as there are many graces and virtues which women ought to be endued with, so you ought more especially to have regard unto those which the sacred scriptures direct you as most proper for your sex. As these more especially:

holiness	meekness	discretion
chastity	modesty	frugality
obedience	sobriety	affability
charity	silence	

Here you see the precepts what you ought chiefly to seek after, by which (as more directly in other places) their contraries are also forbid you: both which will be well worth your labours to example out of the scriptures, so out of your reading and observation elsewhere . . . [Isham (a), IC3415]

England, late 17th century   *Sarah* **Cowper** *copies into her commonplace book two letters of advice, one for each of her sons. These letters are almost verbatim transcripts of Lord Burghley's printed advice to his son.*

A letter collected for my son Will.

When it please God to bring thee to man's estate, use great providence and circumspection in the choice of thy wife for from thence will spring all future good or evil, and it is an action like a stratagem of war wherein a man can err but once. Enquire diligently of her education and how her parents have been inclined in their youth. Let her not be poor how generous soever, for a man can buy nothing in the market for gentility nor choose a base or uncomely creature though wealthy for it will cause contempt in others and loathing in thy self. Neither make choice of a dwarf nor a fool for by the one thou shalt beget a race of pygmies, and the other will be thy daily disgrace and it will irk thee to hear her talk for thou shalt find to thy great grief that there is nothing more irksome than a she-fool.

And touching the government of thy house let thy hospitality be moderate and according to the measure of thy estate, rather plentiful than sparing but not costly, for I never knew any grow poor by keeping of an ordinary table. But some consume themselves through secret vices and then hospitality bears the blame. But banish swinish drunkards out of thy house, that is a vice [which] impairs health, consumes much and makes no show. And I never heard praise ascribed to a drunkard, but the well bearing of drink which is a commendation fitter for a brewer's horse or a brayman than a gentleman. See that thou spend not above three of the four parts of thy revenue, nor above a third part of that in thine house for the other two parts will do no more than defray thy extraordinaries which will always surmount the ordinary by much, otherwise thou shalt live like a rich beggar in continual want and the needy man can never live happily nor content for every one left in an unfortunate estate makes him ready to sell lands and that gentleman that sells one acre of lands sells one ounce of credit, for gentility is nothing but ancient riches so that as the foundation shrinks the building must needs follow after.

Bring thy children up in learning and obedience yet without austerity. Praise them openly, reprehend them secretly. Give them good countenance and convenient maintenance according to thine ability otherwise thy life will seem bondage and what portion thou shalt leave them at thy death, they will thank death for it and not thee. The foolish cockering of some, and the over stern carriage of others causeth more men and women to take ill courses than their own vicious inclinations. Marry thy daughters lest they marry themselves; and suffer not thy sons to pass the Alps, for they shall bring home nothing but pride, blasphemy and atheism, and if by travelling they get a few broken languages it will profit them no more than to have one sort of meat served in divers dishes. Neither by my advice [be] trained up in war for that he that sets his rest to live in that can hardly be an honest or good christian for that every war is of it self unjust, except the cause make it just. Beside it is a science no longer in request than use, for soldiers in peace are like chimneys in summer.

Live not in the country without corn and cattle about thee for he that presents his hands to his purse for every expense is like him that thinketh to seek water in fire, and what provisions thou shalt want prepare to buy it at the first hand for there is a penny in four saved between buying at thy need and when the season and market serves fittest for it.

Be not served with kinsman, friends, or men entreated to serve for they will expect much and do little, nor with such as are amorous for their brains are ever intoxicated, and rather be served by two too few than one too many. Feed them well and pay them with the most and then thou must boldly require duty and service at their hands.

Beware of suretyship for thy best friends. He that playeth another man's debt seeks his own overthrow but if thou canst not choose rather lend thy money thy self upon good bonds though thou borrow, for so shalt [thou] both please thy friend and secure your self. Neither borrow money of a neighbour or friend but of a stranger – where paying for it thou shalt hear no more of it otherwise thou shalt eclipse thy credit, lose thy freedom and yet pay as dear as to another. But in borrowing be precious of thy word for he that hath a care to keep his day of payment is a lord over another man's goods.

Undertake no suit against any poor man without much reason for thou makest him thy competitor and it is base to triumph where there is small resistance. Neither attempt law with anyone before thou be thoroughly resolved that thou have right on thy side. Neither spare for money nor pains, for a cause or two so followed will free thee from suits a great part of thy life after.

Be sure to keep some gentleman thy friend but trouble him not with every trifling complaint. Often present him with many, yet small gifts: and if thou have cause to bestow any gratuity let it be such as may be daily in his sight; otherwise in this ambitious age thou shalt remain like a hop without a pole, live in obscurity and be made a footstool for every insulting companion to spur at.

Towards thy superiors be humbly generous, with thy equals familiar yet respective. Towards thy inferiors show much humility and some familiarity as to bow thy body, stretch forth thy hand and uncover thy head with such popular compliments. The first prepares the way to advancement, the second makes thee known for a man well bred, the third gains a man a good report which once being gotten is easily kept for humility takes such deep root in the mind of a multitude (who are more easily won by unprofitable courtesies than curious benefits) that I advise thee not to affect nor neglect popularity. Trust not any man with thy estate for it is a means thereby for a man to enthral himself to his friends as though if occasion be offered he should not dare to become his enemy.

Be not a scurrilous in thy conversation nor stoical in thy jests; the one will make thee unwelcome to all company, the other will breed quarrels and get thee hatred of thy best friends, for jests when they savour too much of truth leave bitterness in the minds of those that are touched. These nimble apprehensions are but the froth of wit. [D/EP/F37, ff. 49–53]

*Henry **Fletcher** compiled a small booklet on conduct and morals for his*   *Scotland, early*
son. This was divided into sections on general rules, devotion, medita-   *18th century*
tion, love, laziness, attention, business and conversation. This is his
advice on business.

If you would be a man of business, be sincere and upright in all your words and actions. Be diligent, faithful and exact in everything that is committed to you, and in such a manner that they who trust you to do their business, may reckon it surely done, in so far as the nature of the thing will allow. Do nothing superficially, but go to the bottom of every thing you attempt, and do it thoroughly. Let there be no darkness left as to the understanding of it, and no part thereof left unperformed and never delay a thing till the next hour that can be done this hour, for it is always best to be beforehand with your business. Dispatch is of great use and has raised many fortunes, as it did Cardinal Wolsey's and Monsieur Colbert's. Never prefer your pleasure or ease, to your business: there is more satisfaction and refreshment in one hour's sleep or divertisement after your business is over, than in twenty times as much before. Be methodical and regular in all your affairs, and punctual in the times of doing them.

If you observe these things, everyone will delight to have to do with you, and put their business in your hands; and then, as Solomon saith, you shall stand before princes, and not before mean men.

The pamphlet is concluded with the following piece of general advice.

Consider, what a pleasure and support it will be to your mother and me, to see you come back a modest discreet youth, honest and sincere, fearing God, and loving and respecting us, polite in your carriage having profited in your studies.

Consider what true satisfaction this will give to your self; what esteem and applause it will draw from others, remember that time passes quick and cannot be recalled, therefore employ it well, and press forward. If you mispend your time now, it will be bitter to us first, and at last to your self when there is no remedy. Therefore set about your duty with vigour, and acquit your self like a man: the way of virtue is indeed penible in the beginning, but it is pleasant in the progress, and glorious in the end. Remember what pains your mother and I have taken upon you to form you to that which is right, for which you will be one day accountable if you make not a right use of it. [*MS17780, ff. 17, 21*]

*William **Brattle** composed the following set of instructions for his only*   *America, 1716*
son William, who is preparing for university.

    1. Agreeably to what is written I Chronicles xxviii, 9, My dear

son, know thou the God of thy father, and serve him with a perfect heart, and with a willing mind. If thou seek him, he will be found of thee; but if thou forsake him, he will cast thee off for ever.

2. Think often of thine own frailty, and of the uncertainty and emptiness of all sublunary enjoyments. Value not self upon riches. Value not thy self upon any worldy advancement whatsoever. Let faith and goodness be thy treasure. Let no happiness content and satisfy thee but what secures the favour and peace of God unto thee.

3. Remember thy baptism, acquaint thy self well with the nature and obligations of that ordinance. Publicly renew thy baptismal covenant. Renew it seasonably in thy early days with humility and thirsty desire to enjoy communion with God in the ordinance of the Lord's Supper and in all approaches before God therein bringing faith and love and a self abasing sense of thine own emptiness and unworthiness.

4. Prize and esteem the holy word of God infinitely before the finest of gold. Reverence it with thy whole heart, read it constantly with seriousness, and great delight. Meditate much upon it, make it thy guide in all thy ways, fetch all thy comforts from thence, and by a religious and holy walk, establish thine interest in the blessed and glorious promises therein contained. . . .

5. Take care of thy health, avoid all excess in eating and in drinking, in taking thy pleasure, and in all innocent recreations whatsoever. Let not immoderate heat and cold needlessly expose thy body.

6. Beware of passion. Let not anger and wrath infect thine heart, suffer wrong with patience, rather than to right thy self by unchristian methods, or by suffering thy spirit to be out of frame.

7. Labour to establish thy self and beg of God that he would establish thee in the grace of chastity, keep thine heart clean and chaste, keep thine eyes clean and chaste. Never trust to thy self to be thy keeper, avoid temptations to uncleanness of every nature, be watchful over thy self night and day, but in the midst of all let thine heart be with God, and be thou much in prayer. That God would be thy keeper. Let all the incentives to lust as far as may be, be avoided by thee.

8. Speak the truth always. Let not a lie defile thy lips, be content with suffering rather than by telling the least lie to save thy self. Beware of shuffling off by dissimulation.

9. Let pride be an abomination in thy sight. Cloth thy self with humility. Let humility be thine under garment. Let humility be thine upper garment.

10. Despise no man, let the state of his body or mind or other circumstances of his, be what they will, still reverence humanity, consider who made thee to differ.

11. Be just to all men; be thou courteous and affable to all men; render not evil for evil, but recompense evil with good. Owe no man any thing but love.

12. Be thou compassionate, tender hearted, and merciful; do good to all men, be rich in good works, ready to distribute, willing to communicate; for with such sacrifices God is evermore well pleased.

13. Avoid sloth and idleness, give thy self to thy studies; converse with such authors as may tend to make thee wise and good and to forward thy growth in true wisdom and goodness.

14. Acquaint thy self with history; know something of the mathematics, and physic; be able to keep accompts merchant like in some measure; but let divinity be thy main study. Accomplish thy self for the work of the ministry, beg of God that he would incline thine heart thereto, and accept thee therein, and if it shall please God thus to smile upon thee, aspire not after great things; let the providence of God choose for thee, and let the flock have the love of thy heart; be solicitous for their spiritual good, and for the glory of God, and let thy aims be this way in all thy private meditations, and public administrations, all the days of thy life.

My dear child, be of Catholic spirit. [*pp. 284–5*]

The following regulations for conduct were composed by Dr **Gregory** *for the use of his own children. He included sections on religion, conduct and behaviour, amusements, friendship, love and marriage, and stressed the overriding importance of the place of religion in life. His instructions with regard to conduct and behaviour are given.*   *England, mid 19th century*

A Father's Legacy to his Daughters.

One of the chief beauties in a female character, is that modest reserve that retiring delicacy, which avoids the public eye, and is disconcerted even at the gaze of admiration. I do not wish you to be insensible to applause; if you were, you must become, if not worse, at least less amiable women: but you may be dazzled by that admiration which yet rejoices your hearts.

When a girl ceases to blush, she has lost the more powerful charm of beauty. That extreme sensibility which it indicates, may be a weakness and encumbrance in our sex, as I have too often felt; but in yours it is peculiarly engaging. Pedants, who think themselves philosophers, ask why a woman should blush, when she is conscious of no crime? It is a sufficient answer, that Nature has made you to blush, when you are guilty of no fault, and has forced us to love you because you do so. Blushing is so far from being necessarily an attendant on guilt, that it is the usual companion of innocence.

This modesty, which I think so essential in your sex, will

naturally dispose you to be rather silent in company, especially in a large one. People of sense and discernment will never mistake such silence for dullness. One may take a share in conversation without uttering a syllable. The expression in the countenance shows it, and this never escapes an observing eye.

I should be glad that you had an easy dignity in your behaviour at public places, but not that confident ease, that unabashed countenance, which seems to set the company at defiance. . . .

Converse with men even of the first rank with that dignified modesty which may prevent the approach of the most distant familiarity, and consequently prevent them from feeling themselves your superiors. Wit is the most dangerous talent you can possess. It must be guarded with great discretion and good nature, otherwise it will create you many enemies. Wit is perfectly consistent with softness and delicacy; yet they are seldom found united. Wit is so flattering to vanity, that they who possess it become intoxicated, and lose all self-command. Humour is a different quality. It will make your company much solicited; but be cautious how you indulge it. It is often a great enemy to delicacy, and a still greater one to dignity of character. It may sometimes gain you applause, but will never procure you respect. Be even cautious of displaying your good sense. It will be thought you assume a superiority over the rest of the company. But if you happen to have any learning, keep it a profound secret, especially from the men, who generally look with a jealous and malignant eye on a woman of great parts, and a cultivated understanding. . . .

Consider every species of indelicacy in conversation as shameful, in itself, and as highly disgusting to us. All double entendre is of this sort. The dissoluteness of men's education allows them to be diverted with a kind of wit, which yet they have delicacy enough to be shocked at, when it comes from your mouths, or even when you hear it without pain and contempt. Virgin purity is of that delicate nature, that it cannot bear certain things without contamination. It is always in your power to avoid these. No man but a brute or a fool, will insult a woman with conversation which he sees gives her pain; nor will he dare to do it, if she resent the injury with a becoming spirit. There is a dignity in conscious virtue which is able to awe the most shameless and abandoned of men.

You will be reproached with prudery. By prudery is usually meant an affectation of delicacy: Now I do not wish you to affect delicacy; I wish you to possess it: at any rate it is better to run the risk of being thought ridiculous than disgusting. . . .

You may perhaps think that I want to throw every spark of nature out of your composition, and to make you entirely artificial. Far from it. I wish you to possess the most perfect simplicity of heart and manners. I think you may possess dignity withou pride, affability without meanness, and simple elegance without affectation. Milton had my idea, when he says of Eve,

Grace was in all her steps, Heaven in her eye,
In every gesture dignity and love. [*pp. 11–16, 18–19*]

*Christopher **Parker** to his son John Oxley, aged eighteen, after the latter's matriculation at university.*　　　　England, 1830

You are now, my dear Oxley, launched into a new sphere, and much of your future happiness and prosperity depends upon the choice of your associates and in a proper employment of your time, not allowing pleasureable pursuits to improperly interfere with the duties you have to perform. Remember the time, though long in anticipation, is really short, that you will have the assistance of others, to gather that store of useful knowledge which will render you capable of selecting that line in future life that may best suit your taste and inclination, whether in business or profession. I repeat now what I heretofore mentioned in conversation, that I do not wish you at present to fix on the line in life you intend to pursue. You are yet very young and circumstances may alter your opinions. It will be my duty to give advice if I think you are in error, but it had not [been], and I hope never will be, my inclination to dictate that which may make you uncomfortable. I have great happiness in the reflection that up to the present time you have never intentionally caused me a moment's uneasiness. Anxiety I have often felt, but I have always been rewarded by grateful results. I feel confident the same good disposition which has hitherto governed your actions will continue to influence your conduct to the lasting comfort and happiness of us both. [*Parker (3), pp. 236–7*]

Two years later.

You are now at a time of life when every temptation is daily exciting you to join in pleasures and dissipations, many venial, but others that may injure your health and for ever ruin your constitution, and I regret to say, in many instances, lead to premature dissolution. God grant that you may by your own prudence escape danger and you may continue a blessing to me while living and a hope for protection to others when I am gone . . . Pray, my dear Oxley, do consider that others feel more interest in your prosperity that you can be expected to feel yourself at this period of life. I did not during the last vacation tease you by remonstrances for your neglect of books. Too many temptations were daily cast in your way to induce me to hope that my reproofs might avail, but do not think that it was unobserved, and I assure you, painfully so. Resolve but to recover lost time and the end is accomplished. If one idle companion laugh at you, the praise of the more discreet will be tenfold. You have ability, you want nothing but exertion, and pray indulge me by its use. [*Parker (3)*, *p. 237*]

America, 1849   Dr **Hosmer** *writes to his daughter Harriet, aged eighteen.*

My dear daughter, – The allegory so much desired followeth.

'An old man sat before his winter fire, which flickered like his life, to keep the last night of the year, with thought and with memory. His had been an ill-spent life, his character had been moulded by the fierceness of his passions and the obstinacy of his circumstances. He had never secured a position beyond their malignant influences, and his soul had always fluctuated between vice and virtue, the prey of every impulse. As he sat and mused, the wasted years passed before him in procession, and the whole domain of his life lay stretched out like a desert swept by the hot simoon, strewed with good intentions and favouring moments, like rich caravans which never reach their journey's end. On the verge of this desolation lay the green time of his youth, like the first flush of morning, and the old man's seared heart was touched with the memory of its promise and the bitter contrast of its non-fulfilment. Vividly came to him again, those hopes and impulses indulged in so long ago, gradually one after another wrecked and scattered. He felt the ancient time, when virtue was yet a possibility and the lordly structure of a character filled the vista of his wishes; then the dreadful thought that his character had been ruined and his life made a failure forced from him the exclamation, "Return, oh, return years of promise – return, golden opportunities for virtue – give me back my youth that I may yet be good and just." And he had his wish; for it was the New Year's dream of a young man, and he awoke in his hopelessness and all the possibilities of life lay fair and enticing before him, and he could yet make the untried future blossom like the rose. Let us reverence our youth. Let us stand in awe before our opportunities, for there have been lives worse than the horrors of the most painful dream.'

My daughter, read the above with attention, remember it, and make it serve you as a guide and a beacon in establishing a *character*, a good character without which life is a certain failure. [*pp. 7–8*]

Intergenerational Conflict

*Simonds **D'Ewes**, aged sixteen, a student at Cambridge, recalls financial disputes with his father.* England, 1618

Before my return back unto Cambridge, my tutor sending a bill of my expenses there, for my chamber, study and other particulars, (of which a great part was to be repaid at my coming away), although no part of it could well have been prevented, yet my father was so far at first incensed with it, as I was at one time afraid I should have no more gone to Cambridge; neither doubtless, had I, if my silver pot, which was given to the college, my gown, and other necessaries, had not then already been provided and sent thither. But at last he being better appeased, delivered me the money due upon the bill to carry to my tutor. [*vol. 1, pp. 118–19*]

He then discusses the amount of his allowance with his father.

The utmost I desired was but £60; my father conceived £50 to be sufficient; which I was willing to accept, being able to obtain no more, rather than to be at his allowance; because I easily foresaw how many sad differences I was likely to meet with upon every reckoning. I cannot deny but as this short allowance brought me one way much want and discontent, so another way it made me avoid unnecessary acquaintance, idle visits, and many needless expenses. [*vol. 1, p. 119*]

Two years later, while at home before commencing law studies, he comments on the differences between him and his father.

I tasted such full experience of his passion and choleric nature, by his hasty speeches uttered upon very light occasions, as I feared my being so near him at London would produce no good effects; yet this good I found in all my afflictions at this time, that they served for my humiliation, and taught me to set a higher price upon spiritual comforts. [*vol. 1, p. 148*]

*Mary **Rich** recollects her defiance of her father, Richard, Earl of Cork,* Ireland, 1638
over his choice of a Mr Hambletone for her husband.

When I was about thirteen or fourteen years of age, came down to me one Mr Hambletone, son to my Lord Clandeboyes, who was afterwards Earl of Clandeboyes, who would fain have had me for his wife. My father and his had, some years before, concluded a match between us, if we liked when we saw one another, and that

I was of years of consent; and now he being returned out of France, was by his father's command to come to my father's where he received from him a very kind and obliging welcome, looking upon him as his son-in-law, and designing suddenly that we should be married, and gave him leave to make his address, with a command to me to receive him as one designed to be my husband. Mr Hambletone (possibly to obey his father) did design gaining me by a very handsome address, which he made to me, and if he did not to a very high degree dissemble, I was not displeasing to him, for he professed a great passion for me. The professions he made me of his kindness were very unacceptable to me, and though I had by him a very advantageous offers made me, for point of fortune (for his estate, that was settled upon him, was counted seven or eight thousand pound a-year), yet by all his kindness to me nor that I could be brought to endure to think of having him, though my father pressed me extremely to it; my aversion for him was extraordinary, though I could give my father no satisfactory account why it was so.

This continued between us for a long time, my father showing me a very high displeasure at me for it, but though I was in much trouble about it, yet I could never be brought either by fair or foul means to it; so as my father was at last forced to break it off, to my father's unspeakable trouble, and to my unspeakable satisfaction, for hardly in any of the troubles of my life did I feel a more sensible uneasiness than when that business was transacting. [*pp. 2–3*]

Mary later fell in love with a younger son whom she knew would be regarded as unsuitable by her father. Her father sent her two brothers to persuade Mary to end the affair.

I made this resolute, but ill and horribly disobedient answer, that I did acknowledge a very great and particular kindness for Mr Rich, and desired them, with my humble duty to my father, to assure him that I would not marry him without his consent, but that I was resolved not to marry any other person in the world . . .

After my two brothers saw I was unmovable in my resolution, say what they could to me, they returned highly unsatisfied from me to my father; who, when he had it once owned from my own mouth, that I would have him, or nobody, he was extraordinary displeased with me, and forbid my daring to appear before him. But after some time he was persuaded, by the great esteem he had for my Lord Warwick and my Lord of Holland, to yield to treat with them, and was at last brought, though not to give me my before designed portion, yet to give me seven thousand pounds, and was brought to see and be civil to Mr Rich, who was a constant visitor of me at Hampton, almost daily; but he was the only person I saw for my own family came not at me: and thus I continued there for about ten weeks, when I was at last, by my Lord of Warwick and my Lord Goring led into my father's chamber, and there, upon my knees, humbly begged his pardon, which after he had, with great justice severely chid me, he bid me rise, and was by my Lord of Warwick's and my Lord Goring's intercession reconciled to me, and told me I should suddenly be married. [p. 13]

Henry **Oxinden** *writes to Thomas Barrow about his younger brother*   *England, 1641*
Adam, aged nineteen.

My mother received a letter from my brother Adam which hath so troubled her that she is not able to write. She cannot conceive how it comes to pass that my brother giving his Mr Brooks content all the while he lived with him should now be so suddenly changed with his master: which in my opinion may justly give an occasion of belief that the young man his master is in fault. This considera-tion and belief hath caused her to have counsel upon the matter; which hath resolved her thus, that in regard that my brother Adam consented not according to the order of city to serve this man, that Mr Brooks is bound by law to place him according to his liking. She would also that you would entertain counsel upon this matter and follow it till St Mich[aelmas], at which time she intendeth to come on purpose to London and follow the suit herself, being resolved to engage her whole fortune rather than to have her son wronged in this manner. It seems strange to me likewise as well as to her that he should be put from his master and nothing at all that we can hear alleged by his master against him.

If he should be found guilty of any villainous crimes such as were intolerable in a prentice there were some reason for what is done, but as yet we are not informed of any such matters, and till we are, we were extremely to be blamed by the whole world, she to see her son, and myself to see my brother, receive any wrong in the least kind if it is in our fortune to remedy. He writes to my mother to go to sea till the rest of his time be expired, which how he will do we know not; for we have no acquaintance to place him in that course, neither can be at any charges in setting him in a new course, having expended well as we conceive in another. But if it appear that he be in fault and fickle in following the profession he was late in – if he know how to order his matters in that way he speaks of, without trouble or cost to her, I see not but she will give way to it. I find her of my disposition in this, that though she be loving to her children that take good courses, and willing to do what she can for them so long as they do so, yet if they will not be persuaded, to persuade herself not to be exceeding troubled for that cannot be helped.

I do not understand that this is time of year to go for the East Indies. Neither how he will employ himself in the interim: it cannot be thought any ways fit for him to reside in the country, neither to be out of employment wheresoever he be . . .

There is one thing I forgot to certify you of at the beginning of my letter, that the matter my mother insisteth upon is, that she absolutely believeth my brother Adam to be treated [unjustly] in regard that he was promised that he should be with the young man as his Mr Brooks his servant and not as the young man's etcetera, which after he was with him he found no such matter, and this she is able she saith to prove; and truly I conceive that there is no man but would judge this to be very unjust dealings; so that the question will not be whether my brother Adam neglect his shop, or follow drinking or the like; but whether he had his promise fulfilled unto him; and not having it, whether he is not to choose a new master, and his former to be at the cost of binding him for the same and upon the same conditions he was to serve his Mr Brooks. [*Oxinden (a), pp. 210–13*]

Oxinden then asks Barrow the following questions.

First, whether in your conscience you believe that my brother Adam be averse to the course of life I put him in according to his own choice and liking. If he be, all our cares will be vain in re-establishing him in it again. Secondly whether he can now go to sea (which by his letter it seems he hath a mind to) so as it may be three or four year at least before he return. For if his return be sooner I shall find as much trouble with him as now. I desire and that with all my heart he would follow his first course, but if he be averse to it I think no other will be more fitting. [*Oxinden (a), pp. 214–15*]

Adam was eventually allowed to go to sea.

England, 1644   *Anne **Halkett**, aged twenty-one, becomes involved in a clandestine romance with Thomas Howard. Her mother disapproves, since a match has already been arranged for Howard.*

In the year 1644 I confess I was guilty of an act of disobedience, for I gave way to the address of a person whom my mother, at the first time that ever he had occasion to be conversant with me, had absolutely discharged me ever to allow of. [*p. 3*]

Anne will not agree to marry Thomas without the consent of their parents, but she does promise not to marry anyone else. Thomas is sent abroad and Anne hopes her mother will now be mollified.

I was in hopes, after some time that Mr Howard was gone, my mother would have received me into her favour again, but the longer time she had to consider of my fault the more she did aggravate it. And though my Lord Howard (who returned shortly after with his daughter) and my sister did use all the arguments imaginable to persuade her to be reconciled to me, yet nothing would prevail, except I would solemnly promise never to think more of Mr Howard and that I would marry another whom she thought fit to propose; to which I begged her pardon, for till Mr Howard was first married I was fully determined to marry no person living. She asked me if I was such a fool as to believe he would be constant. I said I did, but if he were not, it should be his fault, not mine, for I resolved not to make him guilty by example.

Many were employed to speak to me. Some used good words, some ill; but one that was most severe, after I had heard her with much patience rail a long time, when she could say no more, I gave a true account how innocent I was from having any design upon Mr Howard and related what I have already mentioned of the progress of his affection; which when she heard, she sadly wept and begged my pardon, and promised to do me all the service she could; and I believe she did, for she had much influence upon my Lord Howard (having been with his lady from a child), and did give so good a character of me and my proceedings in that affair with his son, that he again made an offer to my mother to send for his son if she would consent to the marriage; but she would not hear it spoken of, but said she rather I were buried than bring so much ruin to the family she honoured.

My mother's anger against me increased to that height, that for fourteen months she never gave me her blessing, nor never spoke to me but when it was to reproach me, and one day said with much bitterness she did hate to see me. [*pp. 14–15*]

Anne eventually decided to enter a convent, but a family friend persuaded her mother to forget the affair and Anne was again received into her favour. Thomas Howard married another.

*Charles **Hatton** protests to his father about the latter's unfair treatment.* England, 1665

Mr Lord, – Had not my duty obliged me, yet my natural inclination would have compelled me to pay to your Lordship all possible obedience and observance which I have ever studiously endeavoured to do, and think myself only fortunate in this, that I have been so successful therein, that the highest, nay the sole crime, that can·be pretended against me, is not to have been rude to my uncle, your Lordship's own brother, in denying him to lie with me, after that I had by your command invited him into the country, and your self had ordered we should lie together. I can never persuade my self, that you can really account this a crime, much less such a crime, for which I should merit to be turned out of doors and denied your blessing. But it puts me in despair of ever gaining your favour and it fully convinces me, that you have a natural implacable aversion to me, and are resolved never to consider me or provide for me as for your child which I did ever mistrust, for that you have ever denied me, both that education and maintenance fit for your son. As for my education; you never took care I should have any and as for my maintenance, I have been many months, and have had never a shirt to wear, my clothes, so ragged that few beggars have had worse, I have never had a new suit, but when my old one was so worn out, it would scarce hang on my back. I have scarce ever received a penny from your Lordship, to buy any things though never so necessary and have always found servants preferred before me, to every thing whereby I might hope for advancement. Was not all this a sufficient testimony, that you are, and ever have been resolved never to regard me as your child. [*Hatton (b) add. MSS29571, f. 31*]

England, 1670   *Margaret* **Evelyn** *writes to her son John, aged fifteen.*

I have received your letter and request for a supply of money; but none of those you mention which were bare effects of your duty. If you were so desirous to answer our expectations as you pretend to be, you would give those tutors and overseers you think so exact over you, less trouble than I fear they have with you. Much is to be wished in your behalf; that your temper were humble and tractable, your inclinations virtuous, and that from choice, not compulsion, you make an honest man. Whatever object of vice comes before you, should have the same effect in your mind of dislike and aversion that drunkenness had in the youth of Sparta when their slaves were presented to them in that brutish condition, not only from the deformity of such a sight, but from a motive beyond theirs – the hope of a future happiness, which those rigorous heathens in moral virtue had little prospect of, finding no reward for virtue but in virtue itself. You are not too young to know that lying, defrauding, swearing, disobedience to parents and persons in authority, are offences to God and man: that debauchery is injurious to growth, health, life, and indeed to the pleasures of life; therefore, now that you are turning from child to man, endeavour to follow the best precepts, and choose such ways as may render you worthy of praise and love. You are assured of your father's care and my tenderness; no mark of it shall be wanting at any time to confirm it to you, with this reserve only, that you strive to deserve kindness by a sincere honest proceeding, and not flatter yourself that you are good whilst you only appear to be so. [*vol. 4, pp. 21–2*]

*Ralph **Josselin** is frequently disturbed by the behaviour of his nineteen-year-old son John.*   England, 1671

19 February.

A sad week with John, his carriage intolerable, uncertain what to resolve. Lord direct me. A day of comfort in the word, though troubles in my house.

26 February.

Came home opportunely to save a cow cast. Found John within, but as I dreamed high and proud so he was, cast him Lord down as that cow that he may rise up again . . .

John rid away, carried somethings with him, without taking his leave of me, on Wednesday, March 22. God in mercy look after him. [*p. 558*]

5 June.

God good to me and mine at home, only John robbed his mother and sister of near 30s and away. God in mercy break his heart for good. [*p. 559*]

1674. 7 June.

A good week in the providences of God, but afflictive in John's carriage, Lord reclaim him if it may be. [*p. 576*]

30 September.

This day afflictive to us in John, who sets himself on evil. Lord set thyself to overcome him with thy goodness, all our endeavours have the sentence of death on them. [*p. 579*]

23 October.

Offer to John before his mother and four sisters.

John set your self to fear God, and be industrious in my business, refrain your evil courses and I will pass by all past offences, settle all my estate on you after your mother's death, and leave you some stock on the ground and within doors to the value of an £100 and desire of you, out of your marriage portion but £400 to provide for my daughters or otherwise to charge my land with as much for their portions, but if you continue your ill courses I shall dispose my land otherwise, and make only a provision for your life to put bread in your hand. [*p. 580*]

15 December.

John this day owned his debauchery, God give him a true sight of it and heal him. [*p. 581*]

1675. 24 January.

John declared for his disobedience no son; I should allow him nothing except he took himself to be a servant, yet if he would depart and live in service orderly I would allow him £10 yearly; if he so walked as to become God's son, I should yet own him for mine. [*p. 582*]

Ralph did not carry out his threat to disinherit his son.

Scotland, 1675   *Ludovic **Gordon-Cummings** writes to his father Ludovic.*

Dear Father, – I know the report of my coming south will in part surprise you, and I must acknowledge it was rather force than my own inclinations or any desire I had in the least to give you offence made me do it. My birth and education being sufficient ties to oblige me to all the bonds, duties and submission that in conscience or equity a child owes to a parent so kind and provident. But my supposed defects by nature being given out by some to be more in number and of deeper dye than really they may be, and without a further trial can hardly be well determined by any that are indifferent and not altogether unfriendly, wherefore I have resolved to employ a piece of my youth in accomplishing my self not without hope to undeceive those who have so informed you against me of your expectation (I shall not say their desire) and albeit I know you wish what I intend, yet my fear of being retarded till my elder brother came south (which was uncertain, and if at all but in the end of December as he himself declared to me that morning he went to Sutherland) made me presume upon your goodness and fatherly charity in coming south without your knowledge, for which I crave your pardon but for the rest expect your approbation. I intend to spend this session here, and the next vacance also (if by your permission) the session, in hearing the public disputes and examination of witnesses with the Lords interloquitors and reading acts of parliament and sederunt, and the vacance in writing and reading practiques with some pieces of the civil law and collections, which by the blessing of God may effectuate what I design. But since you know that nature is polished by dirt and art attained by pains and industry I hope you

will further my lawful endeavours, for without your help all is to
no purpose. And I assure you in point of spending I shall live in
that measure of sobriety that by your next you shall be pleased to
carve out for me, as your son both in diet and clothes: my
proficiencies (which I know will be your no small comfort) and no
extravagancy. [*dep. 175/1387*]

His father replies.

Your impertinent letter came here to me, but I know the style you
write. Know my mind by what I wrote to your brother George and
others, and will make you repent your foolish course from your
heart. Haste home quickly and by your future carriage strive to
take away your fault, for disobedience is like the sin of witchcraft,
and none of so high a degree as to your parents. I wish the Lord
may convince you of it and grant you repentance, for you dare
not say you had the least ground from me, except that I was too
careful for you; and was on a way of settling you as to what I
judged fittest for you, and it would have become you best to have
been waiting on your father and learning from him. If your own
foolish behaviour both here and wherever you went had not
discovered your folly; I know no friend but did endeavour to
conceal it. Trust not to those foolish fancies that your grandfather
left you anything as I hear you hinted for you will curse them that
put that in your head, or makes you believe it, when you are in
misery, or will help you little, for you need not expect, albeit you
were starving, any thing from me but my curse, if you continue in
your disobedience, besides I will take another course with you
than you imagine. No more but I am your father as you deserve.
[*dep. 175/1387*]

*Ann **Johnson** writes to her son William.*   *England, 1684*

I do perceive that you have still a greater mind to be a soldier than
any thing else nothwithstanding my dislike of it. I did desire you
that that might be your last refuge, I would have you try all your
friends and acquaintance[s] and see if you can hear of any place
either in the custom house or any thing else that you are fit for. If
you can hear of any place that will not cost above one hundred or
one hundred and fifty pound let me know and if all that I can
possibly make will purchase it for you I will do it. I do believe that
my plate and gold watch may fetch above one hundred pound . . .
you may also talk with Tom Congers, it may be that he may help
you, if you would be persuaded I do think it would be your best
way to be put to an attorney. [*DX/827/1, f. 19*]

Honoured Sir   Glasgow the 22 of Sep
                                                    tuar 1697

    I having receved yowr letter am very much gri
ved that I have been the cause of so much greife and trouble
of spirit to yow by my unworthy cariage which I have had since
I cam here I confess that my behaviour towards mr
Andrew hes been very unnaturall but since the first let
ter that yow wrote he can have no resone to compla
ine of any of us for we did not content with him in ane
manner and we shaw hardly any what bot pleassa
mong our selves and as for ours observing of order in
the colledge I am sure he can have no reson to compla
ine of us for there is none in the colledge that either keip
s the classe or the common hall more punctually
then we and we read over and over our lesson whi
ch the regent preschrives to us every day twice or somety
mes thrice and for the unworthy and disgraceful la
nguage which I hid used towards mr Andrew I earne
stly and humbly beseche that yow forgive me it
and with the strength of the almighty god I shall es
vor dare to adventure to commit any such unwor
thy and gracless actions And Ja gaine and againe
confessing my grievous and hainous fault which is hain
ous in the eye of God dod earnestly and humbly suppli
cat and entreated yow that yow would forgive me this
my grevious fault And I with the strength of the
great god shall amend every day yow wrote to me
that yow will cause the regent punish all and the
regents punishing for faults the principall is keip
punish us how ill punysh all the colledge for fa
ults ther for will not punysh us more then any othe
colledge for we must either pay a happeny for
is quated as we are noe otherwise we will be in
trudes out of the colledge I ashure yow we will
ashure as we are here to be extruded if yow dod not or
send some or other to give us money otherwise
we cannot stay here without money so I desire
that yow would be pleased to send and ansue
anent the thing which I have written unto him who
                              Yowr very humble servant
                                William Maxwoll

Letter from William Maxwell, 1697

Honoured Sir
I having receved youre letter am very much greived that I
have been the cause of so much greife and trouble of spirit to
yow by my unworthy cariage which I have had since I came
here. I confess that my behaviour towards Mr Andrew had
been very unnaturall but since the first letter that yow wrote
he can have no reasone to complaine of any of us for wee doe
not contend with him in any manner and wee have hardly any
debats or strifes among oure selves and as for oure observing
of order in the colledge I am sure he can have noe reason to
complaine of us for theirs none in the colledge that either
keepe the classe or the common hall more punctwally then
wee and wee reade over and over our lesson which the regent
prescrives to us evry day twice or sometymes three and for the
unworthy and disgracefull cariage which I had used towards
Mr Andrew I earnestly and humbly beseeche that yow forgive
me it and with the strengthe of the almighty god I shall never
dare to adventure & to commit any such unworthy and
graclesse actions. And I againe and againe confessing my
greivous and hainous fault which is hainous in the eys of God
doe earnestly and humbly supplicat and entreate yow that
yow would forgive me this my grevous fault and I with the
strengthe of the great god shall amend evry day yow wrote to
me that yow will cause the regent principal and the regents
punish us for faults the principall if hee punish us he will
punish all the colledge for faults therfor will not punish us
more then any in the colledge for wee must either pay a
happeny toties quoties as wee are noted otherswise we will be
excluded out of the college I can assure yow wee wi[ll?] assure
as wee are here be excluded if yow doe not ordaine some or
other to give us money otherwise we can not stay here
without money so I desire that yow would be pleased to send
ane answer anent the thing which I have written unto him
who is yowre very humble servant
William Maxwell

National Library of Scotland Acc 7043/1

England, 1716   *Dudley* **Ryder** *agrees with the principle that parents should decide on their offspring's employment.*

Hence I think it is of vast service to children to have parents to choose for them what manner of life to engage in, and parents themselves ought not to leave it to the uncertain unsettled elections of children themselves, who it is impossible should be able to make any settled judgement at all. [*pp. 229–30*]

However, Dudley chose to study law rather than help his father in the family business.

My father this morning took notice of some very little trifling things. I have sometimes wished I had been brought up in my father's business when I look upon the difficulties that meet me in the way of a lawyer, but then it has presently come to my mind that I could not tell how to have led a life constantly under my father's eyes. It would have tired me of life to have had him always teasing me with faults in trifles. It has been much happier for me to be absent. I have enjoyed all the pleasure and love and affection of a kind and loving father without any of the uneasiness that arise from his peculiar temper. If ever I shall have children, I will endeavour to guide them with a much more even and steady hand, never to regard very little faults, or, if they are such as may be of ill consequence, to do it in such a manner as not to be disagreeable to them. It wearies out a child of spirit to be always blamed. [*p. 293*]

America, 1717   *Cotton* **Mather** *is frequently disturbed by the behaviour of his son, Increase. At the age of seventeen, Increase is accused of fathering an illegitimate child.*

Oh! Dreadful case! Oh, sorrow beyond any that I have met withall! What shall I do now for the foolish youth! What for my afflicted and abased family? [*Mather (b), vol. 8, p. 484*]

Mather asks his son to leave home at the age of nineteen.

My miserable son Increase, I must cast him and chase him out of my sight; forbid him to see me, until there appear sensible marks of repentance upon him. Nevertheless I will entreat his grandfather to take pains for his recovery. [*Mather (b), vol. 8, p. 612*]

Three years later.

My unhappy son Increase is again in lamentable circumstances. A vile sloth, accompanied with the power of Satan still reigning over him, ruins him, destroys him. I must not only repeat my solemn admonitions unto the impenitent youth, but (notwithstanding the provocations he has given me) invite him to come again and live with me, that I may have him under my eye continually. [*Mather (b), vol. 8, p. 647*]

*Nicholas **Blundell** sends his daughter Margaret to convent school in France. When the time comes for her return home, she wishes to stay a year longer, and the appropriate arrangements are made. Margaret then changes her mind and persuades the chaplain, Father Daniel, to write to her father on her behalf. Her father replies.*   *England, 1722*

I think I love my dearest child as well as any parent can do, yet am not willing to indulge her in what will be no credit nor advantage to her but on the other side a very great reflection on me, first to say I would go to fetch her, then to say I would defer it one year longer upon her desire and yet after all to have her come all of a sudden is what I can no ways consent to . . . She says how glad she would have been to have seen us this summer, she may assure herself it would have been no small satisfaction to us to have seen her, but as we have deprived ourselves of that comfort so long for her good it is her duty now to comply to us, both in obedience and for our credit as well as her own. I would not have her value herself too much as being an heiress, for if either of my daughters disoblige me, it is in my power to clip their wings, not that I have the least thoughts to do it and hope I never shall have the least provocation for none can be more dear to me than my dearest children are, and when I have a conveniency I shall not fail to settle them in the world to their satisfaction to the best of my power, but would not have them to think I will settle any of my estate on them as long as I live or at least of several years to come. [*Blundell (b), pp. 205–7*]

*William **Byrd** admonishes his daughter Evelyn, aged sixteen, for her encouragement of a suitor.*   *America, 1723*

Considering the solemn promise you made me, first by word of mouth, and afterwards by letter, that you would not from thence forth have any converse of correspondence with the baronet, I am astonished you have violated that protestation in a most notorious manner. The gracious audience you gave him the morning you left town, and the open conversations you have with him in the country have been too unguarded, to be denied any longer. 'Tis therefore high time for me to reproach you with breach of duty and breach of faith, and once more to repeat to you, my strict and positive commands, never more to meet, speak or write to that gentleman, or to give him an opportunity to see, speak or write to

you. I also forbid you to never enter into any promise or engagement with him of marriage or inclination. I enjoin you this in the
most positive terms, upon the sacred duty you owe a parent, and
upon the blessing you ought to expect upon the performance of it.
And that neither he nor you may be deluded afterwards with vain
hopes of forgiveness, I have put it out of my power, by vowing
that I never will. And as to any expectation, you may fondly
entertain of a fortune from me, you are not to look for one brass
farthing, if you provoke me by this fatal instance of disobedience.
Nay besides all that, I will avoid the sight of you as of a creature
detested. Figure then to your self my dear child how wretched you
will be with a provoked father, and a disappointed husband. To
whom then will you fly in your distress, when all the world will
upbraid you with having acted an idiot? and your conscience must
fly in your face for having disobeyed an indulgent parent. I think
my self obliged to give you this fair warning, and to point out to
you the rocks upon which you will certainly shipwreck all your
happiness in this world, unless you think fit to obey my orders.
For God's sake then my dear child, for my sake, and for your own,
survey the desperate precipice you stand upon, and don't rashly
cast your self down head long into ruin. The idle promises this
man makes you will all vanish into smoke, and instead of love he
will slight and abuse you, when he finds his hopes of fortune
disappointed. Then you and your children (if you should be so
miserable as to have any) must be beggars, and you may be
assured all the world will deservedly despise you, and you will
hardly be pitied so much as by him who would fain continue,
etcetera. [*Byrd (b), vol. 1, pp. 343–5*]

*Byrd gave no reason why he disliked the baronet; his daughter never
married.*

America, 1726   *Samuel **Sewall** brought up his grandchildren after their parent's death.
His grandson Samuel, aged twenty, greatly displeased him.*

Samuel Hirst got up betime in the morning, and took Ben Swett
with him and went into the common to play at wicket. Went
before anybody was up, left the door open; Sam came not to
prayer; at which I was much displeased. [*vol. 7, p. 372*]

The next day.

[Samuel] did the like again; but took not Ben with him. I told him
he could not lodge here practising thus. So he lodged elsewhere.
He grievously offended me in persuading his sister Hannah not to
have Mr Turall, without enquiring of me about it. And played fast
and loose with me in a matter relating to himself, procuring me
great vexation. [*vol. 7, p. 372*]

William **Bulkely** *paid the debts of his adult son William although he*   *Wales, 1742*
disapproved of the latter's life-style.

My dear fugitive has been absent from home since Saturday, indulging himself in an indolent sluggish way with very ordinary tipplers, twice before within this month he did of the same, and when I asked him where he had been, would not vouchsafe an answer. I'll give him his own way and say nothing, time may bring him to be sensible of the wrong he does his character, and shame him to a reformation. [*p. 104*]

Stephen **Martin-Leake** *writes to his son John.*   *England, 1761*

I received your letter of the 13th which indeed greatly surprised me, for though you have hardly in anything followed my advice, yet I never thought you could be guilty of such madness and folly, as wantonly to rush upon your own destruction, as you have done, without regarding the consequences, or so much as thinking what was to become of you afterwards . . . as to the being debarred the house of your parents, you have debarred yourself, by an unhappy marriage, are now united to another family, and must follow the fortune of your wife. To see you under these circumstances must doubtless be a great affliction to me, nevertheless I shall be ready to give you my advice as a father, provided you come alone. [*MS 599/84605*]

Thomas **Wale**, *in his diary, desribes the long-term discord between his*   *England, 1771*
wife and his daughter Margaret (Polly). The trouble begins when
Margaret is fifteen.

Mrs Wale in a mild manner talked soundly and freely with her daughter Polly and proposed a reconciliation upon her better behaviour, and a confession of her faults within twenty-four hours, but hearing somewhat in the meantime of her daughter, she relapsed and was so vexed that that she had before said was no more thought of. [*p. 160*]

Three years later.
Daughter Polly having this day behaved rudely and impudently to her Mamma (and that in my hearing) received my reproaches and chastisement. [*p. 168*]

In 1775 it is decided that Margaret should go away to boarding-school at Baddow.
After that Mrs Wale and daughter Polly have long had enmity and ill-will. The mamma too severe and the daughter somewhat as

obstinate and provoking. Have on all sides consented to part. [*p. 175*]

Mr J. Wood, of Catherine College, Cambridge came this day on a visit to me at Shelford, and asked my leave to wait upon my daughter Polly at Baddow in an honourable way, which I could not object to, as I would by no means refuse my daughter her choice, provided that centres in a man of character, honour and such fortune or preferment as will enable him to settle on her and family adequate to what fortune I shall give her, which I proposed should be £2,000. [*p. 186*]

America, 1772   *Landon* **Carter***'s daughter Judy married in opposition to her father's wishes. Two years after the wedding, she writes to him. He records in his diary.*

Yesterday poor Judy wrote to be admitted to see me. I answered her she knew how long ago that, being satisfied of the pains to lead her against her duty, I wrote to her if she came alone, my breast was ready to receive her as usual, and had communicated with her to show I was willing to forget her disobedience on her part; therefore she could not want an invitation to that happiness she expresses; if she did, I bid her in the Lord's name – to come. [*Carter (b), vol. 14, pp. 182–3*]

Yesterday my poor offending child Judy came for the first time since she was deluded away to be unhappily married against her duty, my will, and against her solemn promise. [Her husband has] a poor pittance of an estate. Indeed this fine girl has made a hard bed. Such has been her deception I will contrive that she shall not want for personal necessaries but I will give nothing that either he or his inheritors can claim. [*Carter (b), vol. 14, pp. 183–4*]

Though I resolved not to let nature discover its weakness on seeing her, I was only happy in that I would burst into tears. A poor miserable girl. I could not speak to her for some time. [*Carter (b), vol. 14, p. 184*]

America, 1805   *Leverett* **Saltonstall***, a law student aged twenty-two, asks his father for more money.*

This letter is upon a *law library*. Law books are indeed very expensive owing probably to the small demand for them. A *library* I do not ask for, nor expect at present; only a few books for study, direction in and practice . . . How shall I get these books? I cannot borrow them. As to Mr Tucker he has sold his. I need not tell you I have got no money. I must then hire money or get them on credit. A credit of any considerable length would make a difference of at least fifteen per cent. Should I hire I must call on you as my best friend. On the paper enclosed you will find a list of such books [as] are immediately necessary with their common prices . . .

With some $120 or $130 I can procure as many books as I shall need at present. But how shall I get it? I must call upon my father. He has given me every advantage of education, and he will not withhold I hope the last. But you say you cannot do it. Your finances will not allow it. You are willing to do to the extent of your abilities but cannot impoverish yourself. If so, I say no more. God forbid that I should impoverish my father, or bring a moment's distress on a brother or sister. To prevent this while I have my hands they shall be devoted. I would rather do without books and endeavour to get along 'till I can pick them up one by one. I am sensible that the sum is considerable. After the expenses of my education thus far 150 dollars is a great deal to give, especially when the profession is so poor. [*vol. 2, pp. 245–7*]

His father sent him $200 three weeks later.

Maria **Capel** *(Muzzy), aged eighteen, writes to her grandmother* England, 1815
informing her she has refused an offer of marriage from Edward Barnes.
Her parents had approved the match.

What you heard relative to a Certain Person is true, and though I am well aware that it would, in a *worldy point of view*, have been a desirable thing, yet with all his agremens that I hear *so much* of, he is not indeed the sort of person, that would ever have made me happy. And I am too happy in my present situation to wish to change it unless to be still more so; I know *my* extraordinary *taste*, or rather want of taste, has caused, and does now, much astonishment to every body and more particularly to my own family, which I am very very sorry for. On this subject I am not I think very romantic, for I do not think *violent love* necessary to one's happiness, but I think you will agree with me that a *decided preference* is absolutely so, and that, the preference even, I never could feel. Therefore there was but one way of acting. Now I have begun on the sort of subject, I must acknowledge to you that, General Ferguson suited my taste and feelings *much much* more, but there was one very decided obstacle, in that way, and indeed the *only* one, (which was, *want of that horrid money*). [*pp. 87–8*]

Caroline Capel, Maria's mother, also writes.

It is very true what you allude to of Muzzy and Sir Edward Barnes; I was not aware you had heard of it. I knew you did not know the person, and I never think it fair to tell a thing of this kind, but as you have heard it, I may acknowledge it, and assure you that it is no objection of Capel's or mine that has prevented it, but her own decision. I think a *veto* we have a right to, if unfortunately it ever becomes necessary, but I am afraid of *persuasion* because if the thing did not turn out happily I could never forgive myself. She knows how much Capel and I love and value him. Her sisters quite dote on him and row her from morning till night for her want of taste. [*p. 88*]

England, 1828

John **Skinner** *was almost perpetually at war with his two sons as they grew up, particularly his eldest son Owen. In the following extracts from his diary, Owen is aged nineteen and Joseph seventeen.*

I mentioned to my son, Owen, that I wished him to be very particular in the accounts he kept of Farmer Skuse's agistment stock, as I had seen some oxen which I thought he was fatting and not using as working beasts. He said, if I knew better than he did he would have nothing to do with the concern of taking my tythe for me, and I might do it myself. On my asking him this morning for the list which Skuse had sent in of his stock, he gave it me, and brought me all the papers he had in keeping respecting Skuse's tythe; he also gave me back again the map of the parish, saying he would have nothing further to do with the tythe concern, since he could not give satisfaction. I said, although his conduct formerly had been very reprehensible, I never could have expected such cool, premeditated ingratitude as this. If he would not assist me I must look about for some person as a bailiff, and if it cost me £50 a year there would be less for my children. [*p. 161*]

A few days later trouble arises again.

I spoke to Owen, whose conduct to me since my return home has been very insulting, as far as speaking and rude behaviour will go, and I had determined not to say anything to him; but, as my peace of mind is at stake, and it must be to me a source of continual disquiet to see my son discontented, sulky, and sullen under my roof I went to him and asked what was the cause of his behaviour, and why he chose to insult his Father day after day by his misconduct? I had done everything for him, and when I expected he would be of some service in assisting me in taking the tythe he had refused. I had reason, therefore, to be displeased, not he; that if he felt uncomfortable at home he had better tell me so at once, and what he designed to do with himself, as he did not appear to study for the law with any energy – it was but idling away his time to pretend to that profession. He said he had given up all thoughts of following it, and had other plans. I asked what. He said he should not tell me. I replied that I did not merit this conduct: I have ever assisted him heretofore, and was prepared to mention now I would assist him still if the plans were rational; but I would give up no money to be idled away. He said that he would not tell me his plans, and if I did not let him have some money to forward them, he would take up some on his reversion of what Mrs Manningham had left him: he knew he could do this. Seeing that it was useless to speak to him any longer, I left him. On quitting his room he followed me, and banged and bolted the door against me . . .

I received a note from Owen by the post, wherein he said he was sorry for his behaviour, but declared he did not mean to study for the law, wishing to get into the army, and, if he could not procure a commission, should like to go out to India as an adventurer. This is entirely out of the question. If he can point out any line in which I can assist him, with a prospect of benefit to himself, I will do it, but not throw away money, and have him return a pauper on my hands. [*pp. 163-4*]

The following day.

Owen and his sister went to call on Mr Stephen Jarrett and Mrs Anne Stephens before dinner; the former made an engagement to take a drive with Stephen Jarrett after our dinner. I thought he might have rather assisted me in the tything business, but he has made up his mind to consider solely himself. On my speaking to him I had a repetition of the same unfeeling insults I have of late so much been accustomed to, and, when he was gone with Stephen Jarrett, I went into my study and wrote the following note to him, meaning to leave it, as I had ordered my carriage to drive to my Mother's, finding it impossible to live longer in the same house with so undutiful and ungrateful a son.

Copy of a note to Owen Skinner, dated June 23, 1828.

'After the insults which you have this day coolly and premeditatedly offered to your Father – a Father who has overlooked and forgiven similar insults several times, it is incumbent on that Father to tell his son that his own peace of mind requires that his feelings should not again be put to the trial of fresh insults. He is therefore come to the determination of again quitting his own house; but as he cannot do so for any long period without any great loss – there being no one who will superintend the tything and farming concerns in his absence – he has to request, *nay more, to command his son to leave him.* This Father, however outraged, will still consider the interests of his son as far as the purchase of a commission will go; he moreover will request his Grandmother to receive him for a time till steps can be taken to accomplish this end, and however repugnant it may be to his Father's judgement. But it is decided by his Father never again to be exposed to similar insults from a son who eats of his bread and drinks of his cup, and yet abuses the benefactor who has sustained him from his youth up until now, and was his best and only true friend.'

On going down I found Owen had returned from his drive, and gave him the note. I said it was the last time we should meet, as I could not live longer with him; his behaviour was so contrary to everything that it ought to be that I was going to my Mother's to request she would receive him for a time till something could be done, and asked whether he had any objection to go to her house for a time. He said, 'certainly not'. [pp. 164–5]

John Skinner and his sons were never reconciled.

England, 1832   *Christopher **Parker** to his son John aged twenty, at university.*

You mentioned your pecuniary resources are nearly exhausted. I was in hopes you would not have required any further advances this term. You are aware of the defect of the last year's produce or I should not say a word. Let me know what you really want and I will send it. You state a wish for an allowance. Give me a reasonable hope that it would be beneficial to you or myself, and you shall have it, but between father and son, I at present cannot allow its utility. With guardians or trustees it is necessary to justify them and throw the blame of excess in expenditure upon the ward, who, when of age, has his debts to pay and feels, by embarrassment, the folly of his youth for the remainder of his life. Pay ready money for everything you have, and keep an account of what you expend, and I have no fear that you will injure me or yourself by your expenditure. [Parker (3), p. 239]

England, 1857   *Annie de **Rothschild**, aged thirteen, depicts the angry scene she had with her mother. (Constance is her fifteen-year-old sister.)*

Mamma accused me of having been violent and tempestuous. I have really not been passionate this week and I really think one who has a naturally hottish temper ought to be a little encouraged when she does all in her power to subdue it, but Mamma cannot understand that, however good, sympathizing and kind she is.

When I was in the middle of my letter Mamma came in and I showed her Emmy's letter. Mamma read it, admired it, and then asked me for mine which I refused to give to her. I really could not . . . It pained me to see how angry Mamma looked but I would not show it. I had ci inclu[?], written about Mr H and A —, and on no account would have shown it to anyone else. Mamma called me into the other room and told me angrily that she intended turning over a new leaf, and looking at our letters! that it was our own faults caused by our continual refusal. I was dumbstruck and could not say a word but tearfully left the room; I told it to Connie who continued arguing a long time, about it, saying she intended never writing, that she much preferred not writing at all to being subjected to such a rule. That it was unjust, ridiculous! and we both rose to a pitch of furious indignation which I could hardly restrain. And even when I think of it now, I cannot help thinking it wrong, that young girls may not have secrets together and may not write things forbidden to be seen. Mamma forbad the subject to be again mentioned. I went to bed crying with vexation and could not sleep till late. [*pp. 88–9*]

Edward **Bates** *continually pays the debts of his adult son Richard, always hoping for an improvement in the latter's conduct. Eventually, however, he receives a letter from a friend enclosing a list of Richard's debts.*   *England, 1863*

It leaves me in painful doubt – rather almost full conviction that Dick is utterly lost, hopeless of reform – that he has ceased to strive against temptation, and that he is sinking, without a struggle, into the abyss of voluntary meanness and self-contempt. Till now, I could never believe the possibility that a son of mine could sink so low. He seems beyond the reach of human effort: God's alone can reach his case. [*p. 299*]

Glossary

accidence	the rudiments of any subject, the alphabet
agistment	rate charged upon pasture lands, paid to vicar or rector
agremens	les agremens – agreeable qualities
ague	burning fever
alexiterical	having the power to ward off contagion
anent	about, concerning
attag	attack
balm	anything that heals or soothes pain
balsam	liquid resin
barm	froth of fermenting liquor
battles	meals
bent	of the correct mental inclinations and propensities
besom	bundle of rods or twigs used for birching
bevrie	drink
biggin	a child's cap
blister	plaster applied to raise a blister
bodies	bodices
bolus	large pill
bursten	unable to contain oneself
calomel	mercurous chloride
carduus	thistle
carking	harassing
carminative	medicine to expel flatulence
cast	of a cow, to calf out of due season
chevelure	head of hair, wig
comfrey	rough boraginaceous plant
defluxion	discharge of fluid from the body
diascordion	medicine made of dried leaves of herbs
dodge	to baffle
egrimony	agrimony – genus of plants, often refers to liverwort
erysipelas	inflammatory disease, marked by bright redness of skin
euchre	game of cards of American origin
featherfew	bitter herb
foment	to apply a warm lotion
fraight	freight – to load

froward	self-willed, perverse, unreasonable
gall	painful swelling or sore
glister	clyster – enema
godfrey's cordial	mixture to send children to sleep, laced with opium
hackle-bone	hip bone
hankers	handkerchiefs
hartshorn	aqueous solution of ammonia – possibly obtained from hart's horns.
hire	bribe (?)
hore	hoar – old
hornbook	alphabet and numbers protected by a thin covering of translucent horn mounted on a tablet of wood with a handle
humourous	capricious
husbander	good economical housekeeper
ipecacuanha	emetic produced from roots of a Brazilian plant
issue	ulcer produced artificially
itch	scabies, eruptive disease on the skin
jollop, jolap	jalap – purgative drug
julep	sweet medicated drink
knop	knob, button
knot-grass	weed, an infusion of which was believed to stunt growth
lambitive	medicine taken by licking up with the tongue
lawdirte	perhaps *laudanine*, a white crystalline alkaloid
linings	linens
list	selvage on woven textile fabrics
liverwort	any plant of the Hepaticoe; used medicinally in diseases of the liver
low	a flame, a blaze
maidenhair	type of fern
manchet	finest bread of wheat-loaf
nitre	sodium carbonate
oblation	gift
orts	fragments of left-over food
painful	painstaking
pap	bread moistened with milk or wter for babies

panda	bread boiled to pulp and flavoured with sugar
peccavi	I have sinned
peevers	hopscotch
penible	hardworking
pin and web	eye disease, apparently cataract
plaster	fabric coated with adhesive substance for local application
polypody	fern
polypus	pendunculated tumour growing from a mucous membrane
pompadour	designating a shade of crimson or pink
posset	dietetic drink
pulvis castor	strong-smelling unctuous substance obtained from the beaver
rail	rod
receipts	recipes
red gum	eruption of the skin in teething infants
rue	strong-smelling, shrubby, Mediterranean plant
St John's wort	any type of Hypericum
sal ammoniac	ammonium chloride
sal volatile	ammonium carbonate
sarsaparilla	plant indigenous to tropical America
savoury	of reputable character
scurrilous	of buffoon-like jocularity
sederunt	a sitting of a judicial body
seethe	to boil
sennight	a fortnight
simoon	hot, dry, suffocating sand wind
snakewood	bistort, plant of the dock family with twisted roots
spinnet	keyed musical instrument
stowing	ceasing speech
sublunary	earthly, mundane, material
tamarisk	type of shrub
tansy	bitter, aromatic wild plant
waggler	one who walks unsteadily
whitlow	suppurative sore or swelling in a finger or thumb
working	needlework
wort	liquor boiled with hops
wot	to know
yarrow	strong-scented plant

Sources

Alcott

Amos Bronson Alcott, born 1799, was an author, mystic, transcendentalist and teacher, intent on educational reform. He founded his own school, but his liberal system of education aroused a great deal of opposition and his venture failed. He was the father of Louisa May Alcott, the author of *Little Women*.

(a) *The Journals of Bronson Alcott* (ed. Odell Shephard). Little, Brown and Co., Boston, 1938.

(b) Charles Strickland 'A Transendentalist Father: the Childrearing Practices of Bronson Alcott', *History of Childhood Quarterly*, Vol. 1, 1973.

(c) *The Letters of A. Bronson Alcott* (ed. Richard Hernstadt). Iowa State University Press, Ames, 1969.

Alford

Henry Alford, born 1810, was the Dean of Canterbury, and edited the Greek testament.

Life, Journals and Letters of Henry Alford, DD (ed. F. Alford). Rivingtons, London, 1873.

Allen

Hannah Allen, born 1813, was a Quaker, and belonged to the upper-middle classes.

Hannah Allen, *A Beloved Mother* (ed. her daughter). Samuel Harris and Co., London, 1889.

Bach

Northamptonshire family.

Tibbits of Kelmarsh collection, Northamptonshire Record Office, T(KEL).

Baillie

Grisell Baillie, born 1665 in Berwickshire, was the eldest daughter of Sir Patrick Hume, later the Earl of Marchmont. She married George Baillie whose father Robert was executed for treason in 1684.

'The Household Book of Lady Grisell Baillie 1692–1733' (ed. Robert Scott-Moncrieff), *Scottish History Society*, 2nd series, vol. 1, 1911.

Bates

Edward Bates, born 1793, grew up in the southern states of America. He became a stateman and was considered for presidential nomination.

The Diary of Edward Bates 1859–1866 (ed. Howard Beale). Government printing office, Washington, 1933.

Bayard

Upper-class American family who lived in London 1794–7 and participated in the fashionable social life there.

The Journal of Martha Pinter Bayard (ed. S. Bayard Dod). Dodd, Mead and Co., New York, 1894.

Bishop
Betty Bishop, born 1751, was a Quaker and married to a baker. Diaries of Betty Bishop, The Friends' Library, MS S.83.

Blundell
The Blundells were landed gentry, an old Lancashire, Roman Catholic family. Nicholas Blundell was born in 1669.
(a) 'The Great Diurnall of Nicholas Blundell' (ed. J. J. Bagley), *Record Society of Lancashire and Cheshire*, vols 110, 112, 114, 1968–72.
(b) Nicholas Blundell, *Blundell's Diary and Letter Book 1702–28* (ed. Margaret Blundell). Liverpool University Press, Liverpool, 1952.

Bonham
Well-to-do family from Northamptonshire.
Bonham papers, Northamptonshire Record Office, 2B 556.

Boscawen
Frances Boscawen, born 1719, was the wife of the distinguished Admiral Edward Boscawen and the great-great niece of the diarist John Evelyn.
Frances Boscawen *Admiral's Wife* (ed. Cecil Aspinall-Oglander). Longmans, Green and Co., London, 1940.

Boston
Thomas Boston, born 1677, was the minister for Ettrick, Selkirkshire. He refused to take the oath of adjuration in 1712. His doctrinal views were at variance with the majority of the Scottish assembly.
Thomas Boston, *A General Account of My Life* (ed. George Low). Hodder and Stoughton, London, 1908.

Boswell
James Boswell, born 1740, was a lawyer by profession but is best known for his biography of Samuel Johnson and for his diary, one of the most lengthy and intimate of the eighteenth century.
The Private Papers of James Boswell from Malahide Castle in the Collection of Lt Colonel Ralph Heward Isham (ed. Geoffrey Scott and Frederick Pottle). Privately printed, 1928–34.

Brabazon
Aristocratic family. Mary Brabazon, born 1848, was involved in many philanthropic undertakings.
The Diaries of Mary, Countess of Meath (ed. Reginald Brabazon). Hutchinson, London, 1928.

Bradstreet
Anne Bradstreet, born 1613 in England, emigrated to America with the Pilgrim Fathers in 1630. Her father was steward to the Earl of Lincoln and she married Simon Bradstreet. She is the earliest known female poet in America.
The Works of Anne Bradstreet in Prose and Verse (ed. John Ellis). Peter Smith, Gloucesters, Mass., 1962.

Braithwaite
Anna Braithwaite, born 1788, was a Quaker and married a manufacturer.
Memoirs of Anna Braithwaite (ed. J. Bevan Braithwaite). Headley Brothers,
London, 1905.

Bramston
John Bramston, born 1611, of Essex, was a lawyer and Knight of the Bath.
'The Autobiography of Sir John Bramston kb,' *Camden Society*, 1845

Brattle
William Brattle, born 1662 in Massachusetts, was a Congregational
minister and educator. His son became an eminent lawyer, distinguished
physician and a major-general in the militia.
'William Brattle: Advice of a Dying Father to his Son', *New England
Historical and Genealogical Register*, vol. 3, New York, 1847.

Brockman
Knights of Kent who fought as royalists in the Civil War.
Drake-Brockman papers, British Library, add. MSS 42586–710, 45193–220.

Brooke
Barons Brooke of Northamptonshire.
Brooke of Oakely papers, Northamptonshire Record Office, B(O).

Bulkely
William Bulkely, born 1691 in Wales, was a country squire.
William Bulkely, *Mr Bulkely and the Pirate. A Welsh Diarist of the Eighteenth
Century* (ed. B. Dew Roberts). Oxford University Press, London, 1936.

Burney
Upper-class family. Fanny Burney, born 1752, was a novelist, her first
book being the successful *Evelina*. She married a French refugee, General
D'Arblay.
Diary and Letters of Madame D'Arblay (ed. her niece). Hurst and Blackett,
London (new ed.), 1854.

Burr
Aaron Burr, born 1756, was a revolutionary soldier, lawyer, US senator
and third vice-president of the United States. He was tried for treason for
encouraging the western states to separate from the union.
Memoirs of Aaron Burr with Miscellaneous Selections from his Correspondence
(ed. Matthew L. Davis). De Capo, New York, 1971.

Byles
Mather Byles, born 1706, son of a saddler, Congregational clergyman,
writer and scholar of Massachusetts. He was tried for treason, as a result
of his friendship to the British during the American revolution.
Philip Greven, *The Protestant Temperament. Patterns of Child-rearing,
Religious Experience, and the Self in Early America*. Alfred A. Knopf, New
York, 1977.

Byrd
The Byrd family owned a plantation in Virginia. William Byrd, born 1674, was a planter, colonial official and author.
(a) *The Secret Diary of William Byrd of Westover, 1709–12* (ed. Louis B. Wright and Marion Tinling). Dietz Press, Virginia, 1941.
(b) *The Correspondence of the Three William Byrds of Westover, Virginia, 1684–1776* (ed. Marion Tinling). University Press of Virginia, Charlottesville, 1977.

Byrom
John Byrom, born 1692 near Manchester, was a poet and the inventor of a system of shorthand.
'The Private Journal and Remains of John Byrom' (ed. Richard Parkinson). *Chetham Society*, vols 32, 34, 40, 1854.

Cairns
David Cairns, born 1862, grew up in a Scottish country manse in Roxburghshire. His father adhered to the United Presbyterian faith, which his son later renounced.
David Cairns, *An Autobiography. Some Recollections of a Long Life and Selected Letters* (ed. by his son and daughter). SCM Press, London, 1950.

Calvert
Frances Calvert, born 1767 in Dublin, was married to Nicholas Calvert, Esq. of Hertfordshire, MP.
Frances Calvert, *An Irish Beauty of the Regency* (ed. Mrs Warrenne Blake). The Bodley Head, London, 1911.

Capel
Caroline Capel, born 1773, was the eldest daughter of the Earl of Uxbridge. She married John Capel, the second son of the Earl of Essex.
Caroline Capel, *The Capel Letters being the Correspondence of Lady Caroline Capel and her Daughters with the Dowager of Countess of Uxbridge from Brussels and Switzerland 1814–17* (ed. The Marquess of Anglesey). Jonathan Cape, London, 1955.

Carew
Baronets of Bedington.
Carew papers, British Library, add. MSS 92597–60.

Carswell
Catherine Carswell, born 1880 in Glasgow, was a novelist, and drama and literary critic.
Catherine Carswell, *Lying Awake*. Secker and Warburg, London, 1950.

Carter
The Carter family were very wealthy plantation-owners in Virginia who played an important part in the political life of the state. Landon Carter, born 1707, was a younger son of Robert 'King' Carter and the prolific author of political tracts.

(a) *The Diary of Colonel Landon Carter of Sabine Hall* (ed. Jack Greene). University Press of Virginia, Charlottesville, 1965.
(b) 'Diary of Colonel Landon Carter', *William and Mary College Quarterly Magazine*, vols 13–18, 1905–10.
(c) Edmund Morgan, *Virginians at Homes. Family Life in the Eighteenth Century*. University Press of Virginia, Charlottesville, 1952 (1968 ed.).

Cavendish

Margaret Cavendish, born c.1624, later the Duchess of Newcastle. Margaret wrote poetry, plays and also composed works bewailing the plight of women. She was noted for her outlandish mode of attire. Her husband fought for the King in the Civil War and they spent the Cromwellian era exiled and in poverty.

Margaret Cavendish, *A True Relations of My Birth, Breeding, and Life* (ed. Sir Egerton Brydges). Private press of Lee Priory, Kent, 1814.

Chester

Bedfordshire family.
Chester, MSS, Buckinghamshire Record Office, D/C.

Chesterfield

Philip Dormer Stanhope, fourth Lord Chesterfield, born 1694, was a politician. He was also the author of a notorious advice to his illegitimate son. These letters aroused a great deal of opposition at the time because of the candid nature of the advice.

Lord Chesterfield, *Letters written by the Late Right Honourable Philip Dormer Stanhope to his Son Philip Stanhope esq.* (ed. Eugenia Stanhope). J. Dodsley, London, 1774.

Chitty

Essex family. No more is known about Clarimona Chitty.
'The Will of a Child', *Genealogist's Magazine*, vol. 15, 1968.

Cholmley

Sir Hugh Cholmley, born 1600 in Yorkshire, was a knight and the first baronet of the Cholmley family. He was a royalist and spent the Civil War in exile.
The Memoirs of Sir Hugh Cholmley. Privately printed, 1787.

Churchill

John Churchill, born 1650 in Devonshire, was a leading military commander and was rewarded for defeating the French in 1702 with the title Duke of Marlborough.
David Green, *Sarah, Duchess of Marlborough*. Collins, London, 1967.

Clifford

Lady Anne Clifford, born 1590, was the heiress of the third Earl of Cumberland. She first married Richard, Earl of Dorset, and withstood his pressure to persuade her to relinquish her estates to his control. Her second husband was Philip Herbert, fourth Earl of Pembroke and through him she became Countess of Dorset, Pembroke and Montgomery.

(a) *The Diary of Lady Anne Clifford* (ed. Victoria Sackville-West). Heinemann, London, 1923.
(b) George Williamson, *Lady Anne Clifford, Countess of Dorset, Pembroke and Montgomery 1590–1676. Her Life, Letters and Work*. SR Publishers, East Ardsley, Yorkshire, 2nd ed., 1967.

Cobden-Sanderson
Thomas Cobden-Sanderson, born 1840, was a printer and bookseller. His son Richard founded a publishing firm.
The Journals of Thomas James Cobden-Sanderson. Richard Cobden-Sanderson, London, 1926.

Coleman
Lydia Coleman lived in Boston.
Alice M. Earle, *Two Centuries of Costume in America*. Macmillan, New York, 1907.

Colman
Well-to-do American family.
Alice M. Earle, *Child Life in Colonial Days*. Macmillan, New York, 1899.

Coleridge
Sara Coleridge, born 1802 near Keswick, was the daughter of the poet Samuel Taylor Coleridge. She translated books from Latin and composed works for children such as the fairy tale, *Phantasmion*.
Memoirs and Letters of Sara Coleridge (ed. her daughter). Henry S. King and Co., London, 1873.

Conway
Anne, Viscountess Conway, died 1679, was one of the renowned female intellectuals of the seventeenth-century. Despite suffering from a constant severe headache, she taught herself Latin, Greek and mathematics and was the author of a philosophical treatise. She was in regular correspondence with the Platonist Henry More. Later in her life she joined the Society of Friends.
Conway Letters. The Correspondence of Anne, Viscountess Conway, Henry More and their Friends, 1642–84 (ed. Marjory Nicolson). Oxford University Press, London, 1930.

Cornwallis
Jane Cornwallis, born c.1581, daughter of a minor gentleman of Essex, was first the wife of Sir William Cornwallis and then Sir Nathaniel Bacon, knight.
The Private Correspondence of Jane Lady Cornwallis 1613–44. S. and J. Bentley, Wilson and Fley, London, 1842.

Cowper
Earls of Cowper. Sarah Cowper was the elder daughter of William Cowper, first earl.
Cowper papers, Hertfordshire Record Office, D.

Cumberland
The Cumberland family were landowners in the environs of London. Richard was born in 1752 and George in 1754.

The Cumberland Letters. Being the Correspondence of Richard Dennison Cumberland and George Cumberland between the Years 1771–1784 (ed. Clementina Black). Martin Secker, London, 1912.

Dering
Gentry family from Kent, baronets.
Dering papers, Kent Archive Office, U350.

D'Ewes
Sir Simonds D'Ewes, born 1602, antiquarian writer, was created a baronet in 1641. He kept a detailed diary of his years at Cambridge as a Puritan undergraduate in the early seventeenth century.

The Autobiography and Correspondence of Sir Simonds D'Ewes, Bart (ed. James Halliwell). Richard Bentley, London, 1845.

Dow
Lorenzo Dow, born 1777, was an Evangelist Methodist from 1798 and an itinerant, poor preacher. Peggy was Lorenzo's wife.

Lorenzo Dow, *History of a Cosmopolite.* Joshua Martin, Virginia, 1848.

Doyle
Richard Doyle, born 1825 in London, artist and caricaturist, kept an illustrated diary for the year he was fifteen.

A Journal Kept by Richard Doyle in the Year 1840. Smith, Elder and Co., London, 1885.

Drinker
Quaker family of Philadelphia. Henry Drinker, the husband of Elizabeth, born 1734, was employed in the shipping and importing trade.

(a) *Extracts from the Journal of Elizabeth Drinker* (ed. Henry Biddle). J. B. Lippincott, Philadelphia, 1889.

(b) Cecil Drinker, *Not So Long Ago. A Chronicle of Medicine and Doctors in Colonial Philadelphia.* Oxford University Press, New York, 1937.

Dryden
Northamptonshire gentry family.
Dryden papers, Northamptonshire Record Office, MS D(CA).

Dunbar
Record of a high school in seventeenth-century Dunbar.
Dunbar burgh records, Scottish Record Office, B18/box 1/5.

Dundas
Somerset gentry family.
Phelips papers, Somerset Record Office, DD/PH.

Edwards
Timothy Edwards went as chaplain on an American expedition to Canada.

Alice M. Earle, *Child Life in Colonial Days.* Macmillan, New York, 1899.

Epps
John Epps, born 1806 in Kent, homoeopathic physician. He was brought up in the Calvinist faith.
Diary of the Late John Epps (ed. Mrs Epps). Kent and Co., London, 1875.

Erskine (1)
Ebenezer Erskine, born 1680 in Berwickshire, was the founder of the Scottish Secession Church.
The Life and Diary of Rev. Ebenezer Erskine (ed. Donald Fraser). William Oliphant, Edinburgh, 1831.

Erskine (2)
James Erskine, born 1679, Lord Grange, the second son of the tenth Earl of Mar, was a judge.
James Erskine, *Extracts from the Diary of a Senator of the College of Justice* (ed. J. Maidment). Thomas Stevenson, Edinburgh, 1843.

Evelyn
John Evelyn, born 1670, virtuoso, fellow of the Royal Society and author of a very detailed diary.
Diary and Correspondence of John Evelyn (ed. William Bray). Henry Colburn, London, 1850–52.

Farjeon
Eleanor Farjeon was born in the late nineteenth century. Her family were Jewish and her father worked in the publishing world.
Eleanor Farjeon, *A Nursery in the Nineties*. Victor Gollancz, London, 1935.

Fithian
Philip Fithian, born 1747, was tutor to the Carter family, Virginian plantation-owners. Philip was a Princeton-bred theology student who had received an austere Presbyterian training and disliked much of the gaiety of Virginia.
Journal and Letters of Philip Vickers Fithian 1773–74 (ed. Hunter Farish). Colonel Williamsburgh Inc., Virginia, 1943.

Fitzgerald
Lord Edward Fitzgerald, born 1763, was an Irish rebel who died from wounds sustained during his capture. His wife Pamela was born c.1776.
Gerald Campbell, *Edward and Pamela Fitzgerald*. Edward Arnold, London, 1904.

Fitzhugh
William Fitzhugh, born 1651, emigrated from Bedford c.1670 and became a planter, exporter and lawyer of Virginia.
William Fitzhugh and his Chesapeake World 1676–1701. The Fitzhugh Letters and other Documents (ed. Richard Beale Davis). Virginia Historical Society, University of Carolina Press, 1963.

Fleming

Upper-class family. Marjory Fleming, born 1803, kept a diary, including some of her poetry, from the age of six until her death at the age of nine. Sir Walter Scott, a friend of the family, referred to her as 'Pet Margarie'.
(a) Fleming papers, National Library of Scotland, MS1100.
(b) *The Complete Marjory Fleming*, (ed. Frank Sidgwick). Sidgwick and Jackson, London, 1934.

Fletcher

An upwardly mobile family rising from Dundee merchants to the Lords of Saltoun.
Fletcher papers, National Library of Scotland, MSS 16501–17900.

Foulis

Sir John Foulis, born 1638, baronet of Ravelston. He was involved in public life, holding an official position in Edinburgh.
'The Account Book of Sir John Foulis of Ravelston 1671–1707' (ed. A. W. Cornelius Hallen), *Scottish Historical Society*, vol. 16, 1894.

Freke

Landed gentry family, supporters of the royalist cause during the Civil War. Elizabeth Freke, born 1641, was the daughter of Raufe Freke of Wiltshire and married Percy Freke of Cork.
Mrs Elizabeth Freke. Her Diary (ed. Mary Carberry). Guy and Co., Cork, 1913.

Fry

Quaker family. Elizabeth Fry, born 1780, was a philanthropist, especially active in the campaign for prison reform. She was the daughter of the Norwich banker John Gurney.
Susanna Corder, *Life of Elizabeth Fry*. W. and F. G. Cash, London, 1853.

Gaskell

Elizabeth Gaskell, born 1810 in London, was a novelist, some of whose works depicted the toil and sufferings of the working classes. She married William Gaskell, minister of a Unitarian chapel in Manchester.
Elizabeth Gaskell, *My Diary. The Early Years of My Daughter Marianne* (ed. Clement Shorter). Privately printed, London, 1923.

Gell

Baronets of Derbyshire. Sir John Gell, born 1593, was accused of participating in plots against the commonwealth and imprisoned for treason.
Gell papers, Derbyshire Record Office, D258.

Gordon-Cummings

Scottish gentry family, baronets of Gordonstoun. Roualeyn, born 1820, was an African lion hunter.
Gordon-Cummings papers, National Library of Scotland, dep. 175.

Grafton

Mary Grafton, from Delaware, attended school in Philadelphia.
Alice M. Earle, *Child Life in Colonial Days*. Macmillan, New York, 1899.

Grant (1)

Ann Grant, born 1755 in Glasgow, was married to a clergyman of a Highland parish. After she was widowed she wrote poetry and published collections of letters as well as taking in young lady boarders to make ends meet.

(a) Ann Grant, *Letters from the Mountains*. Luke Hansard and Sons, London (2nd ed.), 1807.

(b) Ann Grant, *Memoir and Correspondence* (ed. J. P. Grant). Longman, Brown, Green and Longmans, London, 1844.

Grant (2)

Elizabeth Grant, born 1797, was the daughter of a Scottish laird and lawyer.

Elizabeth Grant, *Memoirs of a Highland Lady* (ed. Lady Strachey). John Murray, London, 1911.

Gray

Faith Gray, born 1751, was active with her husband in improving York, in particular educational provision for poor children.

Almyra Gray, *Papers and Diaries of a York Family*. Sheldon Press, London, 1927.

Gregory

Dr Gregory, a physician from Edinburgh, was the author of several instruction manuals. He wrote his advice to his daughters when he realised he did not have long to live.

'Dr Gregory: A Father's Legacy to his Daughters', (pp. 1–51) in *The Young Lady's Pocket Library, or Parental Monitor*. John Archer, Dublin, 1790.

Grimston

The Grimstons were a family of country squires of Yorkshire.

M. Edward Ingram, *Leaves from a Family Tree being the Correspondence of an East Riding Family*. A. Brown and Sons, Hull and London, 1951.

Guest

Charlotte Guest, born 1812 in Lincolnshire, is better known as Lady Schrieber, responsible for the china collection deposited in the Victoria and Albert Museum. She was a member of the landed classes and overcame a great deal of opposition in order to marry her first husband, John Guest the ironmaster.

Lady Charlotte Guest. Extracts from her Journal 1832–52 (ed. Earl of Bessborough). John Murray, London, 1950.

Haldane

Mary Haldane, born 1825 in Northumberland, was a Methodist and married to James Haldane, writer to the signet.

Mary Elizabeth Haldane, *Record of a Hundred Years 1825–1925* (ed. by her daughter). Hodder and Stoughton, London, 1925.

Halkett

Anne Halkett, born 1623, was the younger daughter of Thomas Murray, secretary to King Charles I. She married Sir James Halkett.

'The Autobiography of Anne Lady Halkett' (ed. J. G. Nichols), *Camden Society*, new series, vol. 13, 1875.

Hamilton

Mary Hamilton, born 1756, was a lady-in-waiting at court.

Mary Hamilton. At Court and at Home (ed. Elizabeth and Florence Anson). John Murray, London, 1925.

Hamilton-Gordon

Rachael Hamilton-Gordon, aged ten, kept a diary of the journey she took with her parents and brother from London to New Zealand in 1882.

British Library, add MSS 49271, ff. 207-28.

Harley

Brilliana Harley, born c.1600, was the wife of Sir Robert Harley, knight of the Bath of Herefordshire. She successfully withstood a six-week siege during the Civil War from royalist forces.

'Letters of the Lady Brilliana Harley' (ed. Thomas Lewis), *Camden Society*, 1854.

Harrower

John Harrower, born c.1735 in Scotland, sailed to America to become a tutor. One of his pupils was a fourteen-year-old deaf mute, John Edge, who became the first such handicapped person to be instructed in America.

'Diary of John Harrower', *American Historical Review*, vol. 6 (pp. 65–107), 1901.

Harvey

Quaker family. William Harvey's father was a retired businessman with private means.

William Harvey, *We were Seven*, Constable and Co., London, 1936.

Hatton

Gentry family raised to the peerage in 1643, becoming barons and then Viscounts Hatton. Christopher Hatton, born 1632, like his father before him, was governor of Guernsey.

(a) Finch Hatton papers, Northamptonshire Record Office, MSS FH.

(b) Hatton Finch papers, British Library, add. MSS 29550 onwards.

(c) Correspondence of the family of Hatton, *Camden Society*, 1878.

Hayes

Rutherford Birchard Hayes, born 1822, was a lawyer, soldier in the Civil War on Lincoln's side and became the nineteenth President of the United States.

'Diary and Letters of Rutherford B. Hayes' (ed. Charles Williams), *Ohio State Archaeological and Historical Society*, 1922–6.

Head
Caroline Head, born 1852, was a Quaker from the middle classes.
Charlotte Hanbury, *Life of Mrs Albert Head*. Marshall Bros., London, 1905.

Heber
Landed family of Yorkshire and Shropshire. Reginald Heber, born 1728, was rector of Hodnet, and his son Richard, born 1774, became a famous book-collector.
Heber MSS, Bodleian Library, Eng. letters, C.203.

Henry
Landed family of Flinshire. Matthew Henry, born 1662, was a minister.
Henry MSS, Bodleian Library, Eng. letters, E29.

Herbert
Gentry family of Cherbury. Lord Herbert's son was Henry Herbert who became MP for Bewdley in 1709.
Herbert, *Epistolary Curiosities. Unpublished Letters of the Seventeenth Century, Illustrative of the Herbert Family* (ed. Rebecca Warner). Richard Cruttwell, Bath, 1818.

Hill
Quaker family. Sarah Hill was born in 1739.
William Frost, *The Quaker Family in Colonial America. A Portrait of the Society of Friends*. St Martin's Press, New York, 1973.

Holles
Gervase Holles, born 1607, was one of the most foremost antiquaries of his time. He became the mayor of Grimsby and was called to the upper bar in 1639. He lived in exile during the time of Oliver Cromwell.
'Gervase Holles: Memorials of the Holles Family 1493–1656' (ed. A. C. Wood), *Camden Society*, 3rd series, vol. 55, 1937.

Hosmer
Harriet Hosmer, born 1830 in Massachusetts, was a sculptor. She studied anatomy at the University of St Louis, one of the few institutions to admit women into the medical faculty.
Harriet Hosmer. Letters and Memories (ed. Cornelia Carr). John Lane, The Bodley Head, London, 1913.

Housman
Mrs H. Housman, born c.1680, was devoutly religious.
H. Housman, *The Power and the Pleasure of the Divine Life* (ed. Richard Pearsall). J. Oswald, London, 1744.

Howes
Thomas Howes, born 1801, was a student at Rappa Academy, Virginia.
William and Mary College Quarterly Magazine, 2nd series, vol. 22 (p. 415), 1942.

Hughes

Victorian, comfortably-off, suburban family. Mary Hughes was born c.1865.

Mary Vivian Hughes, *A London Child of the Seventies*. Oxford University Press, London, 1934.

Huntington

Susan Huntington, born 1791, was the daughter of a minister and married to a minister.

Benjamin B. Wisner, *Memoirs of the Late Mrs S. Huntingdon*. William Collins, Glasgow, 1828.

Hutchinson

Lucy Hutchinson, born 1620, was the daughter of Sir Allen Apsley and married to Colonel Hutchinson, governor of Nottingham. She and her husband were opposed to the monarchy during the Civil War.

Lucy Hutchinson, *Memoirs of the Life of Colonel (John) Hutchinson* (ed. Rev. Julius Hutchinson). Longmans, Hurst, Rees and Orme, London (3rd ed.), 1810.

Isham

Gentry family of Lamport Hall, Northamptonshire. Sir Justinian Isham, born 1610, was a cultured and learned gentleman, supporter of the King. Thomas Isham, heir of Justinian, was born in 1658 and died at the age of twenty-three.

(a) Isham papers, Northamptonshire Record Office, IC and IL.

(b) *The Diary of Thomas Isham of Lamport (1658–81) kept by him in Latin from 1671 to 1673 at his Father's Command* (ed. Sir Gyles Isham; trans. Norman Marlow). Gregg International Publishers, London, 1971.

Jefferson

Thomas Jefferson, born 1743, was a Virginian estate owner, statesman, diplomat, architect, author, scientist and the third President of the United States. He wished to abolish the privileges of wealth and birth enjoyed by the Virginian aristocracy.

The Domestic Life of Thomas Jefferson (ed. Sarah Randolph). Harper and Brothers, New York, 1871.

Joceline

Elizabeth Joceline, born 1596, feared during her pregnancy that she would die in childbirth. She composed a work of instruction for her unborn child and also secretly bought a winding sheet for her burial. Her fears proved true, and she died nine days after giving birth to a daughter.

Elizabeth Joceline, *The Mother's Legacie to her Unborne Childe* (ed. John Haviland). William Blackwood and Sons, Edinburgh and London, 1852. (This edition is a reprint of the third edition of 1625.)

Johnson

Impoverished gentry family of Buckinghamshire, Thomas Johnson was imprisoned for debt.

Johnson papers, Buckinghamshire Record Office, DX/827.

Johnston
Priscilla Johnston, born 1808, in Norfolk. She was a Quaker and a niece of Elizabeth Fry.
Extracts from Priscilla Johnston's Journal (ed. E. MacInnes). Charles Thurnam and Sons, Carlisle, 1862.

Jones (1)
Upper-class Virginian family.
Jones family papers, Library of Congress. Cited in Daniel B. Smith, 'Autonomy and Affection: Parents and Children in Eighteenth-Century Chesapeake Families', *Psychohistorical Review*, vol. 6, 1977–8.

Jones (2)
William Jones, born 1755, was the curate and rector of Broxbourne and an author.
The Diary of Reverend William Jones, 1777–1821 (ed. O. F. Christie). Brentanos, London, 1929.

Josselin
Ralph Josselin was a Nonconformist minister, farmer and the author of one of the most informative seventeenth-century diaries.
'The Diary of Ralph Josselin' (ed. Alan Macfarlane), *British Academy Records of Social and Economic History*, new series, vol. 3, 1976.

Kildare
Emily Kildare, born 1731, was the Duchess of Leinster.
Brian FitzGerald, *Emily Duchess of Leinster 1731–1814. A Study of her Life and Times*. Staple Press, New York and London, 1949.

Lauderdale
Members of the Scottish peerage. John, second Earl of Lauderdale, born 1616, worked to ensure that the fate of Charles II would not be decided without consulting Scotland.
'Lauderdale letters: Letters from John, second Earl of Lauderdale, to John, second Earl of Tweedale, and others', *Scottish History Society*, 3rd series, vol. 33 miscellany, 1939.

Laurens
Henry Laurens, born 1724, mechant, planter, revolutionary statesman. His daughter Martha married the historian David Ramsay.
Alice M. Earle, *Child Life in Colonial Days*. Macmillan, New York, 1899.

Lawes-Wittewronge
Gentry family of Hertfordshire.
Lawes-Wittewronge papers, Hertfordshire Record Office, D.

Lee (1)
Richard Lee, born 1732 in Virginia, influential planter and president of continental congress. He was an ardent federalist and a rival to Thomas Jefferson.
The Letters of Richard Henry Lee (ed. James Ballagh). Macmillan, New York, 1911.

Lee (2)

Robert Lee, born 1807 in Virginia, had a distinguished military career. He resigned from government service at the onset of the Civil War since he refused to bear arms against the South. He was Commander-in-Chief of the Rebel forces.

'Five Early Letters from Robert Lee to his Wife 1832–35', *Huntington Library Quarterly*, vol. 15, 1951–2.

Legh

Gentry family of Lyme, Cheshire.

Legh Papers, John Rylands Library, Legh MSS.

Leigh

Dorothy Leigh, born mid-sixteenth century, was a gentlewoman.

Dorothy Leigh, *The Mother's Blessing or the Godly Counsaile of a gentle-woman, Not Long since Deceased, Left behind for her Children*. John Budge, London (4th ed.), 1618.

Leith

Harriet Leith, heiress of Alexander Steuart, was the mother of the distinguished General Sir James Leith, born 1763.

Leith Hay papers, Scottish Record Office, GD30.

Livingston

Seventeenth-century well-to-do family from New York.

Alice Morse Earle, *Colonial Days in Old New York*. David Nutt, London, 1896.

Long

John Long, born 1838 in Maine, was the son of a farmer and became the governor of Massachusetts, congressman and Secretary of the Navy.

John D. Long, *America of Yesterday* (ed. Lawrence S. Mayo). Atlantic Monthly Press, Boston, 1923.

Longfellow

Henry Wadsworth Longfellow, born 1807, poet and professor of modern languages at Harvard. His wife Fanny was the daughter of a banker. One of their sons, Ernest, became a painter. Zilpah was Henry's mother.

(a) *Life of Henry Wadsworth Longfellow* (ed. Samuel Johnson). Ticknor and Co., Boston, 1886.

(b) *Mrs Longfellow. Selected Letters and Journals of Fanny Appleton Longfellow (1817–1861)* (ed. Edward Wagenknecht). Peter Owen, London, 1959.

Lovell

Lucy Lovell of Massachusetts, born 1809, was brought up as a Quaker and married a Baptist minister.

Elizabeth Buffum Chace and Lucy Buffum Lovell, *Two Quaker Sisters* (ed. Malcolm Lovell). Liveright Publishing Corp., New York, 1937.

Lucas
William Lucas, born 1804, was a Quaker and a brewer.
William Lucas, *A Quaker Journal* (ed. G. E. Bryant and G. P. Baker). Hutchinson and Co., London, 1934.

Macready
William Macready, born 1793, was a successful actor.
The Diaries of William Charles Macready 1833–1851 (ed. William Toynbee). Chapman and Hall, London, 1912.

Magoffin
Susan Magoffin, born 1827, wrote her diary while travelling to Mexico with her husband and brother-in-law. Their trip was instrumental in preparing the way for the American government to take over Mexico.
Susan Magoffin, *Down the Santa Fe Trail and into Mexico* (ed. Stella Drumm). Yale University Press, New Haven, 1926.

Marshall
John Marshall, born 1755 on the Virginian frontier, was the Chief Justice of the United States and principal founder of the American system of constitutional law.
'Letters from John Marshall to his wife 1773–90', *William and Mary College Historical Magazine*, 2nd series, vol. 3, 1923.

Martindale
Adam Martindale, born 1623, was the son of a carpenter and builder. He became a Presbyterian divine and, when prevented from preaching because of his Nonconformism, taught mathematics.
'The Life of Adam Martindale' (ed. R. Parkinson), *Chetham Society*, vol. 4, 1845.

Martin-Leake
Gentry family of Hertfordshire.
Martin-Leake papers, Hertfordshire Record Office, J99.

Mascall
Elizabeth Mascall, born 1702, was a Methodist. She was married to a pewterer.
Elizabeth Mascall, *Remnants of a Life* (ed. A. Weight Matthews). Privately printed, London, 1902.

Massingberd
The Massingberds were baronets of Lincolnshire.
Burrell Massingberd papers, Lincoln Archive Office.

Mather
Family of Puritan ministers. Increase Mather, born 1639, was a Puritan clergyman, politician and author who worked to establish and strengthen the Congregational church. His son Cotton Mather, born 1663, became before the age of thirty one of the most eminent New England divines. He too was a Puritan clergyman, scholar and author and one of the ringleaders of the

rebellion against the governor of Massachusetts, Sir Edward Andros, supporter of James II.

(a) 'The Diary of Increase Mather', *Proceedings of the Massachusetts Historical Society*, 2nd series, vol. 13, 1899–1900.

(b) 'The Diary of Cotton Mather', *Collections of the Massachusetts Historical Society*, 7th series, vols 7–8, 1911–12.

(c) The letter of Samuel Mather is taken from Alice M. Earle, *Child Life in Colonial Days*. Macmillan, New York, 1899.

Maxwell
Scottish baronets.
Maxwell papers, National Library of Scotland, MS 7043.

Melville
Scottish peers, earls of Leven and Melville.
Melville papers, Scottish Record Office, GD26.

Mildmay (1)
Essex gentry family.
Essex Record Office, D/DMS.

Mildmay (2)
Grace Mildmay, born 1552, gentlewoman, was married to Anthony Mildmay, knight, of Northamptonshire.
'The Journal of Lady Grace Mildmay' (ed. R. Weigall), *Quarterly Review*, vol. 15, pp. 119–38, 1911.

Mill
John Mill, born 1712, was a Scottish minister.
'The Diary of the Reverend John Mill' (ed. Gilbert Goudie), *Scottish History Society*, vol. 5. 1889.

Moore
Thomas Moore, born 1779 in Dublin, was a poet and lyricist. He was of the Roman Catholic faith.
Memoirs, Journal, and Correspondence of Thomas Moore (ed. Lord John Russell). Longman, Brown, Green, and Longmans, London, 1853.

Mordaunt
Warwickshire gentry family.
Mordaunt papers, Warwick Record Office, CR1368.

Morris
Claver Morris, born in 1659, was a doctor.
Claver Morris, *The Diary of a West Country Physician* (ed. Edmund Hobhouse). Stanhope Press, Rochester, 1934.

Newcome
Henry Newcome, born 1627 in Huntingdonshire, was a Nonconformist minister.
'The Autobiography of Henry Newcome' (ed. Richard Parkinson), *Chetham Society*, vols 1–2, 1852.

North
Roger North, born 1653 in Suffolk, of a landed family. He was the author of the biographies of his brothers. Anne was Roger's mother.
Roger North, *The Lives of the Norths* (ed. A. Jessop). George Bell and Sons, London, 1890; facsimile edition (ed. E. Mackinness). Gregg International Publishers, London, 1972.

Oxinden
Kent gentry family on the side of the royalists during the Civil War. As a result, they suffered heavy fines and the sequestration of their estates. Henry Oxinden, born 1609, composed poetry.
(a) *The Oxinden Letters 1607–1642. Being the Correspondence of Henry Oxiden of Barham and his Circle* (ed. Dorothy Gardiner). Constable and Co., London, 1933.
(b) The Oxiden and Peyton Letters 1642–1670 (ed. Dorothy Gardiner). Sheldon Press, London, 1937.

Palgrave
Francis Palgrave, born 1824, was employed in the education department of Whitehall.
Francis Turner Palgrave. His Journals and Memories of his Life (ed. Gwenllian Palgrave). Longmans, Green and Co., London, 1899.

Papendiek
Charlotte Papendiek, born 1765, was employed in the service of Queen Charlotte.
Charlotte Papendiek, *Court and Private Life in the Time of Queen Charlotte: being the Journals of Mrs Papendiek, Assistant Keeper of the Wardrobe and Reader to Her Majesty* (ed. Vernon Broughton). Richard Bentley, London, 1887.

Parker (1)
Ellen Parker, born 1833, was the daughter of Luther Parker, the first white man to be domiciled in the Indian Stream republic in Wisconsin. She taught at a boarding school.
'Ellen Parker's Journal', *Collections of the New Hampshire Historical Society*, vol. 11 (pp. 132–62), 1915.

Parker (2)
Eighteenth-century gentry family of Virginia.
Jan Lewis, *The Pursuit of Happiness. Family and Values in Jefferson's Virginia*. Cambridge University Press, 1983.

Parker (3)
Country squires of Essex. John Oxley Parker was born in 1812.
J. Oxley Parker, *The Oxley Parker Papers*. Berham and Co., Colchester, 1964.

Patrick
Symon Patrick, born 1626, was the eldest son of a Lincolnshire mercer and became the Bishop of Ely.
The Autobiography of Symon Patrick. J. H. Parker, Oxford, 1839.

Penn Charter
School for Quakers in Philadelphia.
J. William Frost, *The Quaker Family in Colonial America. A Portrait of the Society of Friends*. St Martin's Press, New York, 1973.

Pennington
Lady Sarah Pennington, died in 1783, married Sir Joseph Pennington. She left her husband after twelve years of marriage and wrote several conduct books after this separation, seeking to restore her reputation.
Sarah Pennington, *Letters on Different Subjects*. J. Walter, London, 4th ed., 1770.

Perry
Joseph Perry was a minister.
Alice M. Earle, *Child Life in Colonial Days*, Macmillan, New York, 1899.

Phelips
Somerset gentry family.
Phelips papers, Somerset Record Office DD/PH.

Phelps
Caroline Phelps, born about 1807, was married to a fur-trapper.
'Mrs Caroline Phelps' Diary', *Journal of the Illinois State Historical Society*, vol. 23, 1930–31.

Pinckney
Eliza Pinckney, born 1722, took over the administration of her father's three plantations at the age of sixteen. She is identified with the development of indigo as a staple of colonial South Carolina. She married the prominent lawyer Charles Pinckney.
Harriott Ravenel, *Eliza Pinckney. Women of Colonial and Revolutionary Times in America*. John Murray, London, 1896.

Place
Francis Place, born 1771 in London, was a tailor who rose to become a prosperous shop-owner. He was a leading political reformer of the late eighteenth and early nineteenth centuries.
The Autobiography of Francis Place (ed. Mary Thrale). Cambridge University Press, 1972.

Portland
Dukes of Portland, Nottinghamshire.
Portland papers, Nottingham University Library, Cavendish letters, PW1.

Porter
Endymion Porter, born 1587, was employed in the service of Charles I.
Dorothea Townshend, *The Life and Letters of Mr Endymion Porter: Sometime Gentleman of the Bedchamber to King Charles the First*. T. Fisher Unwin, London, 1897.

Post
Frederick Post, born 1819, died from tuberculosis at the age of sixteen.
Extracts from the Diary of the Late Frederick James Post. Privately printed,
London, 1838.

Pratt
Elizabeth Pratt was born in Virginia in 1821.
Julia Cherry Spruill, *Women's Life and Work in the Southern Colonies.*
University of North Carolina Press, Chapel Hill, 1938.

Prentiss
Elizabeth Prentiss, born 1818 in Maine, writer of religious and juvenile
fiction. She was married to a minister of the South Trinitarian church.
G. L. Prentiss, *The Life and Letters of Elizabeth Prentiss.* Hodder and
Stoughton, London, 1882.

Pringle
Walter Pringle, born 1625 in Berwickshire, was a member of the landed
classes and a covenanter.
Memoirs of Walter Pringle of Greenknow. William Hamilton, Edinburgh,
1751.

Revill
Landed family of Derbyshire.
Ashover collection, Derbyshire Record Office, 253A.

Rich
Mary Rich, born 1625, later the Countess of Warwick, was the seventh
daughter of Richard Boyle, first Earl of Cork. She was a devout Christian.
'Autobiography of Mary Countess of Warwick' (ed. T. C. Croker), *Percy
Society*, vol. 22, 1848.

Richards
Caroline Richards, born in 1842, was brought up by her grandparents
after her mother's death, in the village of Canandaigua, New York. Anna
was her younger sister.
Caroline C. Richards, *Village Life in America.* Henry Holt and Co., New
York, 1913.

Rothschild
Family of prestigious Jewish bankers. Annie de Rothschild was born in
1844.
Louisa de Rothschild, *Lady de Rothschild and her Daughters 1821–1931* (ed.
Lucy Cohen). John Murray, London, 1935.

Russell
Lord and Lady Amberley. Kate Russell, born 1842, was the daughter of
Henrietta Stanley, whose letters are also cited in this anthology, and the
mother of Bertrand Russell.
Katherine Russell, *The Amberley Papers* (ed. Bertrand and Patricia Russell).
George Allen and Unwin, London, 1966.

Ryder

Sir Dudley Ryder, born 1691, was a law student when he wrote his intimate diary. He later became Lord Chief Justice of the King's bench.
The Diary of Dudley Ryder (ed. William Mathews). Methuen, London, 1939.

St John

Baronets, then barons of Bedfordshire.
Bedford Record Office, J.

Saltonstall

The Saltonstalls were originally a Yorkshire family who emigrated to Massachusetts and became a leading family in that state. Nathaniel Saltonstall, born 1746, was a doctor and his son Leverett, born 1783, was a lawyer and the first mayor of Salem.
'The Saltonstall Papers, 1607–1815' (ed. Robert Moody), *Massachusetts Historical Society*, 1972.
The letter of Elizabeth Saltonstall was taken from: Alice M. Earle, *Child Life in Colonial Days*. Macmillan, New York, 1899.

Savile

Barons Savile of Nottinghamshire.
Savile papers, Nottinghamshire Record Office, DDSR.

Sewall

Samuel Sewall, born 1652 in Massachusetts, was a merchant, colonial magistrate, and author of a lengthy diary. He was of the Puritan faith and was one of the judges presiding at the witchcraft trials in Salem, 1692.
'Diary of Samuel Sewall', *Collections of the Massachusetts Historical Society*, 5th series, vols 5–7, 1878–82.

Sewell

Quaker family. Mary Sewell, born 1797, was the daughter of a gentleman farmer of Suffolk. She wrote moral tracts and was the mother of Anna Sewell, author of *Black Beauty*.
Mary Sewell, *The Life and Letters of Mrs Sewell*. James Nisbet, London (3rd ed.), 1889.

Shippen

Upper-class family of Philadelphia. Nancy, born 1763, was the daughter of William Shippen, a doctor and pioneer teacher of anatomy and midwifery. She was a leading society belle and at the age of eighteen married the wealthy Henry Livingston. It was to prove a disastrous match.
Nancy Shippen. Her Journal Book (ed. Ethel Armes). J. B. Lippincott, Philadelphia, 1935.

Shore

Emily Shore, born 1819, was the daughter of a doctor. She kept a very detailed diary, in particular recording her interest in natural history, from the age of eleven until her death from tuberculosis at the age of nineteen.
Journal of Emily Shore. Kegan Paul, Trench, Trubner & Co., London, 1898.

Silliman

Benjamin Silliman of New Haven, born 1779, was professor of chemistry and natural history at the University of Yale. He was deeply religious and one of the foremost and most influential scientists in America during the first half of the nineteenth century. Rebecca was Benjamin's mother.

George P. Fisher, *Life of Benjamin Silliman, LL.D.* Charles Scribner and Co., New York, 1866.

Skinner

John Skinner, born 1772, was a rector of a parish in Somerset. He found it impossible to get on with his parishioners or his children and committed suicide in 1839. His diary, which he composed to reveal to posterity the justness of his behaviour, runs to ninety-eight illustrated manuscript volumes.

John Skinner, *Journal of a Somerset Rector* (ed. Howard Coombs and Arthur Bax). John Murray, London, 1930.

Slingsby

Sir Henry Slingsby, born 1601, was the son of a knight and himself became a baronet. He was executed for treason in 1658.

The Diary of Sir Henry Slingsby, of Scriven, Bart (ed. Daniel Parsons). Longman and Co., London, 1836.

Smith

Sydney Smith, born 1771, was Canon of St Paul's and one of the founders of *The Edinburgh Review.*

The Letters of Sydney Smith (ed. Nowell Smith). Clarendon Press, Oxford, 1953.

Spears

Laura Spears, born in 1860, wrote a diary from the age of six as she accompanied her father on a whaling trip round Cape Horn. Her father was captain of the vessel.

Laura Spears, 'A Child's Diary of a Whaling Voyage' (ed. M. W. Jernegan), *New England Quarterly*, vol. 2, 1929.

Stanley

Upper-class family of Cheshire. Henrietta Stanley, born 1808, was active in the campaign for higher education for women and she was also the mother of Kate Russell, extracts from whose diary are included in this anthology.

The Ladies of Alderley being the Letters between Maria Josepha, Lady Stanley of Alderley and her Daughter-in-law Henrietta Maria Stanley during the years 1841–50 (ed. Nancy Mitford). Hamish Hamilton, London, 1967.

Stedman

John Gabriel Stedman, born 1744 in Holland, came to England in 1784. He was a lieutenant-colonel and a writer.

The Journal of John Gabriel Stedman (ed. Stanbury Thompson). Mitre Press, London, 1962.

Steuart
Amelia Steuart was born in c.1770 into an upper-class Scottish family.
Diary of Amelia Steuart, National Library of Scotland, MS 983.

Stirling
Landed Scottish family.
Stratchclyde Regional Archives, Mitchell Library, Glasgow, T-SK.

Sumner
Mary Sumner, a child brought up in the Puritan faith
Alice M. Earle, *Child Life in Colonial Days*. Macmillan, New York, 1899.

Sutherland
Scottish peers, Dukes of Sutherland. Jean Wemyss married a Duke of Sutherland.
Sutherland papers, National Library of Scotland, dep. 313.

Talbot
Earls of Shrewsbury and among the richest of the Elizabethan nobility. George Talbot, sixth Earl, was entrusted with the guardianship of Mary Queen of Scots during the term of her imprisonment. Alethea was the daughter of Gilbert, seventh Earl of Shrewsbury. She married Thomas Howard, second Earl of Arundel, in 1606.
Talbot papers, Lambeth Palace Library.

Taylor
John Taylor, born 1743, was a Baptist minister who had worked down the mines as a child.
Memoirs of the Reverend John Taylor (ed. Adam Taylor). Privately printed, London, 1820.

Thornton
Minor Yorkshire gentry. Alice Thornton, born 1626, was deeply religious.
'The Autobiography of Mrs Alice Thornton of East Newton, County York', vol. 62, *Surtees Society*, 1875.

Tilghman
Molly, born c.1760, and Henrietta, born 1763, in Pennsylvania, were the younger sisters of Colonel Tench Tilghman who had a brilliant military career. Their father was a distinguished lawyer.
'Letters of Molly and Hetty Tilghman', *Maryland Historical Magazine*, vol. 21, 1926.

Timms
Mary Timms, born 1808, was a Methodist, and married to a minister.
Memoirs of the Late Mrs Mary Timms (ed. E. Morgan). T. Whitehorn, London, 1835.

Todd
John Todd, born 1800 in Vermont, was a congregational clergyman and the author of numerous publications.
John Todd, *The Story of his Life* (ed. John Todd). Sampson, Law and Co., London, 1876.

Trench

Melesina Trench, born 1768 in Dublin, married first Colonel St George and after his death Richard Trench. The son of her first marriage became the Dean of Westminster.

The Remains of the Late Mrs Richard Trench (ed. The Dean of Westminster). Parker, Son, Bourn and Co., London, 1862.

Tryon

Thomas Tryon, born 1634, was a London merchant. He began work at the age of six, spinning and carding and taught himself to write while he was employed as a shepherd.

Some Memoirs of the Life of Mr Thomas Tryon. T. Sowle, London, 1705.

Turnbull

George Turnbull, born 1657, was a member of a Fife family of covenanters who had to flee to Holland for a while in 1679. He became a Presbyterian minister.

'The Diary of the Rev. George Turnbull, minister of Alloa and Tyning-hame 1657–1704' (ed. Robert Paul), *Scottish History Society Miscellany*, vol. 15, 1893.

Verney

Family of Buckinghamshire gentry who were on the side of the King during the Civil War. Sir Ralph Verney, born 1613, lived in exile in France for several years. The family was penalized by heavy fines and sequestrian orders on their estate.

(a) *Memoirs of the Verney Family* (ed. Francis Verney). Longmans, Green and Co., London, 1892.

(b) *Verney Letters of the Eighteenth Century from the MSS at Claydon House* (ed. Margaret Maria, Lady Verney). Ernest Benn, London, 1930.

Victoria

Queen of England, born 1819. Vicky was her eldest child, born 1841.

(a) Queen Victoria, *Dearest Child. Letters between Queen Victoria and the Princess Royal 1858–61* (ed. Roger Fulford). Evans Brothers, London, 1964.

(b) *The Girlhood of Queen Victoria* (ed. Viscount Esher). John Murray, London, 1912.

Wale

Thomas Wale, born 1701, was a merchant.

Thomas Wale *My Grandfather's Pocket Book* (ed. Henry Wale). Chapman and Hall, London, 1883.

Walker

Mary, born 1814, and Elkanah Walker were missionaries and among the first pioneers to journey to live in Oregon.

Clifford M. Drury, *Elkanah and Mary Walker*. Caxton Printers, Caldwell, Idaho, 1940.

Wallington
Nehemiah Wallington, born 1598, was a turner and London shopkeeper of the Puritan faith.
(a) Nehemiah Wallington, *Historical Notices of Events in the Reign of Charles I.* Richard Bentley, London, 1899.
(b) Nehemiah Wallington: A Record of the Mercies of God, Guildhall Library, MS 204.

Weeton
Ellen Weeton, born 1776, lost her father at the age of six. Her mother ran a school to provide sufficient income to maintain the family. Ellen was very unhappily married and left her husband, although it meant leaving her only child behind, and became a governess to support herself.
Ellen Weeton, *Miss Weeton. Journal of a Governess* (ed. Edward Hall). Oxford University Press, London, 1936–8.

Williams
Ephraim Williams was a New England farmer.
Alice M. Earle, *Child Life in Colonial Days.* Macmillan, New York, 1899.

Winslow
Anna Winslow, born 1759, was sent from her home in Nova Scotia to a finishing school in Boston. Her family were members of the gentry class. She died before she reached the age of twenty.
Anna Green Winslow, *Diary of a Boston Schoolgirl* (ed. Alice M. Earle). Houghton, Mifflin and Co., Boston and New York, 1894.

Wister
Sally (Sarah) Wister, born 1761 in Philadelphia, was the daughter of a prosperous merchant and reared in the Quaker faith. She kept a diary during the British attack on Philadelphia.
Sally Wister's Journal (ed. Albert Myers). Ferris and Leach, Philadelphia, 1902.

Wood
Frances Wood, born 1812, was the great-niece of Fanny Burney. Her husband was a major.
Frances Wood, *A Great-Niece's Journals* (ed. Margaret Rolt). Constable and Co., London, 1926.

Woodforde
Mary Woodforde, born 1638, was married to a minister.
'Mary Woodforde's Book' pp. 3–35 in *Woodforde Papers and Diaries* (ed. Dorothy Woodforde). Peter Davies, London, 1932.

Woods
Margaret Woods, born 1748, was of a middle-class family.
Extracts from the Journal of Margaret Woods. John and Arthur Arch, London, 1829.

Wynne

Elizabeth, born 1778, and her sister Eugenia, born 1779, were members of an upper-class Catholic family and toured Europe with their parents. Elizabeth married Admiral Thomas Fremantle.

Elizabeth Wynne, *The Wynne Diaries* (ed. Anne Fremantle). Oxford University Press, 1935–40.

Young

Arthur Young, born 1741 in London, was an agriculturalist and author. He owned a small landed estate in Suffolk.

The Autobiography of Arthur Young (ed. M. Betham-Edwards). Smith, Elder and Co., London, 1898.

Further Reading

Introduction

Proponents of the Evolutionary Thesis

Ariès, Philippe, *L'enfant et la vie familiale sous l'ancien regime* (Paris, Librairie Plon, 1960). Translated as *Centuries of Childhood* (London, Jonathan Cape, 1962)

Badinter, Elisabeth, *L'Amour en Plus* (Paris, Flammarion, 1981). Translated as *The Myth of Motherhood* (London, Souvenir Press, 1981)

Demos, John, *A Little Commonwealth. Family Life in a Plymouth Colony* (New York, Oxford University Press, 1970)

Lewis, Jan, *The Pursuit of Happiness. Family and Values in Jefferson's Virginia* (Cambridge, Cambridge University Press, 1983)

de Mause, Lloyd (ed.), *The History of Childhood* (London, Souvenir Press, 1976)

Pinchbeck, Ivy and Margaret Hewitt, *Children in English Society* (London, Routledge and Kegan Paul, 2 vols, 1969)

Shorter, Edward, *The Making of the Modern Family* (London, Collins, 1976)

Slater, Miriam, *Family Life in the Seventeenth Century. The Verneys of Claydon House* (London, Routledge and Kegan Paul, 1984)

Stone, Laurence, *The Family, Sex and Marriage in England 1500 to 1800* (London, Weidenfeld and Nicolson, 1977)

Trumbach, Randolph, *The Rise of the Egalitarian Family. Aristocratic Kinship and Domestic Relations in the Eighteenth Century* (London, Academic Press, 1978)

Opposing Views

Greven, Philip, *The Protestant Temperament. Patterns of Child-rearing, Religious Experience and the Self in Early America* (New York, Alfred A. Knopf, 1977)

Houlbrooke, Ralph, *The English Family 1450–1750* (London, Longmans, 1984)

Laslett, Peter and Richard Wall (eds), *Household and Family in Past Time* (Cambridge, Cambridge University Press, 1972)

MacDonald, Michael, *Mystical Bedlam. Madness, Anxiety, and Healing in Seventeenth-century England* (Cambridge, Cambridge University Press, 1981)

Macfarlane, Alan, *The Family Life of Ralph Josselin, a Seventeenth-century Clergyman. An Essay in Historial Anthropology* (Cambridge, Cambridge University Press, 1970)

Macfarlane, Alan, *Marriage and Love in England. Modes of Reproduction 1300–1840* (Oxford, Basil Blackwell, 1986)

Marshall, Rosalind, *Virgins and Viragos. A History of Women in Scotland from 1080–1980* (London, Collins, 1983)

Ozment, Steven, *When Fathers Ruled. Family Life in Reformation Europe* (Cambridge, Mass., Harvard University Press, 1983)

Pollock, Linda, *Forgotten Children. Parent-child Relations from 1500 to 1900* (Cambridge, Cambridge University Press, 1983)

Wall, Richard, (ed.) *Family Forms in Historic Europe* (Cambridge, Cambridge University Press, 1983)

Wrightson, Keith, *English Society 1580–1680* (London, Hutchinson, 1982)

Wrigley, E. A. and R. S. Schofield *The Population History of England 1541–1871. A Reconstruction* (London, Edward Arnold, 1981)

Working-class Autobiographies

Burnett, John, *Destiny Obscure. Autobiographies of Childhood, Education and Family from the 1820s to the 1920s* (London, Allen Lane, 1982)

Vincent, David, *Bread Knowledge and Freedom. A Study of Nineteenth-century Working-class Autobiography* (London, Methuen, 1981)

Chapter 1

Eccles, Audrey, *Obstetrics and Gynaecology in Tudor and Stuart England* (London, Croom Helm, 1982)

McLaren, Angus, *Reproductive Rituals: the Perception of Fertility in England from the Sixteenth to the Nineteenth century* (London, Methuen, 1984)

Schofield, Roger, 'Did the Mothers Really Die? Three Centuries of Maternal Mortality in "The World We Have Lost" ' in Lloyd Bonfield, Richard Smith and Keith Wrightson (eds.) *The World We Have Gained. Histories of Population and Social Structure* (Cambridge, Cambridge University Press, 1986)

Shorter, Edward, *A History of Women's Bodies* (London, Allen Lane, 1983)

Smith, W. D. A., *Under the Influence. A History of Nitrous Oxide and Oxygen Anaesthesia* (London, Macmillan, 1982)

Trumbach, Randolph, *The Rise of the Egalitarian Family. Aristocratic Kinship and Domestic Relations in the Eighteenth Century* (London, Academic Press, 1977)

Wilson, Adrian, *A Safe Deliverance: Ritual and Conflict in English Childbirth 1600 to 1750* (Cambridge University Press, forthcoming)

Chapter 2

Clark, Gillian, 'A Study of Nurse Children 1550–1750', *Local Population Studies* (forthcoming)

Cunningham, Phillis and Anne Buck, *Children's Costume in England from the Fourteenth to the End of the Nineteenth Centuries* (London, A. and C. Xlack, 1966)

Ewing, Elizabeth, *History of Children's Costume* (London, Bibliophile, 1977)

Fildes, Valerie, *Breast, Bottles, and Babies. A History of Infant Feeding* (Edinburgh, Edinburgh University Press, 1986)

Finlay, Roger, *Population and Metropolis. The Demography of London 1586–1650* (Cambridge, Cambridge University Press, 1981)

Fuller, Peter, 'Uncovering Childhood', in Martin Hoyles (ed.) *Changing Childhood* (London, Writers and Readers Publishing Cooperative, 1977)

Marshall, Rosalind, *Virgins and Viragos. A History of Women in Scotland from 1080 to 1980* (London, Collins, 1983)

Wrightson, Keith, *English Society 1580 to 1680* (London, Hutchinson, 1982)

Chapter 3

Blanton, Wyndham, *Medicine in Virginia in the Seventeenth Century* (New York, Arno Press, 1972)

Cartwright, Frederick, *A Social History of Medicine* (London, Longman, 1977)

Debus, Allen (ed.), *Medicine in Seventeenth-century England* (Berkeley, Calif., University of California Press, 1974)

Hanawalt, Barbara, 'Childrearing among the Lower Classes in Late Medieval England', *Journal of Inter-disciplinary History*, 8 (1977)

Hollingsworth, T. H., 'The Demography of the British Peerage', supplement to *Population Studies*, 18 (1965)

Razell, Peter, *The Conquest of Smallpox: The Impact of Inoculation on Smallpox Mortality in Eighteenth-century Britain* (London, Caliban Books, 1977)

Slater, Miriam, *Family Life in the Seventeenth Century. The Verneys of Claydon House* (London, Routledge and Kegan Paul, 1984)

Trumbach, Randolph, *The Rise of the Egalitarian Family. Aristocratic Kinship and Domestic Relations in the Eighteenth Century* (London, Academic Press, 1977)

Woods, Robert and John Woodward (eds.), *Urban Disease and Mortality in Nineteenth-Century England* (London, Batsford and New York, St Martin's Press, 1984)

Wrigley, E. A. and R. S. Schofield, *The Population History of England 1541-1871. A Reconstruction* (London, Edward Arnold, 1981)

Chapter 4

Brewster, Paul, *American Nonsinging Games* (Norman, University of Oklahoma Press, 1953)

Fawdry, Kenneth and Margaret, *Pollock's History of English Dolls and Toys* (London, Ernest Benn, 1979)

Jewell, Brian, *Sports and Games. History and Origins* (Tunbridge Wells, Midas Books, 1977)

Opie, Iona and Peter, *Children's Games in Street and Playground* (Oxford, Clarendon Press, 1969)

Plumb, J. H., 'The New World of Children in Eighteenth-century England', *Past and Present*, 67, (1975)

Schofield, Angela, *Toys in History* (Hove, Sussex, Wayland Publishers, 1978)

Walvin, James, *A Child's World. A Social History of English Childhood, 1800–1914* (Harmondsworth, Penguin Books, 1982)

Chapter 5

Ariès, Philippe, *Centuries of Childhood* (London, Jonathan Cape, 1962)

Greven, Philip, *The Protestant Temperament. Patterns of Child-rearing, Religious Experience, and the Self in Early America* (New York, Alfred A. Knopf, 1977)

de Mause, Lloyd (ed.), *The History of Childhood* (London, Souvenir Press, 1976)

Pollock, Linda, *Forgotten Children. Parent-Child Relations from 1500 to 1900* (Cambridge, Cambridge University Press, 1983)

Stone, Laurence, *The Family, Sex and Marriage in England, 1500–1800* (London, Weidenfeld and Nicolson, 1977)

Trumbach, Randolph, *The Rise of the Egalitarian Family. Aristocratic Kinship and Domestic Relations in the Eighteenth Century* (London, Academic Press, 1978)

Wrightson, Keith, *English Society 1580–1680* (London, Hutchinson, 1982)

Chapter 6

Cressy, David, *Education in Tudor and Stuart England* (London, Edward Arnold, 1975)

Digby, Anne and Peter Searby *Children, School and Society in Nineteenth-century England* (London, Macmillan, 1981)

Dyhouse, Carol, *Girls Growing up in late Victorian and Edwardian England* (London, Routledge and Kegan Paul, 1981)

Gardiner, Dorothy, *English Girlhood at School. A Study of Women's Education Through Twelve Centuries* (London, Oxford University Press, 1929)

Greven, Philip, *The Protestant Temperament. Patterns of Child-rearing, Religious Experience, and the Self in Early America* (New York, Alfred A. Knopf, 1977)

Stone, Laurence, *The Crisis of the Aristocracy 1558–1641* (Oxford, Clarendon Press, 1965)

Stone, Laurence, 'Literacy and Education in England, 1640–1900', *Past and Present* (1969)

Chapter 7

Canny, Nicholas, *The Upstart Earl: a Study of the Social and Mental World of Richard Boyle, First Earl of Cork, 1566–1643* (Cambridge, Cambridge University Press, 1982)

Cobbett, William, *Advice to young men, and (incidentally) to young women, in the higher ranks of life* (Oxford, Oxford University Press, 1980, first published 1830)

Demos, John, *A Little Commonwealth. Family Life in a Plymouth Colony* (New York, Oxford University Press, 1970)

Gillis, John, *Youth and History. Tradition and Change in European Age Relations, 1770 to the Present* (London, Academic Press, 1981)

Halifax, George, Marquis of, *The Lady's New-year Gift: or Advice to a Daughter* (James Partridge, 3rd ed., 1688)

Macfarlane, Alan, *The Family Life of Ralph Josselin. An Exercise in Historical Anthropology* (Cambridge, Cambridge University Press, 1970)

Stone, Laurence, *The Family, Sex and Marriage in England, 1500 to 1800* (London, Weidenfeld and Nicolson, 1977)

Wright, Louis (ed.), *Advice to a son. Precepts of Lord Burghley, Sir Walter Raleigh, and Francis Osborne*, Folger Documents of Tudor and Stuart Civilization. (Ithaca, NY, Cornell University Press, 1962)

Index

This index lists the main 'dramatis personae' of the book: the authors of the extracts and their relations. It is hoped that the reader will be able to follow the development of particular families.